RESTAURANT SUCCESS

BY THE NUMBERS

A Money-Guy's Guide
to Opening the
Next New Hot Spot

ROGER FIELDS, CPA

TEN SPEED PRESS
Berkeley

Copyright © 2007 by Roger Fields
Front cover photos © by Punchstock/Jupiter Images (top)
and Katy Brown (bottom)

All rights reserved. Published in the United States by
Ten Speed Press, an imprint of the Crown Publishing Group,
a division of Random House, Inc., New York.
www.crownpublishing.com
www.tenspeed.com

Ten Speed Press and the Ten Speed Press colophon are
registered trademarks of Random House, Inc.

Front cover photo (bottom) props courtesy Williams-Sonoma,
Inc., www.williams-sonoma.com

Library of Congress Cataloging-in-Publication Data
Fields, Roger.
  Restaurant success by the numbers : a money-guy's guide to
opening the
next new hot spot / Roger Fields.
     p. cm.
  Includes bibliographical references and index.
  1. Restaurant management. I. Title.
  TX911.3.M27F54 2007
  647.95068–dc22   2007010637

ISBN-13: 978-1-58008-663-9 (pbk.)

Printed in the United States of America

Cover and text design by Katy Brown

11 10 9 8 7 6

First Edition

CONTENTS

Introduction

Recently, I went to a doctor's office to get my eyes checked. After reviewing the patient info sheet and observing that I'd been a restaurant owner since 1992, the ophthalmologist proceeded to tell me how fortunate I was to have lasted in such a difficult business for so long. When I told him that it was not all that bad, he would have no part of it. And when I asked him where he got his information, he told me emphatically, "It's a well-known fact that 80 to 90 percent of all restaurants fail in the first year."

I hate to kick things off on a negative note, but as you'll soon find out, unfortunately this is how most of your early conversations about opening your own restaurant will start, too. I want you to be prepared and, more important, resolute. As you may already know, the restaurant business has a bad rap—one that it definitely does not deserve.

THE 90 PERCENT MYTH

There are actually two myths about restaurant success: the one my not-so-insightful doctor shared and its ugly stepsister, the notion that the 10 percent of restaurants that do succeed, do so only because of luck, otherwise known as the X factor. Let's start with the 90 percent bit.

Yes, your naysayer friends may have seen the caution printed in restaurant textbooks or in industry periodicals, or maybe they heard it on national television when Rocco DiSpirito of *The Restaurant* reality show lamented, "The inventory is highly perishable, the overhead insane—it's no wonder that about 90 percent of all restaurants fail in the first year." But listen carefully (you too, Rocco!): there is absolutely no evidence to support this much-cited failure rate. In fact, evidence points to the opposite.

A recent study found a restaurant failure rate of only 59 percent over a three-year period. The study's author, Ohio State University hospitality management professor, Dr. H. G. Parsa, studied 2,439 restaurants in Columbus, Ohio, using local health department data for the 1996 to 1999 period. Even including restaurants that closed for reasons other than finances—for example, divorce or retirement—Parsa found failure rates of only 26 percent in the first year, 19 percent in the second, and 14 percent in the third. "After an extensive literature review on restaurant failures, I can find no evidence of a 90 percent failure rate anywhere," he concluded.

What? However, those rascally pessimists still aren't satisfied. Columbus, Ohio, doesn't exactly have the same competition as New York or San Francisco, nor even the challenges faced in Washington, D.C., or Portland, Oregon. Well, these findings are consistent with an earlier study by Professor Chris Muller of the Cornell University School of Hotel Administration. He found that approximately 33 percent of *all restaurants in the United States* fail in the first year of operation. That's a far cry from 90 percent. Another 33 percent of those remaining fail in the second year. But once past that crucial starting period, 65 percent of the restaurants that make it through their third year will survive for ten years. Professor Muller's study also found that only 10 percent of franchised restaurants failed in the first year, and 85 percent were still operating under the same ownership after five years.

More encouraging still is the Dun and Bradstreet survey of businesses that went bankrupt or closed with unpaid obligations between 1920 and 1998. The survey found that eating and drinking places had a failure rate of only about 1.06 percent!

The fact is, not only do restaurants *not* have the highest failure rate of all businesses, they actually compare exceedingly well. According to Dun and Bradstreet, apparel, furniture, and camera and electronic stores are all more likely to fail than restaurants. And things just keep getting better. Read on.

AN EVEN BRIGHTER FUTURE

As more and more Americans move to cities, they have less time and space to cook. People need a convenient way to eat when they come home from work. At the same time, meals are still social occasions—times when friends or families get together. But fewer people these days have the energy to cook a big group meal and then actually enjoy it, especially knowing there will be dishes to wash after the guests have gone home. So what do Americans do? They go out to eat, of course!

In the United States, restaurants and food services together make up the nation's largest retail sector. According to the National Restaurant Association, total restaurant-and-food service sales is projected to reach $537 billion at more than nine hundred thousand locations, with the industry experiencing its unprecedented sixteenth consecutive year of real growth.

Consider these facts as well:

- An average restaurant meal now costs only 20 percent more than cooking at home, compared to 93 percent more just ten years ago. "A $10 purchase of groceries a decade ago would have cost a consumer $19 on average at a restaurant. Now the same basket of supermarket food costs $12.50 at a restaurant, making the decision to dine out or get takeout a far more economically sensible one," Paul Westra, an industry analyst at the Robertson Stephens investment bank in San Francisco, told *Nation's Restaurant News*. The popular Zagat restaurant guide has even coined a term for restaurants that cater to customers who choose to go out for everyday meals: Better Alternative to Home, or BATH.

- As the number of American households earning two incomes grows, parents will have less time to prepare meals at home and thus will demand more dining conveniences. Four out of ten adults are cooking fewer meals at home than they did two years ago, according to a 2001 research study conducted by the National Restaurant Association. A similar study reported, "Six out of ten adults (61 percent) indicated that having carry-out or delivery meals means they have more time to spend on other activities." Among eighteen- to twenty-four-year-olds surveyed, an astonishing 77 percent felt the same way.

- McKinsey & Company's "Foodservice 2010" study predicts that restaurants will capture a larger share of the consumer food dollar than grocery stores for the first time as soon as the year 2010. That's just around the corner from tomorrow.

Given these national trends, it is not surprising that, despite economic downturns and high gas prices—which siphon money from people's discretionary spending to basic necessity budgets—the industry continues to experience unprecedented growth. But trends alone do not spur growth; profits spur growth, and unlike the 90 percent story, that's no myth.

DO THE MATH

Joe Vitrano runs J&B Restaurant Partners Inc., which owns thirty-one Friendly's restaurants in Long Island, New York. In an interview in *Total Food Service* magazine, he compares the potential profitability of the restaurant business to that of convenience stores. His conclusion is startling: "In the [convenience] store, you work on a 30 to 35 percent profit margin, while in the food industry the profit margin is over 70 percent. The difference in profitability alone made me do a double take." Though he was referring to gross profits, the numbers for net profits (that is, after overhead, labor cost, cost of sales, and taxes) are also impressive.

According to the Restaurant Seminar Institute, successful, well-managed restaurants can show net profits of 14 percent and higher. Jasper White, a celebrity chef, cookbook author, and co-owner of Jasper White's Summer Crab Shack, says that his two "shacks" run more than a 20 percent profit on annual sales of $15 million.

The National Restaurant Association also reports that most of the restaurants now operating are single-unit or independently owned with average sales of $730,000 for full-service restaurants and $619,000 for limited-service restaurants (those without table service, such as fast food, take-out, or delivery). In other words: you don't have to be a conglomerate to generate meaningful sales in the restaurant business. Think about it: if you can clear a 14 percent net profit from an average full-service restaurant, you would still earn an annual income of $102,000! A lot more than most Americans make!

Bottom line: not only can restaurants be profitable, but demographic and changing lifestyle trends increasingly give restaurants excellent potential as small business opportunities.

THE ROMANCE OF IT ALL

Finally, as I'm sure you know well, the sense of romance in starting up and owning your own restaurant is just as likely to lure you into the business as the *much*-better-than 10 percent success rate and the industry's ongoing growth.

Sir Terence Conran, the famous designer, retailer, and restaurateur responsible for some of England's best restaurants, describes how widespread he believes the dream of opening a restaurant is: "I have a completely unsubstantiated belief that 92 percent of the population have at one time or another entertained the notion of owning and running their own café, restaurant, tea shop, or pub. And in most cases, I am prepared to bet, those dreams have been inspired by the unique sense of well-being that comes from a really good experience of eating out."

Many would-be restaurateurs go into the business thinking that it is sexy. They consider themselves to be experts because they've eaten out a lot. Some excellent home cooks, intoxicated by the joie de vivre of throwing dinner parties, are lured into the business thinking that feeding fifty or more fickle paying members of the public can't possibly be any more difficult than entertaining a few well-selected couples from their close circle of friends. Others are spurred on by the idea of having a "little place of their own," where friends can pop in for something to eat and drink, without the headaches of having to shop or clean up afterward. Some people are enticed by the idea of meeting lots of new and exciting friends and of the possibility of rubbing elbows with celebrities. Many folks get into the business thinking that it's a good way to fulfill the dream of owning their own business.

The good news is that when a restaurant is successful, most of the above romantic elements are possible. Over the years, I have had all of those experiences, and, at the risk of exploiting your own restaurant fantasy, there's an even more powerful seduction: the intoxication that comes from the buzz in a room full of clanking dishes, waiters weaving in and out of tables, and people eating, drinking, talking, laughing, and having the time of their lives, knowing all the while that it was your idea, hard work, and passion that helped to make it all possible. Let's face it; we all love to throw a great party! The good thing about owning a successful restaurant is that you can throw one every night. The bad news is that caught up in the romance of it all, many would-be restaurateurs jump in headfirst without checking to see whether there are rocks in the water. Starting up and running a restaurant is *not easy*—far from it.

Unlike a doctor or lawyer, a restaurant owner is not required to undergo specialized training. If you think you know what good food is and you've done well enough in another profession to have the money to invest, what else is there to know? Even some of the most talented and successful chefs have failed when they opened their own restaurants. Why? They did not understand the basics of running a successful business.

THE X FACTOR

Ever heard about the X factor? Two restaurants open on the same block. Six months later, the one that has X has become very successful: customers stream in the doors, and when they leave, they are happy. The other restaurant, lacking X, is closing its doors and going out of business. Another example of the X factor in action is the restaurant that's off the beaten path, yet somehow people still find their way to its doorstep. What is this mysterious X that makes some restaurants succeed while others fail?

Take heart. The X factor is not just luck or chance, as those naysayers would have you believe. Nor does it have to be mysterious. With careful study and planning, you can increase the probability that your restaurant will have the X factor. In some cases, X might be a great location or the right atmosphere. In others it may be great food. For still others, X may be the right price structure. More often than not, X is a combination of many things: location, food, price, service, atmosphere, and sound operational and financial management.

The X factor, quite simply, is this:

- Understanding your market's needs
- Creating a concept with a strong unique selling proposition
- Consistently delivering value for your customers' money, that is, food, service, and an overall restaurant experience that meets or exceeds their expectations
- Maintaining sound operational and financial management practices

The moral of this story is that if you want to increase your chances of success—particularly since you are going to invest a considerable amount of time, money, and effort into opening a business—you owe it to yourself to be as prepared as you possibly can. The good news is that for most small operations, this is not so difficult—if you're willing to buckle down, put in the time, and ask the right questions.

IF ONLY I'D KNOWN THEN

Take me, for example. Before I opened my first restaurant, I spent ten years as a certified public accountant at large local and national accounting firms. That gave me an advantage in mastering the finance side of the restaurant business. I encountered successful restaurants that were failing as businesses. Although they were busy, these restaurants barely made money, if they had any profit at all. Regardless of why their owners were in the business—for love or money—they all faced the same fact: if a business is not profitable, it will not be worth the owner's time and effort and thus will not last for long. Over the course of those ten years, I learned to identify patterns of success and patterns of failure, and as a result, I thought I knew enough to get into the business myself. Unfortunately, having not started a restaurant from scratch, I did not have the benefit of good advice on the day-to-day challenges of running my restaurant, and I soon learned that there was more to preparing and selling beans than counting them.

While I knew how to price menu items, how much food and beverages should cost, how much to budget for salaries and wages, how much food and beverages to keep on hand to avoid running out or watching them spoil, and how to track inventories, I had difficulties matching my concept to the market, deciding on appropriate menu items and getting them prepared just right, dealing with unsatisfied customers, finding the right purveyors for food and beverages, finding the right chef, hiring and training kitchen and service staff, and attracting the attention of potential customers and then getting them to become regulars.

My first foray into the business came in 1992, when along with several partners, I opened a restaurant in New York City's theater district. After many mistakes and struggling for the first year or so, we changed our concept to meet the market's needs and opened Zuni, an upscale table service restaurant, which became quite successful.

Six years later, encouraged by Zuni's success and armed with the lessons learned from my earlier mistakes, I opened two other takeout concepts in the same neighborhood. The first, a soup and sausage concept, was not as profitable as I had hoped it would be, and I converted it to a wrap sandwich concept, which went on to do quite well; I sold it in 2001 for a nice profit. In August 2004, I sold my interest in Zuni and moved to the San Francisco Bay Area where I am currently working on opening yet another restaurant.

As you can see, many factors determine whether a restaurant will become successful and profitable. Some of them, I was fortunate to be knowledgeable about, while others, unfortunately, I had to learn the hard way.

But after all the ups and downs, I know that opening and running *your* own successful restaurant will bring *you* joy and pride that will outweigh the frustrations that running a business involves. At the beginning, your own restaurant will be very time-consuming and demanding. But hang in there; if you are passionate, dedicated, and have a solid plan, the financial and personal rewards are great. As an owner and operator, you will profit from your efforts at the same time that you bring pleasure and comfort to your customers. I can honestly say that as a business owner, I can think of no greater satisfaction than having satisfied and happy customers come up and thank me personally for a wonderful meal and dining experience. They will let you know instantly when you are doing a good job. I suspect that these experiences, even more than the potential financial reward, is what makes this business so worthwhile for me and other successful restaurateurs.

HOW TO USE THIS BOOK

This book is not only instructional and informative, it's also entertaining. It's not just for people who have dreams of owning their own restaurant; it's also for people who simply want the inside scoop on what it really takes to plan, design, staff, open, and run a successful restaurant. Throughout this book, in addition to practical advice, there are anecdotes of mistakes made and problems encountered, and how they were resolved. I have also included contributed essays from owners, chefs, and other experts from various types of restaurant operations, from hole in the wall to well-known large upscale operators. Their thoughts about their operations and the business in general will provide valuable insight into what it takes to run a successful restaurant.

Because opening and running your own restaurant will require not only a lot of time, dedication, passion, and hard work, but in all likelihood a substantial capital investment, you will need to be as certain as you possibly can that your restaurant idea will have a good probability of success at a specific site in your market area. A good way to test your idea is to conduct a market feasibility study. In addition to evaluating a site location, this will involve gathering and analyzing information about the demographics, psychographics, and competitive environment in your market. If you do not yet have a specific concept in mind, this research will help you identify the types of restaurants that are most likely to succeed in your area.

The early chapters in this book describe how to collect and analyze market data in order to make decisions about a potential concept, and how to quantify that data to decide whether it will make financial sense. Before getting into the meat of concept selection and market analysis, chapter 1, will help to set the table for your future success. For those of you who are interested in the "feel good" or romantic aspects of the business, it will suggest ways to realize them without taking on the responsibilities of ownership. It will also give some of the principal reasons for restaurant failure so that you can avoid them, and give you five rules that will help you to be pragmatic and to set realistic goals for your first restaurant.

Chapter 2, particularly important for those of you who are neophytes, walks through the basics of what constitutes a restaurant concept and outlines some characteristics of several restaurant types, such as, fast food, takeout and delivery, and various types of table service. For example, if you are interested in takeout and delivery, you will learn the three characteristics that are necessary for success in that business. With these fundamentals in hand, you will be able to do more effective research and evaluation.

Chapter 3 will teach you how to do the following:

- Assess the potential number of customers you may be able to capture by looking at population size and potential traffic generators, such as office buildings, apartment buildings, and condominium complexes
- Become familiar with and identify potential target customers—that is, customers you hope to attract to your restaurant—through analyzing their age, income, spending habits, eating-out habits, and so on. With this information you will be able to develop tentative ideas and decisions about the types of food and beverages to serve, design and décor, service elements, and prices to charge.
- Evaluate your overall competitive environment—the number of, or lack of, similar concepts in the area—identify primary and secondary potential competitors, and evaluate their strengths and weaknesses, for example, their parking, food, bar, design and décor, and level of business at various times of the day

Chapter 4 will help you to assess location and site characteristics, such as visibility, proximity to traffic generators, traffic patterns and how they can affect your business, parking, and availability of adequate utilities.

Chapter 5 will show you how to quantify your data in the form of a financial feasibility study, evaluating whether your idea will make money. This chapter will teach you not only how to realistically prepare a budget of the cost to open your restaurant, but also how to realistically estimate sales and expenses and the level of sales you will need to pay yourself a decent wage, pay back your lenders and investors, and still break even.

But opening and running a successful restaurant is not only about gathering and analyzing market data and quantifying it. It's also about food; service; ambience and design; staffing; properly equipping and laying out your kitchen, dining room, and bar areas; attracting customers and keeping them; and much more. That's where the next six chapters come in. Here you'll find all the information and details you need to start fleshing out the concept that you determined is a winner. Chapter 6 will give you some ideas about how to formulate a menu concept to match your target market, discuss the importance of a diverse menu, and teach you how to cost and price your menu items. It also gives tips on menu layout and design. Chapters 7 and 8 will get into some of the specifics of design and decor and give suggestions for how to select an architect or designer. These chapters will also discuss the importance of flow in design, give tips on how to lay out your dining room efficiently, and how to select tables and chairs to maximize your seating capacity. You will also learn how to buy the right amount of starting cutlery, plates, glassware, and so on; how to avoid costly budget overruns; the importance of complying with local and state code regulations; and much more. Chapter 9 will discuss the profitability of selling alcoholic beverages, give details on the various components of a bar, discuss liquor license laws and tell you where to get information, teach you how to prevent employee theft at the bar—almost everything you will need to set up and run your bar. It will also teach you how to price your drinks. Chapter 10 gives an in-depth discussion of kitchen layout and design, discusses the importance of matching equipment with concept, gives descriptions of the key pieces of equipment found in a restaurant kitchen, gives suggestions for how to select good durable equipment, and tells you where to find it. Chapter 11 gives tips on how to match your kitchen staff skills with your concept and gives tips on how to hire a chef and what traits to look for in a good chef. This chapter will also show you the relationship between good service and profits, teach you how to hire and train your service staff, and show you how to prepare a basic service and set up procedures manual.

Once you have determined that your concept is financially viable, you will be ready to make your restaurant dream a reality. The last four chapters will walk you through the rest of your startup tasks. If you are like most entrepreneurs, you will probably need to raise some investment capital or secure a bank loan. With your financial feasibility study, break-even analysis, and capital budget in hand from chapter 5, you will be ready to sell your idea to investors and lenders. Chapter 12 will:

- Introduce you to the SBA (Small Business Administration), the bank of last resort for most first-time restaurateurs, and walk you through the process of applying for a bank loan
- Provide some insights into how to raise capital from investors and alternative sources, such as leasing and getting tenant improvements from landlords
- Present the basics of writing a concise, comprehensive, and convincing business plan, which will demonstrate to investors and lenders not only that your restaurant has the fundamentals to be profitable, but also that you have the necessary skills and know-how to run a successful business

Chapter 13 will teach you how to read and analyze a commercial lease so you will know what questions to ask when negotiating your lease. It will also describe the different types of businesses—corporations, partnerships, limited liability companies and so on—so you will be able to choose the one that is best for you. In this chapter, you will also learn how to obtain a federal tax ID number and how to open business bank accounts.

Chapter 14 will discuss cost-effective ways to market your particular restaurant before it opens, during its early weeks and months, and for as long as its doors are open to the public. You will learn how to identify and use marketing methods that will help to create a memorable brand image for your restaurant and will develop a loyal customer base. For example, you will learn how to get positive word-of-mouth advertising and press write-ups and reviews, the two most powerful forms of advertising.

Chapter 15 will teach you how to identify and eliminate waste, spoilage, and employee theft. It will also teach you how to manage your inventories and labor cost to ensure maximum profitability.

Like every good book, this one has a logical beginning and ending. But you are welcome to read it in whatever order appeals to you. If you do get hooked and decide to take the restaurant plunge, be sure to study and digest chapters 1 through 5.

———

If you've read this far and still want to open or invest in a restaurant, congratulations! You have a realistic idea of the elbow grease that's required. Hard work is the first thing you need to run any successful business, not just a restaurant. This book will tell you the rest of what you need. It will give you the advice that I wish I'd had before I opened my first restaurant.

CHAPTER 1

THE RULES
OF GAME
THE

Over the years, in talking to some of my clients—both successful operators and people whose businesses have failed—I have found that despite all the horror stories about restaurant failure, far too many people still get into the business
because of the romantic aspects. The idea of owning a restaurant encourages these
notions, easily distracting people from the actual day-to-day challenges. You would
think that as a CPA I would have been strictly pragmatic when I got into the business. But the truth is, I had romantic notions floating around in my head, too, which
caused me to get off to a slow, nearly disastrous start. It was only after my first
restaurant became profitable that I was able to really appreciate and enjoy the feel-
good aspects of and fall in love with the business.

Realizing your dream of owning and running a successful restaurant is going
to require equal doses of reality and passion. By definition, being in business for
yourself involves taking a risk, since it requires investing personal resources such
as money and time toward an uncertain outcome. The best approach, when thinking about opening your own restaurant, is to be as realistic as possible. Thus your
dream of owning a restaurant should not be based on romantic notions of entertaining, being popular, meeting lots of people, rubbing elbows with important people,
and that sort of stuff. Instead, base your dream on either a passion for the food and
hospitality business or a passion to succeed as an entrepreneur. If you focus your

passion on realistic goals, you are more likely to ground yourself firmly and make successful choices and decisions as you pursue your dreams.

For those of you who are more interested in the feel-good and entertainment aspects of the business, there are a number of ways to experience them without the responsibilities and challenges of owning and running your own restaurant.

For example, you could find a group of local successful operators and invest in their next venture. You could still call the place your own and would probably get the royal treatment every time you went in with friends and family. It is common for restaurateurs seeking investors to include a certain amount of free meals as part of the return on investment.

If you are not satisfied with a passive role and really have a calling for the hospitality aspects of the restaurant business, you might consider going to culinary school to train as a chef or manager. I have met many outstanding managers and chefs who would not trade their jobs for the responsibilities of full ownership. A possible bonus of being a highly regarded chef or manager is an offer of ownership interests in addition to salary. An additional benefit of being a restaurant manager or a chef is the special treatment that other owners, managers, and chefs give you when you eat in their restaurants. This is a common practice.

PLAN FOR SUCCESS

With your priorities in order and armed with some facts about the restaurant business to quiet those negative nancys and renew your confidence in seeing the day of your grand opening party, are you ready to run out and start your own? Not so fast! Sure, the trends driving the food-service industry suggest it makes sense to open a restaurant. And the potential returns are attractive. But if it were so simple to go out and make money with restaurants, we wouldn't be hearing horror stories about their high failure rate.

The restaurant business is competitive. But that is not the main reason why many restaurants close their doors. The main reason a restaurant fails is because inexperienced owners and investors make many avoidable mistakes. As the old adage goes, "Those who fail to plan, plan to fail."

In any business endeavor, good market research and proper planning help to avoid common mistakes, reduce the amount of time and capital investment needed, and increase the probability of success. That includes the restaurant business. Opening and running a successful restaurant is more than simply buying or leasing property, building it out, designing and decorating it, buying equipment, hiring employees, and selling food and beverages.

Remember, although one out of three restaurants fails in the first year, only 10 percent of franchises go under in the first twelve months. Why are franchises so much more successful than independent restaurants? The answer is simple. Franchise operators put a lot of research into site selection and concept development, and they can rely on the lessons learned by earlier franchises in the same chain. As a result, a franchise comes to the table with proven operating and financial systems.

But, you say, "I don't want to be part of a chain! I want to make my restaurant my own, and I don't want to pay part of my profits to some big corporation." Well, you don't have to open a franchise to be successful. The good news is that you can do this on your own. You merely need to have the right approach, which includes comprehensive and objective market research and analysis and proper planning—just like the chains do.

Consider the most common reasons why independent restaurants fail:

- **Unrealistically high rent and occupancy costs.** All too often, inexperienced restaurateurs take on rent and other occupancy costs that are too high for their budget, making it difficult to sustain viable operations.

- **Undercapitalization and lack of working capital.** Frequently, concepts that would have otherwise been viable, fail because of lack of sufficient funds and working capital to keep the restaurant going until turning the corner to profitability.

- **Lack of attention to details in managing financial resources.** Maintaining proper controls over cash management and handling, controlling portion sizes, controlling food and beverage costs, managing inventory and shrinkage due to theft, and managing spoilage and waste are essential to an operation's success.

- **Poor operational management.** Having a well-trained and happy staff plays an important role in the success of any business. Good management policies help to set the tone, influence employee attitudes and performance, and encourage repeat customer visits.

- **Excessive investment in construction, equipment, renovation, and acquisition costs.** Too many first-time restaurateurs take on too much debt to build or buy their dream restaurant, which results in debt repayments that are too high for their restaurant to be profitable.

- **Poor choice of location.** The right location is very important. It is not unusual for a mediocre business to succeed simply by having a good location, while another well-run operation may fail because of a poor location.

- **Poor choice of concept.** A poor concept for a particular location, or a concept without a unique selling proposition (USP), often fails to attract enough customers to make a restaurant profitable.

- **Poor or inconsistent food and service.** Reliably good food and service are very important to most restaurant guests. Inconsistent food and service negatively impact the overall dining experience and discourage repeat business.

- **Lack of a value proposition.** Customers instinctively seek value, and when they do not get good value for their money, they do not return. They seek it elsewhere. Lacking this understanding, many operators unwittingly price themselves out of their market.

Transforming the Tradition of Takeout

Gregoire Jacquet of Gregoire

In July 2001, after sixteen years of seven-day weeks in kitchens other than my own, I was ready for a change. I resigned my position as acting executive chef for the Ritz-Carlton in San Juan Puerto Rico and headed home with my wife, Tara, who was pregnant with our first child. Those sixteen years began in my native France at age fourteen with a three-year apprenticeship, followed by an intense professional career that included five years as chef de cuisine for Master Chef Jacky Robert at Amelio's in San Francisco and seven years with the Ritz-Carlton.

When we got home, I spent the first four months contemplating which of the many things I wanted to do, made the most sense. The one thing I knew for sure was that I was not going to work for anybody other than myself. Within a few months, I knew my concept: a neighborhood restaurant just like the village eateries found in the countryside of France—a gathering place where you know customers' names and which foods they like—where I would transform the tradition of takeout by serving organic, artisan dishes.

So I set out to find the right space and location. I knew that the space had to be small, as I had a certain amount of capital that I wanted to invest, and I knew that in order to serve organic, artisan food at village prices that I would need to keep overhead low. Takeout also worked in this scheme as I wouldn't need to hire waiters.

- **Poor business acumen.** Many first timers simply lack the ability to run any business, not just a restaurant.

Now that you know some of the principal reasons for restaurant failure, you should have better insight into the research, analysis, and planning needed to fulfill your dream of successfully owning and operating your own restaurant.

PREPARE FOR REALITY

You are now ready to take the first step from dreaming to the reality of owning and operating your own restaurant. Researching and planning for your new restaurant will require lots of hard work, and staying open will require lots of passion and dedication. That said, follow these five basic rules and the whole process, though still challenging, will be rewarding and manageable.

- **Rule #1:** As you move ahead with your plans, keep one foot firmly planted in the realities of business and the other in your passion for your restaurant. Mario Batali put it best in a recent interview. When asked about the relationship between being a passionate chef and running a successful business, he

In January 2002, I found the perfect location: a 600-square-foot hole-in-the-wall just around the corner from the renowned Chez Panisse in the heart of Berkeley's famed Gourmet Ghetto. The location is a densely populated area with over 40,000 residents within one square mile. People who live and work in the area are well-educated, well-traveled foodies with high disposable incomes.

The space had been closed for some time and was in shambles. Thankfully, it was formerly occupied by a bistro, so zoning wasn't an issue. I found a firm of architects and contractors who were familiar with local code regulations and we got to work. My top design priority was an open kitchen so that while cooking, even on the grill, I could talk to customers. My architects were able to do this *and* give me a beautiful country kitchen with two wooden tables and benches right outside my window—and all in time for an opening six months later.

The first day I did $400, $200 from my in-laws. They came, sat down and stayed to make the place look busy. Within a month, I knew I wouldn't have to worry. My first $1,000 day was very hard because it was just one cook, one cashier, and me. After that, I got busier and busier and busier... and had to hire more people.

Nobody can believe it, including myself. At first, Gregoire was just a neighborhood restaurant. But then it got busier. In fact, business doubled every year the first two years, and continues to grow. My Potato Puffs and hexagonal corrugated takeout boxes are now the talk of the town. Four years later, I found a similar space in Oakland and opened another Gregoire!

said, "I tell people that work for me, you have to understand art and you have to understand business, but if you had to choose an address, it would be at the corner of art and commerce."

- **Rule #2:** Consider starting small even if you've had previous experience as a chef or a manager. The road to restaurant failure is littered with the broken dreams of many chefs and managers, celebrity and otherwise. Starting small will require much less start-up capital than starting on a grand scale, and it will give you the opportunity to learn on the job without the stress of running the day-to-day operations of a large business. With the lessons learned from operating a successful small operation, you will be better prepared to go on to build your dream restaurant or restaurant empire, if that is your ultimate goal. Also, do not underestimate the potential profitability and/or satisfaction of owning and running a small operation. I know firsthand that a small operation can be just as rewarding and profitable as a large one. Countless numbers of very successful independent and chain operators got their start with small restaurants. Two that I can think of offhand are Rich Melman of Lettuce Entertain You Enterprises, who started his empire of thirty-seven restaurants with a $17,000 hole-in-the-wall operation in Chicago, and David Overton of The

Cheesecake Factory, whose family got started baking and selling cheesecakes out of their basement in Southern California. Can you think of a city or town that does not have its own popular and successful local operation?

■ **Rule #3**: Set initial realistic goals and objectives. Setting practical goals will help you focus on the appropriate type and size of restaurant for you. For example, if you want to make $150,000, take one or two vacations every year, and retire with a fat nest egg in the bank, chances are that a small, white-tablecloth restaurant in the suburbs will not fit the bill. If, on the other hand, your goal is to have a modest life, cook the best damn food around, mingle with your customers, spend time with your family and friends, pay your bills, and have a small nest egg, such a concept might fit the bill nicely. Setting realistic goals reduces the likelihood that you will get frustrated and lose interest if your profit goals do not come true. With reasonable goals, you can prepare an objective financial feasibility study pro forma profit-and-loss statement; this document will tell you whether your restaurant will be lucrative enough to realize your dreams and your financial goals.

■ **Rule #4**: Recognize from the get-go that the amount of financial resources you have access to will limit the type and size of restaurant you can realistically open. Available capital will depend largely on your personal financial resources (that is, your savings, investments, and equity in your home if you own one) and, if necessary, on your ability to attract investors and lenders. Before you start dreaming, take stock of your financial situation. Then decide how much of it you are prepared to invest in your future restaurant and try to stick with that amount. Do not get carried away and bite off more than you can chew, or you could run out of money before opening day. You would be surprised to know how many first timers make this mistake. Your access to capital combined with your desired income and lifestyle should guide your decision as to what type and size of restaurant to open.

■ **Rule #5**: Make a commitment to find and surround yourself with the right people to help you get the job done. This could include a chef, a manager, or consultants if necessary. Too many early mistakes can cause problems that can doom your restaurant to failure before it has a fighting chance.

One of the most important decisions, if not the most important decision, you will have to make about your restaurant is the concept. No amount of business savvy and management skills can overcome the wrong concept in the wrong location. Chapter 2 will give you an overview of various restaurant concepts and walk you through the process of formulating a tentative concept that you can test later with market research and analysis.

CHAPTER 2

YOUR RESTAURANT CONCEPT

The question potential restaurateurs ask most often is: "How much does it cost to open a restaurant?" If only there were a set answer. There is none, of course. It cost me and my partners ninety thousand dollars to open our first restaurant, but Thomas Keller's restaurant, Per Se, in New York City's Time Warner Center, cost somewhere around eleven million dollars to open.

So you see, starting out by asking how much it would cost to open a restaurant is putting the cart ahead of the horse. A better approach is to start with questions that will help you to identify the many costs of getting a restaurant going and growing. This book is designed to help you ask the right questions before you start the budget process.

Before we go any further, you should note that the models discussed below do not include franchise fees or royalties. That's because this book is primarily for people who are planning to open independent restaurants. A franchisee will not need to make many of the following decisions. In fact, most chains won't even allow franchisees to make such decisions! If, however, you decide to purchase a franchise, you can use most of the concepts in this book to evaluate the soundness of a proposed concept.

Think of building or buying a restaurant the same way that you would approach building or buying a house. Many of the questions are quite similar:

■ What type (or style) will it be?
■ Where will it be located?
■ How big will it be?
■ How will it be furnished, equipped, and decorated?

Before you can make a realistic estimate of how much money you need, you must answer all these questions. One answer may limit other answers. If you want to build a mansion, you'd better find a big enough plot of land (and be able to afford it). If you have a modest-sized plot, you'd better not hire an architect to put up a Taj Mahal there. And if your dream home is an ultramodern ranch style, don't plan to build it in a neighborhood full of Victorian gingerbread houses.

In short, your ideas must make sense and work together. If they do not, it would be wise to change some of your assumptions until you find a set of ideas that makes sense. Some potential home buyers, just like some would-be restaurant owners, start out with a particular concept, only to find that it does not fit their budget or that it is impossible to meet all their priorities. So they go back to the drawing board and change specifications until they have a realistic overall plan. The restaurant business is the same way. That's where your choice of restaurant concept comes in.

A restaurant's concept is the image it projects, the way you present it and the way the public perceives it. Before making the final decision to open your own restaurant, you should develop a tentative concept of what it will be. Until you have a basic concept, it will be difficult to answer crucial questions about your space, equipment, and staffing needs. This initial concept will also help you conduct meaningful market research so you can identify a workable location, prepare a realistic financial feasibility study, and work through your business plan to see if it makes financial sense.

Restaurants come in all types and sizes, from a local diner or greasy spoon to a Chinese place, a fancy French restaurant where couples get engaged, a sidewalk café, or a family-style Italian joint. Each of these cater to a specific kind of customer. A burger joint can be an upscale "grille" or a down-at-the-heels "dive." The local Chinese place may be an informal take-out enterprise with little décor beyond a calendar in Mandarin. Or it may be a fancy affair with table linens, silk-swathed waitresses, potted bamboo, and exotic menu items. A sidewalk café may serve traditional sandwiches and lemonade, or imported cheeses on fancy breads with fine wines and sparkling water on the side.

But wait a minute, you may say, "I've already found the perfect location, yet you say I need a concept first!" This may sound like a chicken-versus-egg dilemma; does the concept come first and then the location? Or the site and then the concept? Even if you think you have already found the perfect location for your restaurant, the location is only ideal if you have a concept that fits your site.

In other words, the process of deciding on a concept is the same whether or not you've already chosen a location. If you've got your heart set on a location, you'll have less flexibility in finalizing your concept. Likewise, if you have a concept that you are convinced is a winner, you'll want to be extra certain to choose the right location for that particular concept. For example, if you want to open an upscale bistro, you would probably not choose a location in a moderate- to low-income neighborhood, even if the real estate were cheap. A concept with low to moderate prices and generous portions will increase your chances of success in that area.

A restaurant's concept involves all the aspects of operating a restaurant, particularly the following:

- Service style and restaurant type
- Atmosphere and ambience
- Menu
- Price range
- Possibility of a bar and selling alcohol
- Restaurant size

In later chapters, we'll discuss each of these issues—all of which can affect your final cost—in greater detail. For now, however, let's focus on what kind of restaurant you want to open, that is, your service style and restaurant type. This decision will affect everything else, particularly your space requirements, labor costs, average check size, and seat turnover.

SERVICE STYLE AND RESTAURANT TYPE

Whatever the motif, there are three basic choices for a restaurant format:

- Fast food with no table service. Just as its name suggests, fast food means quick preparation and quick counter service. Parts of most fast food menu items are prepared in advance, and then kept warm or cold until it's time to finish them to order. These establishments use many disposable items—paper napkins, food containers, plastic knives, forks, spoons, and so on—whose costs add up quickly.

- Takeout and delivery. In these restaurants, customers order food to eat elsewhere, so space requirements for customers and décor costs are not critical. But you'll have to leave room in the budget for storage and purchase of extra disposable items, delivery staff wages, and whatever you use for delivery—carts, bicycles, scooters, cars, or mileage reimbursement.

- Table service à la carte. In this type of restaurant, wait staff take individual food orders, give them to the kitchen (where the food is prepared and plated), and then deliver food to the table. This level of service is generally found in upscale restaurants, diners, coffee shops, and other casual full-service (waiter service) restaurants. Typically, this is a more expensive kind of place to open and run.

Deciding on the style of service and type of restaurant you want will help you make initial ballpark estimates of what you will need in terms of space, supplies, staff, and furnishings.

Your choice of restaurant format is closely related to the kind of food you decide to serve. Certain types of cuisine—Chinese and other Asian foods, for example—are particularly suited to the takeout and delivery format. Pizza—which cooks fast, is inexpensive, and can be delivered intact—is a classic takeout and delivery food. Conversely, a fancy French-inspired meal, assembled so the colors combine perfectly and every garnish is in the right place, is more suited to full table service in a restaurant designed to make the guests feel pampered.

As you read the following sections about the three main restaurant types, consider what the major requirements for your chosen format will be. Here are some questions to ask yourself:

- Is experienced wait staff available in your city?
- Is the population in your area spread out or dense enough that delivery service is practical?
- What is the cost and availability of restaurant-zoned space? Is it practical to build in your area?
- Will the space you're considering accommodate the staff and other needs of your dream restaurant?

FAST FOOD, WITH NO TABLE SERVICE

In a fast-food format, the working space needs are most important at the counter. At a typical fast-food restaurant, customers usually line up to place their orders with counter workers who act as cashiers, deliver the orders to kitchen workers who assemble food, and then give the completed orders to the customers. During rush periods, it can get very busy behind the counter, so there must be enough space to allow counter workers to move around easily without crashing into each other!

Storage needs are high in fast-food operations. These businesses use lots of disposable service items—paper napkins, plates, and cups; plastic knives, forks, plates, and spoons; paper or plastic containers; individual seasoning packets; bags or boxes; and so on. As a result, they require lots of storage space for new items and used disposables. This is particularly true in rural and suburban areas where deliveries to restock these disposables are infrequent.

Floor space is at a premium in a fast-food restaurant. In fast food and in some table-service formats, seats with hard, durable surfaces can encourage high table turnover and make cleanup faster and easier.

As you will note in the following sections, a fast-food format has both the storage and working space requirements of a delivery operation and the floor space needs of an à la carte restaurant. Thus, a fast-food restaurant may have higher space rental costs than the other two formats. However, there are typically no delivery or waiter payroll costs.

TAKEOUT AND DELIVERY

More often than not, delivery operations also offer takeout and vice versa, so we will address these two styles together. These restaurants differ substantially from fast-food shops in terms of floor space requirements and menu offerings. Most takeout restaurants provide little or no seating for their customers, and they generally have a wider range of menu items than fast-food operations. Perhaps the best example of a tiny takeout is Al's Soup Kitchen International, made famous by the Soup Nazi on the sitcom *Seinfeld*. Al's operation was so small that customers had to stand on the sidewalk to order their soup.

Successful takeout and delivery restaurants share these characteristics:

- **Low to moderate prices.** The typical customer looking to order takeout or delivery does not want to spend much more than it would cost if they had to prepare a meal for themselves; in other words, they are looking for what Zagat calls a Best Alternative to Home (BATH). These customers are not looking to spend the kind of money that a typical table-service restaurant might charge.

- **Speedy preparation.** Convenience and speed of service are important in these restaurants, particularly in urban areas with a fast-paced lifestyle. Customers on a one-hour lunch break, for example, cannot afford to wait long for their food. Others want their food to be ready in less time than it would take them to prepare a home-cooked meal. Customers on their way home, or at home waiting for delivery, do not want to wait for their food. They want it quick, fresh, and hot. To meet their needs, these menus should include items that can be prepared, cooked, and served quickly. Asian food using bite-sized ingredients that cook quickly in a wok, pizza, or rotisserie chicken with batch-prepared side dishes are possibilities.

- **Menu items that cannot be easily prepared at home.** According to the National Restaurant Association, half of all customers who dine in or order takeout or delivery prefer foods that have flavor and taste sensations not easily duplicated at home.

What does this mean in terms of costs for your restaurant? Like fast-food restaurants, takeout and delivery places need a lot of storage space. They rely heavily on disposable items, quick service, and ingredients prepared ahead of time. Depending on the concept, takeouts can offer items assembled or cooked ahead of time in batches, items prepared to order, or a combination. Supplies must include sturdy leak-proof packaging, which may require extra storage space.

Unlike most fast-food operations, which only need to place and prepare orders quickly, takeout and delivery restaurants must be able to deliver as well. This adds another cost item. In delivery operations, most orders are received by telephone, cooked to order, and then delivered by foot or bicycle in urban areas and motor vehicle in suburban areas. Delivery operations are best suited to heavily populated urban areas, where high volume will offset higher transportation costs.

Certain types of equipment and furnishings can make a world of difference to takeout and delivery restaurants, and they pay for themselves in time saved, customers retained or attracted because of better service, and higher average check size. A comprehensive telephone ordering system with caller ID, for example, can track a customer's past purchase records and display the customer's address and telephone number, reducing the time needed to take orders. Such a system can be invaluable in reducing the demands on staff and increasing speed of service, thus saving labor costs and enhancing the customer's experience. Similarly, reach-in refrigerators for bottled or canned drinks and snack items, placed near the cash register, can help to increase the average check size by attracting impulse purchases.

Don't forget to factor these into start-up costs. I'll get into more specific cost estimates in chapter 11 about how to design your operating and capital budgets.

TABLE SERVICE À LA CARTE

Table-service restaurants tend to require many more decisions than do simpler takeout and delivery places or fast-food restaurants. All these elements will affect the total start-up cost. You must consider dining room space and layout requirements, turnover rate at tables, the type of seating, the cost of table-service items, and the required skill level for kitchen and service staff.

Table-service restaurants offer a variety of styles of service: plate service, platter service, cart service, or a combination of the three. Floor space needs vary for each style. In plate service, the food is plated in the kitchen, and wait staff delivers it to the tables. This requires the least amount of tabletop and dining room floor space. Platter service, in which the food is delivered to the tables on platters and served in front of the diner, generally requires larger tables and more floor space. Cart service, which is common in Chinese restaurants that serve dim sum, requires the most space since carts must be maneuvered in and around the dining room. (See chapter 8 for more on designing your restaurant space.)

At lower-end restaurants, where service may be so minimal as to resemble a fastfood joint, owners need a high volume of business to make up for the low check averages and often the low gross profit margin that each order generates. Such a restaurant will have relatively low service and décor costs—in part, to be sure that customers are not too comfortable to give up their table to the next waiting customers!

In casual and upscale restaurants where the emphasis is not only on food but also on comfort, seating should be comfortable. The more sophisticated a restaurant is, the nicer its china, silverware, and glassware must be. The better restaurants use real table linen instead of paper napkins. Similarly, the more formal restaurants will require skilled wait staff who may need to know how to properly set out tableware for a fancy French setting or be comfortable talking about upscale menu and bar items. All of these amenities cost money. However, they also allow restaurants to charge more.

CAN YOU HAVE IT ALL?

In certain geographic locations, many casual, moderately priced operations offer table service, takeout, *and* delivery. In very competitive table-service markets, takeout and delivery can contribute substantially to revenues. In fact, indications are that demand for takeout, even from mid-range restaurants, is growing. According to a 2002 National Restaurant Association survey, takeout increased 34 percent between 2001 and 2002 in table service restaurants where the average check was over $25. Six out of ten restaurant operators report that their customers have become more interested in higher quality takeout foods than they were two years ago.

If your business is primarily table service, then takeout and delivery should be limited to your off-peak hours unless your kitchen is staffed and equipped to handle the additional business. Your ability to offer all three levels of service will be greatest when you have a steady predictable flow of business during all hours of operation.

Restaurants that are not designed to handle all three levels of service often end up compromising the quality of food and service offered in their dining room during peak hours. Once you have customers seated in your restaurant, go to great lengths to make sure that the quality of food and service makes them want to come back.

UNIQUE SELLING PROPOSITION

No matter what restaurant type and market segment you choose, chances are that you will face competition. Your challenge will be to convince target customers that your restaurant is a better choice. The best way to do this is to develop a concept that has a strong *unique selling proposition*, or *USP*. Put simply, your USP will set your restaurant apart from your competitors. Because this concept is all too often misunderstood and overlooked, I think it is important to discuss why it is important to the success of your new restaurant.

Economists and marketing experts often classify products as either *homogeneous* or *differentiated*. Homogeneous products are so similar to each other that customers choose mainly based on price. A good example of a homogeneous product is orange juice. Because most brands are perceived as very similar to each other, most sell for the same price in supermarkets, and when one brand goes on sale, customers purchase more of it. Differentiated products, by contrast, are perceived as unique when compared to other similar products; customers develop strong preferences and may even pay more for a favorite item. Cosmetics are a good example of differentiated products, with name brands pulling in much higher prices than generic brands. For example, when I practiced public accounting, one of my clients operated a chain of high-end barber salons that also sold its own brand of private-label shampoos. To my surprise, I discovered that my client and most, if not all, of the other major brands purchased their product from the same contract manufacturers. In most cases, the only differences between these products were the fragrance and

Crafting a Unique Concept

Ann Gentry of Real Food Daily

While living in New York City in the early 1980s and funding my acting dreams waiting tables at Whole Wheat and Wild Berrys, one of the leading vegetarian restaurants in Greenwich Village, I met the cook Roger Leggat who took me to open-air markets and taught me how to select the freshest ingredients and how to treat them in the kitchen. In addition to Roger, some of my best teachers about food were the customers that I waited on. It was around this time that I started to think I could someday open my own restaurant, one that served my own version of vegetarian cuisine.

Still determined to become an actor, I moved to Los Angeles where I expected to find lots of natural foods restaurants. To my surprise, there were only two serving balanced healthful cuisine and one closed shortly after I arrived.

I started taking home cooked meals to the set on my acting gigs. People would taste and love them and request samples. The demand was such that I set up a real kitchen in my apartment. My growing reputation landed me a job as Danny DeVito's private chef while he was acting in and directing *Throw Mama from the Train.*

After my job with Danny ended, I was convinced that there was a market for my food so I started a home delivery service, which grew to over thirty people a day. I was still acting,

the packaging. Yet my client was able to charge a premium because customers saw a perceived value in being associated with that private label.

In reality, few products are truly homogeneous. Most are differentiated in some way. Nevertheless, research has shown that a product that customers perceive to have the greatest difference will develop the greatest demand and the most loyal customer base. Research also shows that customers seeking differentiated products—destination restaurants, for example—are often prepared to travel longer distances, and in some instances, pay more to get them. Think about Hard Rock Café, Chez Panisse in Berkeley, or Commander's Palace in New Orleans.

This brings us to the relationship between how distinctive your restaurant is and the prices you can charge. In the restaurant business, the more homogeneous the concept—burger joints and pizzerias, for example—the more resistant the menu items are to price increases. Fine dining or upscale restaurants, however, can charge more because customers differentiate their products by identity, not by price. This explains why a McDonald's franchisee may have a hard time getting an extra nickel for an order of McNuggets, but an upscale restaurant will have no problem getting an extra five dollars for its pan-seared duck breast. Keep this in mind as you are thinking about your concept; the concept you choose will have a direct impact on the prices you can charge.

but I knew I had to make a choice. I knew I had to do what was giving me such an enormous amount of satisfaction. I gave up acting and immediately started making plans to open my own restaurant serving the vegan dishes I had been perfecting for years. It was around this time that I met my husband Robert Jacobs an experienced retailer who helped me to put together a business plan, and together we made my dream come true.

Although I knew that it might be difficult, I also knew that featuring a vegan menu using organic and locally grown products would set my new restaurant apart from all of the other vegetarian restaurants. I also knew that I had to be just as passionate about running a business as I was about my food and the service I provided to my customers.

When I started talking about my Real Food Daily restaurant idea, so many people said it couldn't be done. "Who would go to a restaurant that serves only plant based cuisine?" they asked. "You should at least put a little fish or chicken on the menu," my well-intentioned friends advised. But, I knew I could prove them wrong. I just knew that there was a market in Los Angeles for my type of food and cooking. I was right, people started coming from day one and more and more are coming fifteen years later.

My restaurants have exceeded my wildest dreams; they are experiencing double digit sales growth every year and attracting a wide diversity of customers. I can safely say that at least half of our customers are not vegetarians or vegans. They are simply well informed customers who want satisfying and delicious food prepared innovatively and creatively with high quality fresh ingredients. They want my version of real food.

Just how different should you be? This will depend on your concept. If you want to open an upscale restaurant in a competitive market, you should strive for something distinctive, since customers seeking gourmet foods and upscale restaurants are typically seeking something out of the ordinary. The more convenience-oriented your concept is, on the other hand, the less your menu will have to stand out. Customers who frequent convenience-oriented, low-priced restaurants are not usually looking for vastly different or unique products, although they will appreciate small specialty items. If you want to open a burger joint, for example, you do not have to reinvent the burger. But you should offer something that will set you apart from other burger joints: lower prices, faster service, or perhaps a USP side-menu item, such as spicy fries (like Arby's curly fries), a special dessert or milk shake (like Wendy's Frosty), or a promotional item (like McDonald's Happy Meals).

Think about how you decide where to eat. How often would you frequent a restaurant that did not offer something that made it special? That element could be a bargain, convenience, food quality, portion size, service, unusual menu items, or atmosphere. Whatever makes your restaurant unique should be something that your target customers can easily recognize and value.

Now that you understand how important it is to differentiate your product, it should be clear that your chances of succeeding will improve greatly if you start out with a good USP. Sadly, most first-time restaurateurs do not think in these terms. They seem to think like Kevin Costner's character in the movie *Field of Dreams*, who built a baseball field in a distant cornfield: "If I build it, they will come."

I should know! I made the same mistake when I opened my first restaurant, Poco Loco. I'll tell you more about that in the next chapter. In the meantime, learn from the poor USP choice made by TropiGrill, a Florida regional chain that tried to expand beyond its customer base to the Northeast—specifically to Long Island suburban communities that were set in their ways and not terribly adventurous in their eating habits.

How will you choose a USP for your restaurant? The first step is to write down, using as few words as possible, why your restaurant concept stands out from your potential competitors. The next step is to find out whether your concept is something that your target customers will value so much that they will choose your restaurant over your competitors. In fact, this brings us to a crucial term as people dine out more and more: *value.*

The perception of a restaurant's value is especially important during economic downturns; restaurants perceived as offering good value for the customer's money are more likely to survive a slump.

But how do you figure out what customers value?

You find out as much as you can about your target market and competitors. Market research will play a big part in determining whether your unique concept will appeal to your customers. This brings us to the subject of the next chapter: your target market, that is, your customers. A good restaurant will never stop asking itself the questions: Who are our customers? Are we doing everything to make them happy?

The odds that your concept will succeed go way up when you understand the demographics of the location you are considering. Your objective is to stack the deck in your favor, and you need information to do that. A proper market study can confirm whether your concept is likely to work in the location you have chosen. Although some restaurateurs have succeeded without thoroughly analyzing their target market, you can be sure that many more have failed because they did not conduct a proper market study. This is not to suggest that you should not start with a hunch or gut feeling, but it is meant to encourage you to follow up your hunch with solid research.

After you have read chapter 3, reread this chapter and ask yourself if the service style that you have in mind is the one that best meets the needs of the customers you want to attract to your restaurant. Will your concept work?

CHAPTER 3

YOUR TARGET MARKET

In 1992, my partners and I opened a sixty-seat full-service restaurant in New York City's Theater District, right near Times Square, with an initial investment of about ninety thousand dollars. The neighborhood demographics were changing for the better and rents were reasonable. To save the headache of starting from scratch, we leased a location where a fully equipped restaurant had gone out of business. At the time, Mexican cuisine was becoming very popular. We thought that if we found a location with the right rent, all we had to do was open a Mexican restaurant and customers would come. We also thought that our food, combined with a kitschy Day of the Dead motif, would be a big attraction for the neighborhood's actors and musicians. In keeping with this theme, we called the restaurant Poco Loco.

Despite our high hopes, we struggled at the beginning. Why? We had a catchy concept, a great neighborhood, good demographics, relatively low costs, and a full kitchen and restaurant all ready to go. We had a lot going for us, except for one crucial thing. We had made the biggest mistake that most first-time restaurant owners make: we had failed to read our market.

My partners and I were not alone in misreading our location on 43rd Street at Ninth Avenue, a 1,900-unit housing complex in the shadow of Manhattan Plaza that looks upscale—perfect, most budding restaurateurs might think. They would think wrong. In reality, Manhattan Plaza is a subsidized housing complex for actors, musicians, and low-income long-time neighborhood residents. In the sixteen years since I began doing business in that neighborhood, I have seen many businesses open and close because their owners did not take the time to investigate the average household income of the housing complex residents or to remember how often the word "struggling" precedes "actor" or "musician." The residents of the surrounding neighborhood were mostly middle- to lower-income baby boomers, empty nesters, and struggling actors with families.

No matter how good or how trendy our food was, the actors who lived nearby could not afford to eat at our place as often as we needed them to if our business was going to thrive. The boomers and nesters had fairly conservative tastes. So did the people who came in from out of town and caught a bite to eat before the 8:00 p.m. shows started. A competitor, who also happened to be a friend, told me as tactfully as possible that theatergoers probably did not want to sit through a three-hour show in a crowded theater after having eaten beans for dinner!

Slowly, we learned. We looked at the menus of our nearby successful competitors and watched who ate at those restaurants. Once we understood who our customers were most likely to be, we went to work. Our first priority was not to lose the customer following we had attracted with our festive atmosphere. But we knew we had to come up with an approach that would appeal to the more conservative neighborhood boomers and theatergoers. At the time, chefs Mark Miller in New Mexico, Dean Ferring in Texas, and Bobby Flay at Mesa Grill in New York were attracting national attention with inventive Southwest cuisine. I set out to research this new trend.

My visit to Mesa Grill reminded me that one of the best parts about the restaurant business is doing research. The food was bold, very tasty, mildly spicy, sophisticated, and beautifully presented. It was so good that I came back again and again for more research. I was thrilled to discover that the atmosphere was lively and that the profile of many of the customers eating there was similar to that of my immediate competitors' customers.

This was it! Switching our concept to Southwest would broaden our market appeal even as it would allow us to keep our existing customer base. More important, we would be the only Southwest-style restaurant in the Theater District, giving us an all-important unique selling proposition.

We changed our name to Zuni. We upgraded our dining room by painting the walls in warm, welcoming reds, oranges, and yellows and reupholstering the furniture in bright colors that complemented the walls. We added whimsical lighting and hung attractive paintings. Finally, we hired a chef who not only was knowledgeable about the cuisine but also had a flare for dramatic presentation. All these details, we knew, would appeal to affluent boomers who go to the theater regularly.

The first sign that we had done the right thing was when more pretheater patrons began filling our tables. Soon, more locals began to eat at our restaurant regularly also. Shortly after that, the press followed with favorable reviews.

The lesson? Your restaurant's concept—its menu range, cuisine, atmosphere, and price structure—should be selected to attract the particular type or types of customers who are most likely to patronize your restaurant (primary target customers).

Your analysis of target customers' needs will help you to decide what type of food to serve and what prices to charge. (We'll talk more about this later in chapter 4.)

This chapter will teach you how to assess your market so you can determine whether there will be enough customers on a regular basis to support your new restaurant *and* the competition. Try not to fall in love with a concept or a location—especially not both at once—before you have completed your market studies.

You will be gathering demographic and lifestyle information. This will give you some indication about your potential customers' eating habits, the types of restaurants they like, the types of food and beverages they prefer, their income levels, and, consequently, the prices you will be able to charge.

Understanding people's eating habits will help you to identify potential regular customers, that is, customers who will come to your restaurant at least three to five times per month. At Zuni, a good 35 to 40 percent of post-theater customers are regulars. The higher the percentage of regulars in your customer base, the more predictable your business will be.

Finally, you will need to assess the competitive environment so you can determine whether the market is saturated, whether your tentative concept is already overrepresented, whether there are population groups or market segments who are underserved by existing restaurants, and whether there is a need for a particular type of restaurant or cuisine in your area.

Don't let the idea of a market feasibility study scare you. Much of the demographic data you need is readily available online, and you can find out some of what you'll need to know just by using your eyes, ears, and common sense.

ANALYZING THE MARKET'S DEMOGRAPHICS

Let's start out with an overview of how to gather the information you need to identify potential customers. The first thing to look at is who lives, works, or visits the city, town, or market area where your restaurant will be located, that is, its demographics. As we have already seen, overall demographic trends in the United States are very favorable for restaurants. Not every single city or location, however, has the right mix of potential customers for every conceivable concept. That's where the homework comes in.

Because markets vary in diversity and complexity, the amount and types of demographic data you will have to gather and analyze will also vary. You should therefore be careful not to generalize when analyzing your data. For example, although studies show that, overall, boomers earning more than fifty thousand dollars per year eat at table-service restaurants more than other demographic groups, this does not mean that urban boomers will have the same spending or eating habits as rural boomers. The average fine-dining check in Biloxi may be fifteen dollars, but in New York or Chicago you're getting away cheap if it's fifty dollars.

The amount of research you will have to do depends on how familiar you are with your market area and how comprehensive you want your research to be. Obviously, the more familiar you are with the market area, the less research you will have to do. Some detail-oriented would-be restaurateurs may prefer to conduct extensive studies, while others may intuitively make assessments based solely on observation. Many successful restaurateurs, in fact, rely mostly on personal observation or on the observations of real estate professionals who live and work in a particular market area. Remember: it is the quality, not the quantity, of information you gather and how you interpret it that will matter. The important thing is to be objective and thorough in your investigation regardless of the method you choose.

IDENTIFYING DEMOGRAPHIC GROUPS

Factors you can use to identify specific demographic groups and potential target customers in your area include the following:

- Average age
- Marital status
- Average disposable income
- Average household size
- Home ownership
- Education level
- Average rent and prices of houses, condominiums, and apartments
- Population trends
- Food and beverage sales
- Major employers and industries

You can get this kind of information from local libraries, chambers of commerce, economic development and city planning offices, local business improvement districts (BIDs), and real estate brokers. Most major U.S. cities provide excellent demographic data on the Internet. In New York City, for example, using census data, the city demographics are broken down into various primary metropolitan statistical areas (PMSAs), each of which is defined specifically according to streets and blocks. An Upper West Side PMSA, for example, could encompass the blocks from 63rd to 72nd streets between Central Park West and Columbus Avenue. The city provides information for each PMSA, including the average income, average rents, the average educational level, and the average number of adults.

Combining this data with relevant psychographics and lifestyle information about various population groups will allow you to draw valuable inferences. For example, if you discover that a large percentage of the population in your target area is made up of males between the ages of eighteen and thirty, an age group that typically includes heavy beer drinkers, this could be a sign that you should think about investing in a bar with a large tap system for your proposed restaurant. Other demographic groups also tend to show restaurant spending patterns:

- Singles and empty nesters eat out more than families with children.
- People eat out more as their income increases.

- Eighteen- to twenty-four-year-olds eat out more often than other groups.
- Households with a working female eat out more than those without.
- A 2002 survey conducted by Madison Direct Marketing found that 82 percent of parents with kids under five eat takeout or delivered meals at home at least three times a week.

If you want to delve deeper, American Express and other major credit card companies sell information about the dining habits of cardholders in a particular zip code, detailing how often a group of potential customers eats out; the average amount they spend for each meal; and the types of restaurants they tend to frequent.

When researching demographic information, use the most current data available, since neighborhood demographics change over time—often dramatically. Understanding your market area's demographic profile will also provide valuable information on the following considerations:

- The types of customers you are likely to attract
- The type of food to serve
- The prices to charge
- Specific and effective marketing and advertising campaigns
- The hours of business and meal periods to serve

You don't have to know exactly how you make these decisions yet, but you should have a rough idea. We'll come back to these decisions in later chapters.

DETERMINING MARKET SATURATION

Good demographic and other market studies can also help you to estimate how many restaurants a market area can support. For example, if the number of restaurant seats in a location seems high compared to its population, the market may well be saturated. (These numbers will vary depending on a particular area's demographics. In other words, an urban area with high incomes and many two-income couples without children would support many more restaurant seats per capita than a lower-income area populated by families.) A saturated market could mean that a new restaurant would have a tough time making a go of it and would be extremely vulnerable if the local or overall economy turned sour.

Think about San Francisco. According to 2002 state and U.S. Census Bureau reports, San Francisco had a density of one restaurant for every 216 residents of the city and surrounding county. This ratio was more than twice as high as in Los Angeles County or the New York metropolitan area, two of the nation's greatest restaurant cities. This restaurant density level was supported by high levels of disposable income generated by the large number of dot-com companies concentrated in the San Francisco Bay Area, business travelers with generous expense accounts, and a robust tourist industry. Sure enough, San Francisco's demographic reality meant that the city's restaurants got hit hard when the dot-com boom turned into an economic bust. The sharp drop in tourism after 9/11 compounded matters. Restaurant receipts fell by 30 percent, and between June 2001 and February 2003, the city lost

161 restaurants, about 4 percent of the total number. Other indicators of a saturated market are high rates of restaurant closings compared to openings and high rates of change of ownership. You can obtain information on restaurant openings and closings from local real estate brokers specializing in restaurants, and from state and local restaurant associations.

Some cities, like Berkeley, California, provide information on whether sales taxes collected from restaurants are rising or falling. Flat or decreasing sales taxes may be an indication of saturation or a slowing local economy. This does not mean that a well-conceived concept in a crowded location will not succeed. After all, we have all seen a new restaurant come along and succeed where others have failed. The key component for success in competitive markets is usually a concept's uniqueness.

CONSIDERING TRANSIENT VERSUS PERMANENT POPULATIONS

In doing demographic studies, it is important to distinguish between an area's *transient population* and its *permanent residents*. The transient population is made up of the total number of people who live elsewhere but come to the area to work, shop, visit various recreation and cultural centers, and attend sports and entertainment events. In New York City, for example, the Theater District attracts millions of visitors every year to attend the many Broadway and Off Broadway plays and shows. Many restaurants in this district, including Zuni, rely on theatergoers—that is, the transient population—for 50 percent or more of their business.

How do you know where to draw the borders of your target market area? This is a tough question, especially if you have a large transient population.

Your answer will partly depend on your chosen *meal period* and your *restaurant concept*. For example, fast-food restaurants and diners draw from small areas for dinner. In busy cities where parking is scarce and expensive and traffic is heavy, the distances that customers are prepared to travel for breakfast or lunch are even shorter. In these cases, the market area may be a matter of blocks, or five to ten minutes' walking distance. Jeff Hunger, vice president of marketing for the Columbus, Ohio-based casual chain Damon's Grill, summed up this point for *Restaurants and Institutions* magazine: "All the research I have shows that the main drivers of lunch traffic are proximity to the restaurant and how long it takes to get in and out."

Interestingly, more specialized restaurant concepts can attract customers from a broader geographical area. For example, customers will travel longer distances to eat at an upscale restaurant than they will to get to a fast-food establishment. According to the National Restaurant Association, a fine-dining establishment can draw customers from as far away as twenty or thirty miles. It is not unusual for residents of Long Island and New Jersey—known to New Yorkers as the "bridge and tunnel crowd"—to travel long distances in heavy traffic to eat at one of New York City's many upscale restaurants. Confirming this phenomenon, the *Oakland Tribune* rates restaurants not by a star system, but by whether or not the reviewer thought that the restaurant was "worth the drive." Four cars indicate that the restaurant was "worth the drive—even if there's traffic," and one car indicates that the reviewer thought that you should "stay parked." By contrast, National Restaurant Association studies show that in most suburban areas, the standard table-service restaurant has a market area encompassing a one-mile radius. Other anecdotal evidence suggests that 60 to 80 percent of a restaurant's customer base lives within a five-mile radius.

THINKING OUTSIDE THE BOX

Chef Tom Valenti got the idea for Ouest, an upscale bistro-inspired restaurant on Manhattan's Upper West Side, while he was chef at Butterfield 81 in downtown Manhattan. After a friend tried to convince him to open a restaurant on the Upper West Side, he started paying attention to Butterfield 81's reservation book. From the telephone numbers, he could tell that a high percentage of guests were coming from the Upper West Side. This bucked the conventional wisdom that the Upper West Side was not a good place for upscale restaurants, and it made him think that his friend was right. "It seemed that maybe the demographics had changed for the better in terms of a want or need for fine dining," he told *Entrée* magazine.

Valenti took an entire year to do his market research, and it paid off. From the time Ouest's doors opened, it was a hit. Since then, more upscale restaurants have followed his lead, and Valenti opened another restaurant in the neighborhood, 'Cesca, which serves Italian cuisine with French and American influences.

BURNING SHOE LEATHER

In addition to doing formal demographic studies, you'll need to burn some good old-fashioned shoe leather. Visit the area or location you're thinking about to observe the traffic volume; the population density; the types of residential homes and the kinds of cars parked in the garages or on the streets in front of them; the types of commercial, retail, and industrial businesses; and the types of restaurants in the area. Visit or eat at as many kinds of restaurants as you possibly can, particularly those that are busy and unique. Collect menus from the restaurants that you visit, and study the price ranges the market is willing to pay for different sorts of restaurants and levels of service.

Some locations, like downtown areas of large cities, may be good for breakfast and lunch but not for dinner, since most people work between the hours of 8:00 a.m. and 5:00 p.m. In some instances, the window of opportunity to do business may be extended if your concept will appeal to people who remain in the area or visit after hours to shop and socialize.

When deciding on the type of restaurant and a price structure, you should examine the local workforce demographics to determine whether customers will have enough disposable income to support your concept. For example, if the proportion of executives to secretarial staff is small, a restaurant that offers more affordable fare will be more appropriate. If you are planning a concept based on breakfast and lunch in a location with a large numbers of corporations, you should find out whether these companies provide in-house cafeterias for their workers.

UNDERSTANDING YOUR CUSTOMER MIX

Let's say that your chosen location is a college town and your primary target customers will be college students. To attract and keep these students as regular customers, your average menu price will have to be low enough that they can afford to eat at your establishment frequently. Your choice of seating and atmosphere should also appeal to students—comfortable and casual. But wait; students will not be your only customers. What about local residents, faculty, staff, visiting parents, and friends? Schools with successful athletic programs and large stadiums will also provide opportunities to cater to sports fans, whether they are coming in for an event or watching it on television with friends.

The key to formulating the concept for your restaurant is understanding your potential *customer mix*: how will you keep your principal customers happy while making sure to satisfy less frequent, but still important, customers? In this case, the goal is to position your concept to appeal to as many different demographic groups and meal periods as possible. In situations like the college town example, you need to understand subtle differences in market demographics, such as tastes at Ivy League and other colleges known for high academic achievement or colleges known for their sports teams. At a big enough campus, there may be enough brainy students *and* enough jocks for each crowd to have its own favorite hangout.

This brings us to another important point about demographics: the bigger the population, the more room there is for you to specialize. For example, in large cities like New York, Houston, and Chicago, the populations are so large and demographically diverse that there is ample room for many different concepts.

SIZING UP YOUR COMPETITION

Once you have a good idea of your market area's overall demographic characteristics and who your potential target customers are—where they live and work; where they are coming from or going to; how old they are; their average incomes; how much they spend on breakfast, lunch, and dinner; and how often they get take out or order delivery—your next goal is to find out the types of food and beverages they like, the sorts of places they like to go to, and the dining atmospheres that make them feel comfortable. The best way to answer these questions is to shop the competition. Sam Walton, founder of Wal-Mart and perhaps the most successful retailer ever, wrote in his autobiography, "I didn't just learn from reading every retail publication I could get my hands on, I probably learned the most from studying what John Dunham was doing across the street." Confirming her husband's focus on shopping the competition, Helen Walton added, "It turned out there was a lot to learn about running a store. And, of course, what really drove Sam was that competition across the street—John Dunham over at the Sterling Store. Sam was always over there checking on John. Always. Looking at his prices, looking at his displays, looking at what was going on. He was always looking for a way to do a better job." Follow this lead and it will work for you too.

If you love food and restaurants like I do, I promise that this will be the most enjoyable part of your market research. Not only will you have a grand old time, you can include these expenses as part of your tax-deductible start-up costs when you finally open your restaurant. Just imagine Uncle Sam subsidizing your enjoyment!

Here are some questions to keep in mind when shopping the competition:

- What is their unique selling proposition, or USP? How will your concept be different enough to appeal to the competition's customers and attract and keep new customers?
- Which restaurants serve the same or similar menu items as yours at similar prices?
- Do your competitors have a full bar, service bar, or no bar at all? (For those with bars, talk to bartenders to find out which foods and drinks are popular.)
- Are competing restaurants formal or casual?
- What do customers like or dislike about the competition's food and ambience? (Eat at these restaurants and talk to the customers. Ask them how often they come and why.)
- What are your competitors' food and service reputations? (Read local newspapers and restaurant guides, like the Zagat Survey, when available, for reviews and read postings on food blogs.)
- How close are competing restaurants to your potential location?
- Are competing establishments easy to find and get to? If applicable, is there enough parking?
- What are atmospheres and decors like at competing restaurants? (You may want to serve similar food at similar prices but in a different atmosphere, or create a unique identity altogether.)
- Is the competition offering fair value for their price?
- What are the occupancy levels of waiting areas and parking lots at competing establishments during the hours you intend to be open? (Long lines are a good sign that there is room for another similar concept in the area.)
- Do your competitors offer delivery or takeout?

The number and types of restaurants you research will depend on your proposed concept. Generally, your potential competition will be made up of primary and secondary competitors. *Primary competitors* are those restaurants near your site that offer similar service styles (takeout and delivery, fast food, or table service), menu items, prices, service level (casual or upscale), and atmospheres and decors. According to the National Restaurant Association, all similar restaurants within a fifteen-minute drive should be considered primary competitors. As we discussed earlier, upscale and destination restaurants tend to have a much wider market area than other concepts.

Secondary competitors are all the other restaurants in your immediate market area, such as diners, coffee shops, takeout shops, or fast-food establishments, particularly those with a similar check average. Interestingly, the January 5, 2004, issue of *Nation's Restaurant News* reported that the National Restaurant Association projected that 2004 quick-service restaurant (QSR) sales would grow more slowly than full-service restaurant sales because QSR operations face stronger competition from grocery and convenience stores as well as from takeout orders from other types of restaurants.

Your competition's proximity will depend on whether your restaurant will be located in a rural, urban, or suburban area. In urban areas, proximity may be measured in terms of city blocks. In suburban and rural areas, where people must use their cars to eat out and shop, it may be measured in miles or the amount of time it takes to travel there. In New York City, where delivery is done either on foot or by bicycle, delivery is typically limited to a ten-block radius. In the suburbs, however, delivery is done by car and may extend several miles. Some years ago when I lived in Norfolk, Virginia, Domino's Pizza was offering no charge for any pizza that was not delivered hot within twenty minutes. Since then, Domino's has expanded to New York City, where it limits its delivery to a ten-block radius or half a mile.

In some instances, your competitors won't be who you think they are. For instance, moderately priced and inexpensive, casual table-service restaurants could compete with other fast food, quick service, and takeout operations, such as coffee shops, diners, and delicatessens for lunch but not for dinner, because lunch is a very price- and time-sensitive meal period. For example, while most people eat dinner out a few times a month, most workers (except for the few who have the time to brown bag it) have to buy lunch every day, with one hour to eat it. The point here is that if you plan to open a casual bistro in a neighborhood with many different types of fast food and other quick-service concepts, chances are your lunchtime competition will not be limited to other table-service restaurants with concepts that are similar to yours.

Whenever possible, try to figure out why successful restaurants are successful and why failing restaurants are failing. It has been said that Sam Walton, Wal-Mart founder, never had an original idea in his life; he simply observed what competitors were doing well, copied it, and did it better. "Sam phoned to tell me he was going to start a wholesale club. It was no surprise. He is notorious for looking at what everybody else does, taking the best of it, and then making it better," observed Bud Walton in Walton's autobiography.

Competitor research will also help you in your search for the right location, which we will cover in the next chapter.

CHAPTER 4

LOCATION, LOCATION, LOCATION

You've heard it before: three of the key requirements for any successful restaurant or retail business are location, location, and ... location. But what makes a good location? Remember: a location is only perfect if you have a concept that will fit your site. How many times have you seen one restaurant concept come along and succeed at the same location where another endeavor had failed? Concept and location are like the chicken and the egg. One or the other has to come first. Market and demographic research will help you to identify the right concept or location, and then the other can follow.

That said, there are some rough guidelines that you can follow in picking your ideal location. Ideally, the best location for a restaurant is one that has a high concentration of potential customers, day and night. This might be a central business district near a residential area, or, say, large parts of San Francisco! Many restaurants, of course, are successful serving just one or two meal periods; you don't have to plan on being open from breakfast through nightcap time. But wouldn't it be nice to know that you could, if you wanted to? In reality, to get such a place, you probably would have to stay open 24/7 to afford the rent! These prime locations attract lots of competitors and tend to be very expensive, that is, *if* they are available. But with the right concept for the neighborhood, that high rent pays off.

Good Concept, Bad Location

Leon Ellis of Moca Bar and Lounge

When I opened my first restaurant in 1994, there was a definite need for a nice, table service restaurant in Harlem—its residents were traveling elsewhere to socialize with family and friends at good restaurants. What's more, there were very few casual yet upscale soul food restaurants in all of Manhattan. I found a location just on the border of the very affluent upper Fifth Avenue neighborhood and decided to open Emily's, a white tablecloth, soul food restaurant. Emily's food concept was based on the great relationship I had with my mother and her love of preparing delicious meals for the family.

The immediate neighborhood was moderate to low income. There were no large business, but there was lots of talk about pending gentrification and development including a bank and an upscale supermarket. I decided to take a chance and get in before the development started. Emily's was well received, favorably reviewed by the *New York Times* and had a small, loyal following. But in the end, to my dismay, there was just simply not enough disposable income in the immediate neighborhood to support a white tablecloth restaurant.

The one aspect of Emily's business that did well was the bar. I noticed that on Thursdays through Saturdays there would always be quite a few urban professionals between the ages of 25 and 55 coming in mostly for drinks. After observing and talking to them

In 1998, I opened a take-out wrap shop in the Times Square area named Wrapsody. The store was 370 square feet at the street level, with 120 square feet in basement space. Rent and utilities were $6,000 per month, and it cost another $150,000 to remodel and equip the space. Why would anyone pay this much rent for such a small space and spend so much money to build it? The answer is simple. It was the quintessential prime location. Because it was central to businesspeople, theatergoers, shoppers, tourists, and local residents living in the many nearby high-rise apartment buildings, there was heavy pedestrian traffic morning, noon, and night, seven days a week. A few months after we opened, business was so good that it was taking up far too much of my time (I wasn't kidding about 24/7!). Shortly after I sold Wrapsody at a nice profit, I ran into the very happy new owner. He told me that he was grossing sixteen thousand dollars per week.

Clearly, prime locations are not for everyone. However, non-prime locations, which boast the significant advantages of low rents and little or no competition, may be ideal for *your* restaurant. In a neighborhood that is on its way up, there's no substitute for being the first in the door. When I opened Zuni in 1992, our rent was $3,500 per month. In more upscale neighborhoods, our rent would have been at least three times as much. At that time, Times Square and most of the areas west of Midtown Manhattan were not very desirable neighborhoods, and at least 20 percent of

over a number of years, I learned that a formal white tablecloth environment was not conducive to drinking, snacking, and relaxing. They said that the presence of tablecloths made them feel that they would have to sit for a full dinner. These customers, mostly Harlem residents, wanted to be in an environment that was upscale, sexy, and nicely designed but less formal and, once again, there weren't any around. That's when the idea for my next venture, Moca Bar and Lounge, was born.

As a member of this demographic group, I had a good idea about their design aesthetic, but I wanted to be sure. I spent the next several months visiting successful lounges all over Manhattan to get design and cocktail ideas.

Although the area around Emily's did not develop the way I hoped it would, other parts of Harlem did. During my years running Emily's, I formed strong relationships with local small business and civic organizations. As fate would have it, a local developer was looking for an upscale restaurant to anchor the corner of his new building on a busy block in Harlem and approached me. We negotiated favorable lease terms and a very generous free rent period to do build-out. My contractor was able to give me the look I was looking for on a tight budget and after 6 months, I opened Moca Bar and Lounge.

Moca is now quite successful, and Harlem has continued to develop and grow. It's a completely different place than it was ten years ago. The demographics have changed dramatically and we now have residents with a lot more disposable income, yet there are still not many nice restaurants and bars. To fill this gap, I have put together a business plan and I am well on the way to opening a much larger version of Moca which I plan to call Chocolat.

the commercial space in the area was vacant. But I had a hunch that the tremendous demand for housing in New York City would soon push development westward—a hunch that I confirmed by attending local community board meetings. Remember the importance of market research? Within two years after we signed the lease, the redevelopment of Times Square started, and the neighborhood began to change. If we had to sign a new lease today, our rent would be approximately $20,000 per month. Fortunately, we signed a long-term lease, which helped us to get our footing while rent was affordable and now adds a tremendous amount of underlying equity to the business.

How do you do find out about future prime locations? Ask local authorities and real estate developers what future developments are planned for a particular market area. Using your intuition, visit and observe neighborhoods that you think may be in transition and talk to residents and small business owners. Look for the emergence of an anchor tenant such as a new housing development or a successful, upscale or unique restaurant. If you choose this third approach, timing will be very important. Study the market closely to determine whether there will be enough potential customers while the neighborhood is still in transition and whether you can create a concept with a strong enough unique selling proposition (USP) to draw people from other neighborhoods. Three well-known examples of restaurateurs who chose non-prime locations are Drew Nieporent with Montrachet in New York City, Paul Kahan with Blackbird in Chicago's Market District, and Thomas Schnetz and Dona Savitsky with Doña Tomás in the Temescal district of Oakland. Not only did these restaurateurs choose locations off the beaten path, their restaurants became instrumental in revitalizing formerly downtrodden neighborhoods. This scenario has been repeated in several cities and towns across the country.

As commercial real estate becomes increasingly expensive in densely populated ethnically diverse suburbs and cities, an interesting development is immigrant restaurateurs choosing strip malls as their location of choice. Because these stores tend to be small with low rents, they are ideal for immigrant entrepreneurs with limited capital to get a start. Strip malls require far less red tape than building in cities, and they have abundant parking. Be aware, however, that mall leases can be full of hidden costs such as percentage rents and high common area charges for maintenance and utilities. (We'll go into more detail on signing a commercial lease in chapter 13.)

One strategy for choosing a location with guaranteed traffic is to select one that is known for its concentration of restaurants before it becomes saturated. This phenomenon is known as *clustering*. In New York, for example, there's Restaurant Row in the Theater District and in the Bay Area there's Chinatown in San Francisco and College Avenue in Berkeley. These locations are known for having a large number and variety of restaurants, which in turn generate heavy traffic. However, in a cluster it's going to be hard to stand out, so a good USP will be important.

Convenience-oriented restaurants like diners and fast-food operations, which rely on heavy volume for profitability and cater to a wide range of customers, may be located almost any place that has high pedestrian or vehicular traffic. On the other hand, trendy upscale restaurants and ethnic cuisine are better suited to large, densely populated urban areas like New York, Chicago, San Francisco, Los Angeles, and other communities with a diverse mix of people and cultures.

Destination restaurants, as mentioned previously, attract people from long distances. Market research shows that these restaurants tend to have the broadest market appeal even though they are not always situated in highly trafficked locations. In fact, a good reason for creating a concept with destination characteristics is that you won't necessarily have to choose a location in a high-rent district. Destination restaurants typically offer one or more USPs. They may have a marquee chef, a celebrity owner, and a reputation for exceptional or unique food, ambience, or people watching. Good locations for destination restaurants include historic buildings or districts, or sites with spectacular views or bucolic surroundings. They also tend to receive heavy media coverage in local and national print publications and on radio and television. Think of Brooklyn's River Café, with its spectacular view of downtown Manhattan; The French Laundry in Yountville, California; or Salt Lick in Driftwood, Texas, a barbecue joint southwest of Austin.

When deciding whether a potential location will work for your restaurant, once you've researched its demographics, evaluate the following factors:

- Access to utilities
- Zoning and codes
- Site visibility and accessibility
- Traffic patterns
- Parking availability

ACCESS TO UTILITIES

Access to utilities is critical for any restaurant. Large urban areas usually have an abundance of electric power and natural gas lines. In rural districts, however, only bottled gas, which puts out 25 percent less heat than natural gas, may be available. Electrical equipment runs on 110-volt or 220-volt single phase, which is not a problem in most locations. However, should you need three-phase 220-volt power lines, you may run into trouble; these are not always readily available, and upgrading your electric service can be very costly. Also be aware that older buildings may need extra lines installed to accommodate your needs.

If you will need to make upgrades, factor this into your budget. You may also be able to negotiate a lower rent or get the owner of the space to cover some or all the upgrade costs. (For more on leases, see chapter 13.)

ZONING AND CODES

Zoning laws vary from city to city and state to state. These can affect the cost and availability of a space dramatically. Before you commit to a space, verify that it is zoned for your specific type of establishment and your desired occupancy levels. Complying with zoning laws can be very costly and time consuming, particularly if you need to get a variance (that is, approval of uses other than those specified by the zoning laws). If you must apply for a variance in order to use a site, you should seriously consider finding another place. Stay away from locations with restrictions on the sale of alcohol unless you do not plan to sell alcoholic beverages and can still make a profit without the contribution of these high-margin menu items.

In addition to local zoning ordinances, you will have to meet fire, health, and building department codes. If you build your new restaurant from scratch or make structural improvements or other improvements costing over a certain dollar amount to renovate an existing restaurant, any work performed will have to pass specific plumbing and electrical inspections from local building and fire departments. You must meet codes such as maximum occupancy limits, proper amount of and placement of fire exits, properly lit exit signs, fire extinguishers, smoke alarms, sprinkler systems, and proper grease extraction and fire suppression systems in the kitchen.

In addition, your facility will have to pass an inspection by the local health department. For example, all equipment and storage racks must be six inches above the floor to allow for proper cleaning. All dishwashing sinks must be NSF (National

Sanitation Foundation) certified, and kitchen and bathroom floors must be tiled. Refrigerators and freezers must maintain specified temperatures and countless other sanitary requirements to help ensure that you will serve safe food and beverages. For this reason, and despite many claims to the contrary, most restaurant kitchens are much cleaner than the average home kitchen.

Complying with all of the state and local rules, codes, and regulations, though frustrating at times, will be well worth it. So hang in there. The best and quickest way to get a license is to familiarize yourself with all the requirements, make sure you meet them, and then hire the right people early in the process to get you through the approval maze.

One of the biggest advantages of buying an existing restaurant, where a license was already established, is that you won't have to go through most of the local zoning and community approval investigations. Chapters 7, 10, and 9 all give specific applications of zoning and code regulations.

SITE VISIBILITY AND ACCESSIBILITY

Assess your site's visibility and accessibility. Visibility to pedestrians and motorists is a free source of advertising. If your restaurant is not in a location where it can be seen easily, you may have to spend more in advertising to attract customers. Ideally, your restaurant should be visible from both sides of the street. Is it on a corner or in the middle of the block? Corner locations are more visible, typically require less signage than those in the middle of a block, and are easier to give directions to. Just try sending someone to "the northeast corner of Fourth and Main," as compared to saying, "It's on Main Street, a few buildings up from Fourth, maybe the third or fourth building." Corner locations have another benefit in that cars almost always have to stop or slow down at intersections and so are more likely to see your restaurant.

The faster the traffic on your street, the more difficult it will be for passing motorists to notice your restaurant. Check to see how visible your proposed restaurant site will be when driving by at the speed limit. While you don't want nearby traffic to be too fast, it shouldn't be too slow, either. Customers need to be able to enter and exit your restaurant easily. Because any interruption in the flow of traffic in front of your business can be disastrous, it is essential to find out whether any major public works projects are pending—say, new highways or road repaving—that may direct traffic away from where you want it to go: straight to your front door!

Ask local trade groups and authorities whether there are restrictions on the types and sizes of signage that will be allowed in your area. If you are considering a location in a historic district or building, prepare to comply with restrictions and deal with nit-picking bureaucrats. Some building owners are very specific about the types and sizes of signage and changes to the facade that they will permit. This may or may not affect how you show off your concept. If your restaurant will offer an upscale, relaxing experience, you probably won't want a large, highly visible neon sign. Instead, you may want the building itself to make your statement.

Even the New York Restaurant Group, which also owns Smith & Wollensky, one of the most successful upscale steak houses in the country, could not overcome poor visibility. Alan Stillman, president of the New York Restaurant Group in Manhattan, learned the hard way that a thin line separates a bad location from an unfamiliar brand name, especially for a restaurant expanding in a new market. Although his Maloney & Porcelli dinner house was very popular elsewhere in the country, he had to close a Washington, D.C., branch after just one year in operation. Although the restaurant had a Pennsylvania Avenue address, it was accessible primarily from the less-traveled Indiana Avenue and thus was hard to see. Customers didn't know it was there.

TRAFFIC PATTERNS

Visibility and traffic patterns go hand in hand. Once you have chosen a potential site, make sure to check it out to avoid Maloney & Porcelli's fate. The volume and patterns of pedestrian and vehicular traffic in front of your proposed site will be good indicators of your potential to attract customers. (Here's a tip: for a quick way to narrow down your search for a heavily trafficked block, look for large national and regional chain stores like The Gap or Eddie Bauer, since they tend to choose high-traffic locations.) Stand at the location and count pedestrian and vehicular traffic at various times of the day, particularly during the hours that you plan to be open for business. Watch the traffic in all directions and on both sides of the street. Who makes up the traffic? Are they office workers, affluent shoppers, factory workers, and event goers?

While you want people to pass in front of your restaurant, you don't want it to be so crowded that people can't get to it. Drive along the routes people will take to and from your proposed site at various times of the day, particularly the times you think will be your peak hours. How long does it take? The shortest distance can take seemingly forever to traverse if traffic is heavy and congested. Is the traffic too jammed to make it convenient to get in and out of your restaurant's parking lot? Again, this will be especially important if your concept stresses convenience and even more so if your main meal period will be breakfast and/or lunch.

If your site will be located near a freeway exit or off a busy highway, take traffic patterns into consideration when deciding which meal periods to target. If you want to target breakfast customers, you should find a location on the inbound side of the road leading into a major metropolitan district or industrial park. For dinner customers, by contrast, choose a site on the outbound side of the roadway. Check how easily traffic can enter and exit highways leading to your restaurant; this will play an important role in determining whether your site will be a success.

The closer you are to the following landmarks, the higher traffic you are likely to see:

- Residential areas
- Shopping centers

- Schools
- Recreational facilities
- Central business districts
- Industrial centers
- Parking facilities
- Mass transportation stops
- Entertainment centers
- Freeway exits

In rural and suburban areas, where residents use their cars to shop and dine out, an increase in traffic counts (the number of cars traveling a street) may be a good indicator that the outlook for restaurant sales is good.

If you are going to prepare a business plan to obtain financing, it is always helpful and often necessary to present third-party lenders with official traffic counts. When available, official traffic counts can also be used to substantiate your own observations. The following are good sources for obtaining local traffic counts:

- Commercial and residential real estate developers
- Local city planning and zoning departments
- Local chambers of commerce
- Local economic development offices
- State transportation departments

PARKING AVAILABILITY

Depending on your concept, geographic location, and the meal times you plan to serve, you should determine whether parking will be adequate, particularly during your anticipated peak hours. If your restaurant will be located in a large, densely populated urban city where taxicabs, parking garages, and public transportation systems are readily available, parking will not be as crucial an issue. However, a location near a commercial parking lot still can be a big advantage for attracting suburban customers. Some of the more upscale restaurants in medium to large cities often provide valet parking utilizing nearby parking garages.

In suburban and rural locations, the more convenience-oriented your concept, the more important it will be to have parking nearby. Office and factory workers in suburban and rural locations looking for a quick breakfast or lunch will need access to fast parking. By contrast, fine dining and casual establishments in both urban and suburban areas rely on off-premise parking, parking in neighborhood streets, and valet parking. That being said, the availability of convenient parking can add significantly to the success of the very time-sensitive lunch and breakfast meal times, even at upscale restaurants.

Some cities require parking plans before they will issue restaurant permits. For example, in Berkeley, California, local ordinances may require large restaurants to provide on- or off-premise parking in order to avoid parking congestion in local neighborhood streets. If a potential restaurateur cannot find the space for enough parking, he or she will not be permitted to open a restaurant in that location.

If you will need to provide parking, your first step should be to investigate local parking ordinances. Most local city ordinances regulate the amount of parking that will be permitted and set a specific size for each parking space, typically 7½ feet by 16 feet for compact cars and 10 feet by 18 feet for larger cars. When calculating your space needs, you should provide for a traffic lane to allow cars to enter and exit the parking lot easily.

If your off-premise parking will be located adjacent to another building, local ordinances will generally require that you get permission and a written agreement from the building owner. *Do not* assume that your patrons will be able to use the parking lots of nearby businesses. Parking lot owners can and do have unauthorized parked cars towed at their owners' cost. If there is a tempting off-site lot nearby that belongs to another business and is likely to result in tickets, see if the owner of the site will allow you to post a sign warning your customers away.

CHAPTER 5

DOLLARS AND SENSE:

A Feasibility Study

Congratulations! You are now ready to determine whether the amount of money, time, and effort that you have to invest in your dream restaurant will be worth it. If you did an objective competitive analysis of your immediate market area and determined that concepts similar to the one you have in mind are so busy that there are long waiting lines, or that there is a need for your concept that is not being met, you can be reasonably confident about your new restaurant's chances of attracting customers. However, you still need to determine whether your projected number of customers times the prices you plan to charge less your costs of food, labor, and overhead will equal a financially viable operation.

To determine whether your operation will be financially viable you need to prepare a pro forma operating budget, also known as a financial plan or financial feasibility study. A pro forma operating budget is a forecast of sales and an estimate of the expenses you will incur in order to produce those sales and generate a profit. Although it will not be 100 percent accurate, a pro forma budget will help you to quantify your market research enough to know whether your odds of succeeding are worth the risk; that is, it will tell you whether your operation is likely to be profitable. It is also the document that you will show to potential investors, enticing them to invest in your restaurant venture. Obviously, the more profit it shows, the more likely you are to attract investors.

In addition to forecasting potential profitability, you can also use a well thought out and objective pro forma operating budget to monitor your operations in the crucial opening weeks and months. You can use it to track ongoing progress by comparing budget projections—your initial estimates of sales and expenses—to actual results, determine whether your operating objectives are being met, and make the proper changes if they are not. You can also use a pro forma operating budget to identify opportunities to improve profits. For example, say your sales volume estimates are just about right, but your targeted food costs are running 5 percent higher than your initial estimates. In this case, you may be able to lower the costs of your menu ingredients and/or increase prices ever so slightly to make up the difference. These adjustments may seem like small changes, but operationally they could make the difference between getting into the black and closing your restaurant's doors. Having good cost controls in place early on will save valuable operating cash flow until you can turn the corner to profitability.

To help put things in perspective as you prepare your financial feasibility study and capital budget, reread chapter 1.

Okay, so let's get started.

ESTIMATING INCOME

Developing a pro forma operating budget is an opportunity to estimate your potential profitability and to create a very useful planning tool. As mentioned at the outset, "Those who fail to plan, plan to fail." The information you use to prepare your pro forma operating budget should come from your market research and analysis, and it should be as comprehensive, objective, and realistic as possible. Obviously, the better your market research, the greater the likelihood of achieving useful results. Combine your research and analysis with a good dose of common sense.

All too often new restaurateurs get carried away with romantic notions of the business and end up preparing pie-in-the-sky financial projections, only to end up with pie-in-the-face results. Some people don't bother to prepare projections; they simply make grandiose assumptions. They start out with a dream only to end up with a nightmare. I can't tell you the number of financial feasibility studies I have seen over the years that had little or nothing to do with reality. Avoid this mistake by estimating your sales conservatively and your expenses realistically and objectively. It is much better to underestimate sales and overstate expenses than the other way around!

FORECAST SALES VOLUME

With your head firmly on your shoulders, the first step in preparing your financial plan is to *forecast sales volume*. Use the information you gathered when researching your target market: your competitors' prices, your USP, market saturation of concepts similar to yours, the spending habits of your target customers, and your seating capacity. (This last one, of course, does not apply if you are planning only takeout and delivery.)

Once you have a reasonable estimate of potential sales factors, complete your forecast of potential sales volume by establishing the following:

1	The days of the week that you will open for business
2	Your hours of operation and the meals you will serve: breakfast only; breakfast and lunch; lunch only; lunch and dinner; dinner only; or breakfast, lunch, and dinner
3	Your estimated average food and beverage check size per customer per meal period
4	Your restaurant's seating capacity or number of seats
5	Your estimated number of customers, or seat turns, per meal period
6	Measurement periods: daily, weekly, monthly, and yearly

You should determine your hours of operation based on your concept, your location, and the demographics of your market and your competition. A good way to gauge your initial hours of business is to look at the hours your immediate competition keeps, combined with your market research, to determine whether there is a need for a late-night bar, early morning breakfast, and so on. (See top of table 5-1 business hours.)

Since you don't have a final menu, gauge your average check size per customer by estimating what prices your target customers are willing to pay for similar food and beverages in a similar type of setting. You should also estimate the average amount each customer will spend for food and beverages respectively at each meal period and at the bar. Your starting point should be other concepts in the area—especially those that will be your immediate competitors—that have similar design, décor, and service elements as well as similar food, menus, and prices. Remember: the goal is not to simply copy your competition's prices, but to assess the competitive pricing environment in your market, that is, to find out what the market will bear. The best way to get estimates of per-person food and beverage check averages is to ask owners, managers, waiters, and bartenders at similar local concepts. You would be surprised how many of them will divulge this information. It may be helpful here to jump ahead and skim chapter 6.

When estimating your restaurant's average check size, it is important to differentiate average checks for each meal period because prices, portion sizes, and customers' eating habits often differ according to the meal period. For example, at Zuni, while we offered the same lunch and dinner menu, the lunch portions were smaller and the menu prices were lower. Similarly, the average check at dinner was higher than at lunch, not only because of bigger portion sizes and higher menu prices, but also because more customers drank alcoholic beverages and ate desserts at dinner. It's really amazing the difference the sale of a few additional desserts and drinks can make in an average check and your bottom line. If your concept will include a bar or lounge, estimate separate average check sizes for food and beverages. Unlike lunch and dinner food and beverage checks, bar and lounge average checks typically remain the same for each meal period.

One way to estimate customer counts is seat turnover. Seat turns are the number of times each seat in your restaurant will be occupied during each meal period. For example, if you served one hundred customers during dinner, and your restaurant had fifty seats, your seat turnover would be one hundred divided by fifty, that is, two.

When estimating customer counts or seat turns, do not assume that your business will experience the same level of business every day, week, and month of the year. When forecasting revenues, it is important to consider seasonal fluctuations and the daily business patterns in your market area.

- **Seasonal fluctuations.** In cities, like New York, many neighborhood restaurants experience a decline in business from mid-July to mid-September, when local residents take vacation and leave town. During your market research, talk to restaurateurs in your area about seasonal fluctuations in their business. Other good sources of information are the local chamber of commerce, the local restaurant association, and local vendors and food and beverage purveyors.

- **Daily patterns of business in your market area.** Different markets or locations have varying patterns of business on different days of the week. Some locations are busier for breakfast and lunch Monday through Wednesday than they are Thursday through Sunday. Similarly, some locations are busier for dinner Thursday through Saturday than they are Sunday through Wednesday, and so on. Again, the patterns of business will vary according to your concept and your market. Studying your competition is the best way to gauge levels of business on different days of the week. This is not only a good way to estimate revenues, but also expenses, since you will schedule staff and food and beverage purchases and deliveries accordingly.

In order to monitor your operations, measure your progress, and make meaningful comparisons of data, you need a financial measurement period. A measurement period can be any period of time that you want it to be. It's important to have both short-term and long-term measurement periods. In the short term, you want to identify both positive and negative trends and respond quickly. In the long-term you want to be able to plan. While short-term pro forma operating budgets are great management tools, they do not take into consideration seasonal fluctuations or other local events, like conventions or festivals, which could influence your business. Also, most investors and lenders will want to see forecasts and projections that cover both short-term and long-term periods.

Use the above factors to prepare a forecast of daily sales volumes by multiplying your estimated food and beverage average check sizes per customer by the number of customers per meal period for each day of the week that you will open for business. For example, if you expect your average lunch food check per customer to be $9 and you are projecting 35 customers for lunch on Mondays, your projected food sales would be $9 times 35 or $315. To arrive at weekly sales, you would simply total the estimated daily lunch, dinner, and bar sales. (See table 5-1.)

COMPARATIVE FORECASTING

To determine the average lunch, dinner, or bar check for any given day, divide the total sales by the number of customers. For example, the average lunch check on Monday would be $350 ($315 plus $35) divided by 35 customers, or $10. While these average numbers don't seem to be very useful now, they will become important later on to track your business and spending trends. For example, if your average check sizes decrease, you should investigate the reasons for changes in your customers' spending habits. Possible reasons could be poor service or customer dissatisfaction with food and beverage quality or portion sizes. You can also periodically compare your average check sizes with those of your nearest competitors to see how competitive your overall prices are.

Once you are up and running, you may want to do daily, weekly, monthly, and yearly forecasting and budgeting, but for your initial pro forma operating budget the most meaningful measurement periods are weekly, monthly, and annually. Weekly and monthly numbers are important because they factor in slow days and busy days in overall successful weeks and months. Also some of your major expenses—such as payroll, rent and occupancy costs, and utilities—are determined and paid weekly and monthly. You may have a few slow days but still generate enough sales by the end of the week or month to pay all of your bills and have some cash left over. After you have estimated a week's activity, you can then project a month's and a year's activity by multiplying by 4.33 and 52 respectively. Why 4.33 you ask? That's because for business purposes, there are actually 4.33 weeks in a month; that is 52 weeks divided by 12 months. Therefore, if you agreed to pay an employee $500 per week, your annual cost for that employee would be $500 times 52 weeks or $26,000 per year. If your calculation were $500 times 4 weeks times 12 months, the result would have been $24,000 per year, or $2000 less on an annual basis. Now try this, $500 times 4.33 weeks times 12 months; the result ($25,980) is much closer to $26,000.

ESTIMATING EXPENSES

Once you have an idea of what your income will be, the next step is to estimate expenses. It is very important to differentiate between fixed and variable costs and to understand the relationship between profits, sales volume, and costs, which help to determine your break-even point. Differentiating between fixed and variable costs will also be required to do your break-even analysis.

Fixed costs, also referred to as overhead, generally remain the same whether your business is open or closed. True examples of fixed costs are rent, insurance, licenses, fees, and loan payments. No matter how busy you are, these costs will remain the same. For example, it is generally not possible to renegotiate rent after a lease has been signed. In the restaurant business, other costs that tend to remain fixed over the short term include trash removal, utilities, managers' salaries, and telephone.

The good thing about fixed costs is that they are predictable. That said, they change over time. For example, most leases will call for annual escalations. Also, periodically you will want to give raises to yourself, your manager, and salaried staff.

Variable costs vary directly with your volume of business. As business volume increases, so will your variable costs and, similarly, when your business volume decreases so too will your variable costs. Examples of variable costs are food, beverages, and labor. For instance, every time you sell a burger you will incur the cost of a hamburger patty, a bun, and so on. You can increase or decrease your food costs by increasing or decreasing portion sizes, changing recipe ingredients, or changing the quality of menu ingredients.

While your manager's salary (this may be your own salary if you do not have a manager) may remain fixed, a certain amount of labor costs may vary with sales volume, most notably service and kitchen staff. During the slow season, many restaurants reduce the number of kitchen and service staff, and then increase them again when business picks up. The number of hours staff work each day, raising or lowering pay rate, or hiring more or fewer skilled or unskilled kitchen staff also change labor costs. That said, a certain level of service and kitchen staff will remain

TABLE 5-1: SAMPLE SALES FORECAST

Assumptions: Seating capacity = 50			
	Lunch	Dinner	Bar
Business hours	12–4	4–10	4–10
Average entrée	$5.00	$13.95	$13.95
Average appitizer	4.00	5.00	4.50
Average dessert	3.50	3.50	3.50
Average beverage	5.00	5.00	5.00
Soft drink/sodas/juices	2.50	2.50	2.50

		Average check	Covers	# of orders	Total sales	TOTAL FOOD SALES	TOTAL BEVERAGE SALES
MONDAY	Lunch		35				
	food	$9.00		35	$315.00		
	beverage	5.00		7	35.00		
	Dinner		45				
	food	17.00		45	765.00		
	beverage	6.00		36	216.00		
	Bar/lounge		30				
	food	8.00		15	120.00		
	beverage	7.00		30	210.00	$1,200.00	$461.00

(continued)

TABLE 5-1: SAMPLE SALES FORECAST (continued)

		Average check	Covers	# of orders	Total sales	TOTAL FOOD SALES	TOTAL BEVERAGE SALES
TUESDAY	Lunch		45				
	food	$9.00		45	$405.00		
	beverage	5.00		9	45.00		
	Dinner		55				
	food	17.00		55	935.00		
	beverage	6.00		44	264.00		
	Bar/lounge		40				
	food	8.00		20	160.00		
	beverage	7.00		40	280.00	**$1,500.00**	**$589.00**
WEDNESDAY	Lunch		50				
	food	$9.00		50	$450.00		
	beverage	5.00		10	50.00		
	Dinner		60				
	food	17.00		60	1,020.00		
	beverage	6.00		48	288.00		
	Bar/lounge		40				
	food	8.00		20	160.00		
	beverage	7.00		40	280.00	**$1,630.00**	**$618.00**
THURSDAY	Lunch		60				
	food	$9.00		60	$540.00		
	beverage	5.00		12	60.00		
	Dinner		85				
	food	17.00		85	1,445.00		
	beverage	6.00		68	408.00		
	Bar/lounge		50				
	food	8.00		25	200.00		
	beverage	7.00		50	350.00	**$2,185.00**	**$818.00**

		Average check	Covers	# of orders	Total sales	TOTAL FOOD SALES	TOTAL BEVERAGE SALES
FRIDAY	Lunch		60				
	food	$9.00		60	$540.00		
	beverage	5.00		30	150.00		
	Dinner		150				
	food	17.00		150	2,550.00		
	beverage	6.00		120	720.00		
	Bar/lounge		80				
	food	10.00		40	400.00		
	beverage	7.00		80	560.00	**$3,490.00**	**$1,430.00**
SATURDAY	Brunch		125				
	food	$11.00		125	$1,375.00		
	beverage	5.00		63	312.50		
	Dinner		150				
	food	17.00		150	2,550.00		
	beverage	6.00		120	720.00		
	Bar/lounge		75				
	food	10.00		38	375.00		
	beverage	7.00		75	525.00	**$4,300.00**	**$1,557.50**
SUNDAY	Brunch		150				
	food	$11.00		150	$1,650.00		
	beverage	5.00		75	375.00		
	Dinner		50				
	food	17.00		50	850.00		
	beverage	6.00		40	240.00		
	Bar/lounge		25				
	food	8.00		13	100.00		
	beverage	7.00		25	175.00	**$2,600.00**	**$790.00**

WEEK TOTALS
Food sales $16,905.00
Beverage sales..$6,265.50
Overall $23,168.50

fixed. Just to stay in business, you are going to need a skeleton crew with a few waiters, cooks, dishwashers, and so on.

Taken together, food, beverage, and labor costs—including payroll taxes (Social Security, Medicare, federal unemployment, and state unemployment) and benefits like workers' compensation insurance—make up the largest portion of total costs of almost all restaurant operations. These costs will usually consume 60 to 65 percent of a typical restaurant's budget. That's the bad news. The good news is that, unlike fixed costs, they can be changed relatively easily. Your ability to manage and control your variable costs while holding your fixed costs steady in the short term can make the difference between profit and loss.

FIXED COSTS

Estimating expenses is not nearly as subjective as projecting sales. In fact, after doing the right homework, you should be able to come up with fairly reliable expense estimates. For example, you can determine fixed costs such as rent and other occupancy costs by talking to local commercial real estate brokers and property owners. You can estimate loan payments, if applicable, by talking to your banker about current interest rates or by looking them up in any major newspaper, such as the *Wall Street Journal*. Once you have the rates, go to www.score.org, click on Business Tools, and then on Loan Amortization Schedule. There you will find a calculator that will help you figure out monthly payments on different loan amounts. Similarly, you can get good estimates of utility costs simply by calling up local utility companies and telling them the number of, type, and size of ranges, ovens, fryers, refrigerators, lighting fixtures, and HVAC systems you plan to use, along with your hours of operation. You could also ask the owner of a local similarly sized operation what their approximate monthly costs are. Better still, if you plan to take over a closed restaurant operation or buy an existing one, the local utility company can provide estimates of the previous tenant's average bills by season.

Estimates of other fixed expenses such as trash removal, telephone, extermination, insurance, licenses, and fees are all easily obtainable by making a few phone calls to the respective brokers and service providers. Accountants or lawyers with restaurant experience can estimate licensing and fee expenses. Many will eagerly provide these estimates at no charge if they think they have a chance of picking up a new client!

VARIABLE COSTS

Estimating food and beverage costs, which are variable expenses, can be tricky since at this stage you probably have not developed a final menu. The best approach is to select a food and beverage cost percentage that is reasonable and consistent with other similar successful local concepts. For these estimates, ask your local restaurant association or an experienced local accountant with similar restaurant clients, or construct a hypothetical menu and price it out. Avoid using national estimates; ingredient prices vary widely from state to state and from season to season.

To estimate weekly payroll, your other major variable expense, use your projected daily and weekly sales forecast to prepare a labor schedule. On your projected busy days, schedule more kitchen and server hours, and likewise on projected slow days schedule fewer. The number of staff required and therefore labor hours will vary with your concept. To get some ideas about staffing levels, ask owners of local restaurants that are similar in size and concept, or talk to a local consultant. You can obtain estimates of pay rates by calling local restaurant employment agencies or by talking to other local restaurateurs (see table 5-2). To estimate your payroll taxes and benefits, you can have your accountant do it based on your manpower schedule, you can do it yourself using a good bookkeeping software package such as Quick-Books, or you can have a payroll processing company do it for you. Many payroll companies will provide these estimates in return for the chance at winning your business. Information about payroll tax and benefit rates is usually available form local restaurant associations. Most towns have business advisory centers that will provide this information. A good source for this type of information, and for help preparing operating budgets, is www.score.org, the website for the Service Corps of Retired Executives (SCORE), which provides free training and one-on-one counseling. A big mistake many first-time owners make is failing to estimate payroll taxes, which can add an additional 12 to 14 percent to payroll costs depending on the state.

Many first-timer restaurateurs leave their personal salaries out of their projections. They usually assume that they will get paid when their business makes money. Do *not* do this. Plan for your own success. As an owner, your time, effort, and hard work should be rewarded with a reasonable weekly or monthly salary. Besides, if you show banks or investors a pro forma that does not include your salary, they will want to know why.

Estimates of other types of variable costs such as laundry and linen, cleaning supplies, paper supplies, tableware, glassware, and flatware replacement—will vary according to concept and volume levels. Again, with determined homework these can be estimated fairly accurately. For laundry, linen, and paper supplies, ask local providers for guesstimates based on your weekly estimated number of customers. For tableware, glassware, and flatware, talk to owners or managers of restaurants that are a similar size and type or an experienced restaurant accountant or consultant in your area. Do the same for cleaning supplies. The local municipal authority usually bills water and sewer charges. To get estimates, ask operators of similarly sized establishments or the local authority. In some towns and cities, the water and sewer fee is included in rent and occupancy charges. Obviously, if your concept is fast food or takeout and delivery, items such as laundry, linen, glassware, and so on would not apply, but you will probably have fairly hefty paper supplies costs. If you plan on accepting credit cards, don't forget to include a variable cost line item for credit card processing fees. Credit card companies take a small percentage of each sale as a fee. As of this writing, American Express charges around 4 percent and Visa and MasterCard charge between 1.5 and 2 percent.

Use the following I.R.S publications for help with payroll expenses: *Tax Guide for Small Business* (Publication 334); *Employee's Daily Record of Tips and Report to Employer* (Publication 1244); *Reporting Tip Income* (Publication 531); *Tips on Tips— A Guide to Tip Income Reporting for Employees in the Food and Beverage Industry* (Publication 1872); and *A Guide to Tip Income Reporting for Employers in the Food and Beverage Industry* (Publication 1875).

DEPRECIATION EXPENSES

An expense that deserves special mention is depreciation. It is an unusual expense because it does not require an actual cash outlay. Instead, it is what accountants call a cost-allocation expense, since it takes the cost of equipment, furniture, and building improvements and allocates them over a number of years. By law, namely the IRS, you can depreciate different types of equipment and tenant improvements over different periods of time. For example, if your equipment cost is twenty thousand dollars and the applicable depreciation period is ten years, then you would deduct two thousand dollars in depreciation expense on your income statement and on your taxes every year for the next ten years, even though you would not have actually spent two thousand dollars on equipment each of those years. This is a complicated expense, so the best thing to do is have an accountant help you with the calculation.

CALCULATING YOUR PROFIT OR LOSS

This is where the rubber hits the road. Remember, the primary reason to open and run any business, not just a restaurant, should be to make a profit. Profit is what's left over from sales after paying all of your fixed and variable expenses. For example, after you have compiled all of your figures and checked them twice, the next step is to subtract estimated total variable and fixed costs from estimated total sales; the difference will be your profit or loss. If the net result is zero, a negative number, or a very low number and your sales projections were conservative and your cost estimates were objective and realistic, then your restaurant idea is not likely to be financially viable and you should not pursue it.

This is probably not what you wanted to hear, but that is why it's called a feasibility study; it's meant to determine whether your idea is feasible! Besides, to the extent that your research is thorough and your sales and expense estimates are realistic and objective, why would you want to take the risk if the results are unprofitable? That said, you may want to revisit the sales and the food, beverage, labor, and rent and occupancy costs in your pro forma. Check to see if you could realistically increase your prices and still be competitive. As mentioned earlier, food, beverage, and labor costs consume 60 to 65 percent of a typical restaurant's budget. Review these costs to see if you can reasonably lower them without significantly altering your concept. For rent and occupancy costs, consider looking for less expensive space in the same neighborhood. Rent and occupancy cost is a major fixed cost for most restaurants. A quick way to review these costs and other fixed and variable costs is to do a break-even analysis, which we will get to a little later. If your review does not yield satisfactory results, your only option at this point is to go back to the drawing board, do more market research, and try to identify another concept that is unique and will generate more sales or will be less costly to operate. That's the bad news; the good news is you already have done quite a bit of the necessary marketing research for your original concept.

If, though, you end up with a number that shows your idea is a winner the potential profits convince you that your restaurant will be worth your time, effort, and money and/or will attract investors—then you are ready to figure out how much capital you will need to make your restaurant a reality! For example, if your restaurant will cost $290,000 to open and if your pro forma shows $100,000 in net profits the first year, this amount may be enough to attract potential investors and lenders since it suggests a good return on their investment. To calculate return on investment, simply divide the net income by the total amount invested. (See table 5-3.)

However, you won't know the potential return on your investment until you have prepared an objective and conservative capital requirements budget. A capital requirements budget is the budgeted amount of capital (money) that will be required to open your restaurant. We will talk more about preparing a capital budget later in this chapter. For example, assume that your capital budget shows that your restaurant is going to cost $290,000. (See table 5-5). Assume also that you will require $240,000 of investor capital; you are going to invest the other $50,000 of your own money. Now further assume as shown in table 5-3, that your pro forma shows a net income of $125,963 in your first year of operation; you will pay $100,963 to your investors, and in addition to your salary of $75,000 you will keep the other $25,000 as your share of the profits. In this scenario, investors' return on investment after the first year of operations would be $100,963 divided by $240,000, or 42 percent. By any standard, that's a very attractive return and would increase your probability of attracting investors.

Obviously, if your restaurant continued to generate such good profits you would want to either keep a larger share of the net profits for yourself or increase your salary, *after* the investors get back their $240,000. At $100,963 per year, it would take about two and a half years for them to get their investment back. In fact, a good strategy for attracting investors is to do exactly this. If investors know that you plan to give priority to returning their investment (money) quickly, they would be more likely to invest. However, after returning their initial investment you should plan to continue to give them a good return on their investment. They deserve it, they took a risk on you! Because restaurants are seen as risky investments, most restaurant investors other than close family and friends look for a return on investment of at least 25 percent. That said, some investors looking to experience the "romantic" or "feel good" aspects of the business might settle for a lesser return.

There are many ways to distribute profits between you and your partners. Profit distribution is out of the scope of this book, but your attorney or your CPA will help you to structure an equitable deal that makes financial sense. Details on the distribution of net profits, would then be spelled out in your partnership, corporation, or LLC agreement. In chapter 12, we discuss these various forms of business.

TABLE 5-2: LABOR SCHEDULE AND COSTS

		HOURS	covers	HOURS	covers	HOURS	covers	HOURS	covers
	Lunch/Brunch		35		45		50		60
	Dinner		45		55		60		85
	Bar		30		40		40		50
	JOB TITLE		MON		TUES		WED		THURS
Kitchen staff	Chef		off		10 a.m.–8 p.m.		10 a.m.–8 p.m.		10 a.m.–8 p.m.
	Sauté/prep cook # 1	8	8 a.m.–4 p.m.	0	off	0	off	8	8 a.m.–4 p.m.
	Grill/prep cook # 1	8	10 a.m.–8 p.m.	8	8 a.m.–4 p.m.	8	8 a.m.–4 p.m.	0	off
	Pantry/prep cook # 1	8	8 a.m.–4 p.m.	0	off	0	off	8	8 a.m.–4 p.m.
	Dishwasher/ porter # 1	8	8 a.m.–4 p.m.	8	8 a.m.–4 p.m.	8	8 a.m.–4 p.m.	8	8 a.m.–4 p.m.
	Dishwasher/ porter # 3	7	4 p.m.–11 p.m.	0	off	0	off	0	off
	Pantry/prep cook # 3	6	4 p.m.–10 p.m.	8	8 a.m.–4 p.m.	8	8 a.m.–4 p.m.	7	4 p.m.–11 p.m.
	Sauté/prep cook # 2	6	4 p.m.–10 p.m.	7	4 p.m.–11 p.m.	7	4 p.m.–11 p.m.	0	off
	Grill/prep cook # 2	0	off	7	4 p.m.–11 p.m.	7	4 p.m.–11 p.m.	7	4 p.m.–11 p.m.
	Pantry/prep cook # 2	6	4 p.m.–10 p.m.	7	4 p.m.–11 p.m.	7	4 p.m.–11 p.m.	7	4 p.m.–11 p.m.
	Dishwasher/ porter # 2	0	off	8	4 p.m.–12 p.m.	8	4 p.m.–12 p.m.	8	4 p.m.–12 p.m.
TOTAL		**57**		**53**		**53**		**53**	
Servers (lunch)	Busser	5	11 a.m.–4 p.m.	5	11 a.m.–4 p.m.	5	11 a.m.–4 p.m.	5	11 a.m.–4 p.m.
	Server	5	11 a.m.–4 p.m.	5	11 a.m.–4 p.m.	5	11 a.m.–4 p.m.	5	11 a.m.–4 p.m.
	Server	4	11 a.m.–3 p.m.	4	11 a.m.–3 p.m.	4	11 a.m.–3 p.m.	4	11 a.m.–3 p.m.
	Server								
Servers (dinner)	Server	6	4 p.m.–10 p.m.	7	4 p.m.–11 p.m.	7	4 p.m.–11 p.m.	7	4 p.m.–11 p.m.
	Server	5	4 p.m.–9 p.m.	6	4 p.m.–10 p.m.	6	4 p.m.–10 p.m.	6	4 p.m.–10 p.m.
	Server								
	Busser								
	Busser	6	4 p.m.–10 p.m.	7	4 p.m.–11 p.m.	7	4 p.m.–11 p.m.	7	4 p.m.–11 p.m.
TOTAL		**31**		**34**		**34**		**34**	
	Bartenders	7	4 p.m.–11 p.m.	7	4 p.m.–11 p.m.	7	4 p.m.–11 p.m.	8	4 p.m.–12 p.m.

HOURS	covers 60 / 150 / 80 FRI	HOURS	covers 125 / 150 / 75 SAT	HOURS	covers 150 / 50 / 25 SUN	TOTAL HOURS	pay rate	total cost	
	10 a.m.–8 p.m.		10 a.m.–8 p.m.		off		N/A	Salaried	
8	8 a.m.–4 p.m.	8	8 a.m.–4 p.m.	8	8 a.m.–4 p.m.	40	$11.00	$440.00	
0	off	8	8 a.m.–4 p.m.	8	8 a.m.–4 p.m.	40	$10.00	$400.00	
8	8 a.m.–4 p.m.	8	8 a.m.–4 p.m.	8	8 a.m.–4 p.m.	40	$9.00	$360.00	
0	off	0	off	8	8 a.m.–4 p.m.	40	$7.00	$280.00	
8	8 a.m.–4 p.m.	8	8 a.m.–4 p.m.	6	4 p.m.–10 p.m.	29	$7.00	$203.00	
0	off	7	4 p.m.–11 p.m.	0	off	36	$9.00	$324.00	
7	4 p.m.–11 p.m.	7	4 p.m.–11 p.m.	6	4 p.m.–10 p.m.	40	$11.00	$440.00	
7	4 p.m.–11 p.m.	6	4 p.m.–10 p.m.	6	4 p.m.–10 p.m.	40	$10.00	$400.00	
7	4 p.m.–11 p.m.	0	off	6	4 p.m.–10 p.m.	40	$9.00	$360.00	
8	4 p.m.–12 p.m.	8	4 p.m.–12 p.m.	0	off	40	$7.00	$280.00	
53		60		56		385		$3,487.00	(1)
5	11 a.m.–4 p.m.	5	11 a.m.–4 p.m.	5	11 a.m.–7 p.m.	35	$5.00	$175.00	
5	11 a.m.–4 p.m.	5	11 a.m.–4 p.m.	5	11 a.m.–4 p.m.	35	$5.00	$175.00	
4	11 a.m.–3 p.m.	5	11 a.m.–4 p.m.	5	11 a.m.–4 p.m.	30	$5.00	$150.00	
		5	11 a.m.–4 p.m.	5	11 a.m.–4 p.m.	10	$5.00	$50.00	
7	4 p.m.–11 p.m.	7	4 p.m.–11 p.m.	5	4 p.m.–9 p.m.	46	$5.00	$230.00	
6	4 p.m.–10 p.m.	6	4 p.m.–10 p.m.	5	4 p.m.–9 p.m.	40	$5.00	$200.00	
6	4 p.m.–10 p.m.	6	4 p.m.–10 p.m.			12	$5.00	$60.00	
5	4 p.m.–9 p.m.	5	4 p.m.–9 p.m.			10	$5.00	$50.00	
7	4 p.m.–11 p.m.	7	4 p.m.–11 p.m.	5	4 p.m.–9 p.m.	46	$5.00	$230.00	
45		51		35		264		$1,320.00	(2)
9	4 p.m.–1 a.m.	9	4 p.m.–1 a.m.	5	4 p.m.–9 p.m.	52	$5.00	$260.00	(3)

TOTAL WEEKLY PAYROLL (1) + (2) + (3) $5067.00

TABLE 5-3: PRO FORMA OPERATING BUDGET

	Weekly	Monthly	Annually	% of sales
REVENUES				
Estimated food sales	$16,905.00	$73,198.65	$878,383.80	73%
Estimated beverage sales	6,263.50	27,120.96	325,451.46	27%
Total sales	23,168.50	100,319.61	1,203,835.26	100%
Food cost (30%)	5,071.50	21,959.60	263,515.14	22%
Beverage cost (20%)	1,252.70	5,424.19	65,090.29	5%
Cost of sales (1)	6,324.20	27,383.79	328,605.43	27%
Gross profit	**16,844.30**	**72,935.82**	**875,229.83**	**73%**
FIXED OPERATING COSTS				
Rent/occupancy	$1,847.58	$8,000.00	$96,000.00	7.97%
Utilities	692.84	3,000.00	36,000.00	2.99%
Telephone	57.74	250.00	3,000.00	0.25%
Advertising	115.47	500.00	6,000.00	0.50%
Insurance	96.23	416.67	5,000.00	0.42%
Exterminator	34.64	150.00	1,800.00	0.15%
Chef/kitchen manager	961.54	4,163.46	50,000.00	4.2%
Owners salary	1,443.42	6,250.00	75,000.00	6.2%
Manager	750.00	3,247.50	38,970.00	3.2%
60% kitchen and service wages	3,040.20	13,164.07	157,968.79	13.1%
Payroll taxes	743.42	3,219.00	38,628.04	3.2%
Workers' compensation insurance	309.76	1,341.25	16,095.02	1.3%
Licenses and fees	69.23	300.00	3,600.00	0.3%
Trash/garbage hauling	173.08	750.00	9,000.00	0.75%
Fixed costs (3)	**10,335.14**	**44,751.95**	**537,061.85**	**45%**

	Weekly	Monthly	Annually	% of sales
VARIABLE OPERATING COSTS				
Repairs and maintenance	$92.31	$400.00	$4,800.00	0.40%
Water and sewer	57.69	250.00	3,000.00	0.2%
Credit card charges	347.53	1,880.99	22,571.91	1.9%
Cleaning supplies	250.00	1,082.50	13,000.00	1%
Laundry	200.00	866.67	10,400.00	1%
Paper supplies	100.00	433.33	5,200.00	0.4%
Tableware and glassware replacement	50.00	216.67	2,600.00	0.2%
Miscellaneous	100.00	433.33	5,200.00	0.4%
40% kitchen and service wages	2,026.80	8,782.80	105,393.60	9%
Payroll taxes	243.22	1,053.94	12,647.23	1%
Workers' compensation insurance	101.34	439.14	5,269.68	0.4%
Social security and medicare tip taxes	305.24	1,321.71	15,872.74	1%
Variable costs (2)	**3,874.13**	**17,161.08**	**205,955.16**	**17%**
Operating profit before depreciation	$2,635.03	$11,022.79	$132,212.82	13.5%
Depreciation (4)	120.19	520.43	6,250.00	
Net income	2,514.84	10,502.36	125,962.82	10.5%
Investment in restaurant (table 5-5)			290,000.00	
Overall return on investment			$\frac{125,962.82}{290,000.00}$	43%

CALCULATING YOUR BREAK-EVEN POINT

Once you have completed your pro forma operating budget and your profit-and-loss statement, your next step is to do a break-even analysis. As you might suspect, break-even is the point at which your total sales and expenses are equal, meaning there is no profit or loss. By doing a break-even analysis, you will be able to determine the daily sales level your restaurant would need to achieve to break even or, put another way, before you can make your first dollar of profit. A break-even analysis will also help you to make "what if" decisions without having to redo your entire pro forma statement. (See the following section for examples of "what if" scenarios.)

A full and complete discussion of break-even and cost, volume, and profit analysis is outside the scope of this book. However, you can use the following formula to calculate your break-even point:

Break-even point equals total fixed costs divided by (one minus variable costs as a percentage of sales). See formula in table 5-4.

Don't worry about the math supporting this formula; just use it and it will work magic for you.

Using the pro forma operating budget from table 5-3, you are now ready to calculate weekly, monthly, and yearly break-even sales points. See table 5-4. The following walks you through a weekly sample calculation.

1	Total fixed costs are made up of the fixed operating costs of $10,335.14 plus the depreciation expense of $120.19 for a total of $10,455.33
2	Total variable costs are made up of the cost of sales of $6,324.20 plus the variable operating costs of $3,874.13 for a total of $10,198.33.
3	Variable costs as a percentage of sales is calculated by dividing the total variable costs by the total sales, or $10,198.33 divided by $23,168.50 equals .44, or 44 percent.
4	One minus variable costs as a percentage of sales (the contribution rate) is one minus .44, or .56.
5	The weekly break-even sales is the total fixed costs divided by the contribution rate, or $10,198.33 divided by .56, which equals $18,676.26.

To determine the monthly break-even sales point, divide the monthly total fixed costs by the contribution rate (one minus the monthly variable costs as a percentage), or $45,272.38 ÷ .56 = $81,429.47. In this example, the yearly break-even point is $543,311.85 ÷ .56, or $977,263.89.

To determine your daily break-even point, simply divide your weekly break-even sales by the number of business days each week, which in this case is seven. The daily break-even sales in this example, therefore, is $18,676.26 ÷ 7 = $2,668.04.

This means that before you can make *a single dollar of profit* at the current projected sales and operating costs levels, your restaurant would need to have average sales of $2,668.04 each day. You could also divide monthly break-even sales by thirty days and yearly break-even sales by the number of days you will be open each year to arrive at daily break-even sales.

DOING "WHAT IF" SCENARIOS AND SPOTTING POTENTIAL PROBLEMS

According to the sample pro forma (see table 5-3), weekly sales are $4,492.24 above breakeven (total sales minus the weekly break-even point, or $23,168.50 minus $18,676.26), and prospects are looking good for this new restaurant, but what if projected sales are lower than break-even sales? If that were the case, it could mean any of the following:

- Your prices are too low
- Your fixed costs are too high
- Your variable costs are too high
- Your concept may not be a fit for the market

By simply plugging in different amounts of sales and fixed and variable costs into your break-even formula, you will quickly see what level of sales are required to break even and make a profit. For example, let us assume that the person in the example missed the opportunity to get their lease at $8,000 per month, but a larger corner location became available at $10,000 per month. Here's how to figure a new weekly break-even: $10,4555.33 (total fixed costs) + $2,000.00 = $12,455.33; $12,455.33 (new total fixed costs) ÷ .56 = $22,241.66.

In other words, to cover the additional $2,000 in rent and still make the original weekly profit number of $2,514.84 (net income), weekly sales would have to increase by $3,565.40 ($22,241.66 [new break-even point] minus $18,676.26 [previous break-even point]).

Similarly, what if, instead of having to pay additional rent the person in the example was able to reduce variable costs from 44 percent to 41 percent? In this case, the new variable cost percentage would be .41, and the new weekly break-even point would be $10,455.33 ÷ (1 - .41), or $10,455.33 ÷ .59 = $17,720.98. The savings would be $18,676.26 (previous break-even point) - $17,720.98 (new break-even point) = $955.28 less per week.

With a slight modification to the break-even formula, you will also be able to calculate the level of additional sales necessary to generate a certain amount of profit. The modified formula that you would use is as follows: (total fixed costs plus profit) ÷ 1 - (cost as a percentage of sales) = desired sales.

Let's assume that in order to attract a certain group of investors the sample restaurant must show annual net profits of $200,000 instead of $125.962.82. To determine the first year's required amount of sales, the calculation would be:

$$\frac{\$543,311.85 + \$200,000 \text{ [or } \$743,311.85]}{1 - .44 \text{ [or .56]}} = \$1,327.342.50$$

TABLE 5-4: BREAK-EVEN ANALYSIS

	Weekly	Monthly	Yearly
VARIABLE COSTS			
Costs of sales (1)	$6,324.20	$27,383.79	$328,605.43
Variable costs (2)	3,874.13	17,161.08	205,955.16
Total variable costs	10,198.33	44,544.87	534,560.59
FIXED COSTS			
Fixed costs (3)	$10,335.14	$44,751.95	$537,061.85
Depreciation (4)	120.19	520.43	6,250.00
Total fixed costs	10,455.33	45,272.38	543,311.85
Break-even formula	$$\frac{\text{fixed costs}}{1 \text{ minus variable costs as a \% of sales}}$$		
Variable costs as a % of sales	$$\frac{\text{total variable costs}}{\text{total sales}}$$		
Variable costs as a % of sales	$$\frac{10,198.33}{23,168.50}$$	$$\frac{44,544.87}{100,319.61}$$	$$\frac{534,560.59}{1,203,835.26}$$
Variable costs as a % of sales	44%	44%	44%
1 minus variable costs as % of sales or (1 – .44)	56%	56%	56%
Break even	$$\frac{10,455.33}{56\%}$$	$$\frac{45,272.38}{56\%}$$	$$\frac{543,311.85}{56\%}$$
Break even	18,676.26	81,429.47	977,263.89

TABLE 5-5: SAMPLE CAPITAL REQUIREMENTS BUDGET

First month's rent	$8,000	Pots, pans, and cooking utensils	$3,500
Rent security	16,000	China, glassware, silverware, etc.	5,500
Utility deposits	3,000	Logo, menu, and awning design	3,500
Architect's fee	8,000	Initial insurance	4,500
Permits (plumbing, fire, health)	1,500	Opening food inventory	3,000
Liquor license	10,000	Opening beverage inventory	2,500
Attorney	5,000	Opening cleaning supplies	1,000
Renovations, design, and décor	100,000	Opening payroll	10,000
Furniture and fixtures	25,000	POS system	20,000
Kitchen and bar equipment	20,000	Working capital	40,000

TOTAL: $290,000

In other words, in order to show net profits of $200,000, your annual sales would have to increase from $1,203,835.26 to $1,327,342.50 or an increase of $123,507.30.

With your pro forma operating budget and break-even analysis in hand, you are now ready to prepare your capital budget, but first, let me give you one caveat. It is very important to recognize that projected sales and expenses seldom match actual results in the first few weeks and months of operation. Sales often take a few months to build to your projected levels. Meanwhile, all of your fixed costs and some of your variable costs will be running from day one. With this understanding you can plan your capital requirements budget accordingly, particularly your working capital. Working capital, is extra capital, a reserve fund if you wish, to meet any unforeseen expenses and to keep the business afloat during the early months until it becomes profitable.

ESTIMATING CAPITAL REQUIREMENTS AND ESTABLISHING A BUDGET

Now we've finally gotten to a would-be restaurateurs' favorite question: how much does it cost to open a restaurant? Once you've got numbers showing that you have a viable concept, the next step is to estimate how much capital (money!) you will need to open your restaurant.

The way to do this is to prepare a *capital requirements budget*. It is critically important that this budget is as accurate and realistic as possible, particularly if you plan to get loans or investor capital. Having to go back to lenders and investors for additional capital will quickly erode their confidence in you.

Lacking a realistic budget or preparing a budget and not sticking to it are among the most common reasons for early restaurant failure. It is easy to get carried away with your dream and underestimate start-up and build-out costs. For example, when we opened our first restaurant, our unrealistic dream budget was $30,000 short. A better example can be seen in the 2003 documentary film *Eat This New York*, which is about the travails that faced starry-eyed John McCormick and Billy Phelps, who left Minneapolis to open a restaurant in New York City. Their pain, anguish, and frustrations illustrate the horrors of underestimating start-up costs. To their credit, and despite the film's ominous warning about restaurant failures, John and Billy stuck with it and realized their dream of owning a successful neighborhood café in New York. The moral of the story is, what is now a successful restaurant could easily have been a disaster due to lack of poor budgeting. This mistake is common, even among seasoned veterans.

Your goal is to prepare a realistic capital budget that will allow you to open your restaurant with a minimum of heartaches and hassles and on time. Being on time is almost as important as being on budget since most of your fixed costs—rent, insurance, and loan payments—will continue to run while you're setting up even if you're not ready to open. Delays in your restaurant opening will also result in a loss of business, particularly if you will be operating in a seasonal market and plan to catch the high season.

The best way to avoid early cash flow problems is to include a contingency or allowance in your budget to cover capital cost overruns and/or construction delays. The budgeted amount for contingencies will depend on the size of your restaurant and the scope of the work to be done. The recommended amount is an additional 20 percent of your final budget.

Use the following checklist as a guide when preparing your preliminary capital budget (see table 5-5 for an example of a capital requirements budget):

- Rent and rent security deposits (realtor)
- Design, décor, and layout fees, if necessary (architect, engineer, contractor)
- Construction costs, *including taxes and delivery charges of materials* and, where applicable, compliance with Title III of the Americans with Disabilities Act of 1990 (contractor)
- Legal, accounting, and other professional fees related to the following (accountant or attorney):
  - Negotiating a lease
  - Registering a legal and DBA name
  - Obtaining federal and state identification numbers and state and local sales tax identification numbers
  - Drawing up partnership and shareholders agreements if necessary
  - Obtaining business permits, such as building permits, fire department permits, health permits, and liquor licenses
  - Paying the actual cost of all permits
- Liquor license cost (state liquor authority)
- Insurance premiums for the following (insurance broker):
  - Workers' compensation
  - General liability
  - Liquor liability
  - Fire
  - Flood
  - Business interruption
  - Burglary
  - Contents
  - Sprinkler damage
- Furniture, fixtures, and equipment costs, *including taxes, delivery, and installation*, such as the following (vendors and contractors):
  - Kitchen equipment
  - Dining room furniture
  - Bar furnishings
  - Point-of-sale systems and other computer and related software
  - Utility deposits (utility companies)
  - China, glassware, flatware, and kitchen utensils, *including taxes and delivery* (vendors)
  - Opening inventory of food, beer, and wine (vendors,)

- Designing and printing menus costs (professional printers or your own computer and printer)
- Opening payroll and related payroll taxes (an accountant or your own estimate)
- Initial marketing and promotional expenses (professional, local PR firm, or yourself)
- Working capital: extra capital to meet any unforeseen expenses and to keep the business afloat during the early months until it becomes profitable; this should be a minimum of three months' worth of fixed costs (from your pro forma statement; see table 5-3)

NOW WHAT?

If your feasibility study and break-even analysis show that your concept is a winner, the next step is to decide whether you have the financial resources to open a restaurant yourself or whether you will need to borrow money or get investors. If you need a loan or investment capital, prepare a business plan (which should include your pro forma profit-and-loss statement, break-even analysis, and your capital requirements budget) and shop it to banks and investors. (See chapters 12 and 13.)

Having gotten this far, you are now ready to get into more specific details of what is involved in actually making your restaurant dream a reality. The following chapters will teach you how to develop and price your menu, design and lay out your dining room, set up a bar, design and equip your kitchen, and select and train your staff. A lot of the information in these chapters will be very useful in helping to prepare your final pro forma operating and capital requirements budgets. You should therefore read and study them carefully.

CHAPTER 6

CONSTRUCTING
THE MENU

One of the most important decisions you will have to make early
on is what kind of food to serve. French, American, Italian, Mexican, fusion? Of all
the elements within your concept, none defines it more than the type of food you
offer. Think about it: whenever a group of Americans are deciding where to go out to
eat, the first question is usually, "What kind of food are you in the mood for?" This is
why most, if not all, restaurant guidebooks list establishments by cuisine type.

When creating your menu concept, you need to consider your target market, your
potential competitors, and current food trends. Deciding what kind of food you want
to serve is only the start of the process of creating a menu. You'll then need to decide
how many items to offer and at what price and be sure that you have the resources
you need—staff, equipment, ingredients, and time—to make that menu a reality. It's a
great moment when all this comes together and you have an actual customer menu
that you can hold in your hands. This may seem like a lot of work, but don't worry.
This chapter will walk you through the steps one at a time.

YOUR TARGET MARKET

What are your target customers' tastes? Are they on the go and looking for fast service? Young and wanting something exciting? Or a conservative meat-and-potatoes
crowd? Are they affluent with disposable income and enough time to enjoy it at a

fancy place? Casual and budget conscious? Or all of the above? If you did your market research using the techniques outlined in chapter 2, you know the answers. You have an idea of a unique selling proposition that will appeal to these customers. You also have identified cuisines, cooking methods, or other food trends that are over- or underrepresented or have not yet occurred to anyone in the neighborhood you're considering.

When I was thinking of changing my concept early in 1994, there were at least twenty-five Italian restaurants within a seven-block radius of my restaurant. I knew that in order to compete successfully, I had to do something other than Italian. As I mentioned earlier, there was no Southwest cuisine, and, as they say, the rest is history. You would not believe how many other entrepreneurs came along and opened Italian restaurants anyway, each one thinking that they could beat the competition. Most failed.

Getting a general idea of the kind of food you will serve is just a start. The next challenge is to refine your idea. Let's say your target market is young and looking for something different, so you've decided to serve an ethnic cuisine. But how adventurous are your target customers? Will they want authentic flavor and atmosphere with lots of spices and unfamiliar menu items, or will they prefer an Americanized version that is milder and at least passingly familiar?

Ethnic restaurants constantly wrestle with the question of how spicy to make their hot foods. Many Americans' idea of "hot" would be considered mild in the dish's home country. If food is too spicy, Americans will not eat it. But if it is too mild, a restaurant risks alienating customers who are seeking a more exotic experience. Take the example of Yan Can, a California-based Pan-Asian fast-food chain. Chef Martin Yan's team, which spent eighteen months developing the menu, couldn't picture Americans handling a real traditional Chinese kung pao chicken, which is full of hot oil, chilies, and Szechuan peppercorns. So they toned down the spices. But look at what a reviewer for *Metro*, a Silicon Valley weekly newspaper, said: "When I dine at an Asian restaurant, I expect sizzle and pop; I expect rousing contrasts between hot and cool, rich sauces and deep smoky infusions. The food at Yan Can proved listless and stripped intentionally of flavor, or as the manager said, 'tweaked down' for the American masses. Large doses of sugar pummeled spices into submission, making the dishes we tasted sweet, not sassy, as they should have been." This review drove away pickier dinnertime customers.

In another scenario, let's say that your unique selling proposition is a celebrity chef. Is your chef's vision in line with what your customers want?

There's a great scene in the movie *Big Night*, which illustrates the problem of reconciling a chef's taste to a customer's. A couple not familiar with risotto, an Italian rice dish, wants to have noodles with their risotto even though the two starch dishes are not meant to be eaten together. Then the wife complains because the chunks of seafood in her seafood risotto are not large. The chef throws a tantrum because the difficult customers do not understand how his food is supposed to be served! In the end, however, he ends up agreeing to make them the spaghetti they want because he realizes that they are too unsophisticated to appreciate fine dining.

This goes back to the challenge of finding a unique selling proposition that matches your target customers' tastes and is broad enough to attract enough of them to make your restaurant a success.

NEW TRENDS

Luckily, people's tastes are broadening. There has been an explosion of books, magazines, and television shows related to food and dining. Consider the following: the Food Network now reaches 80 million households, up from 6.5 million when it was launched in 1993, and there are currently more than three hundred culinary schools in the United States with more than fifty-five thousand students studying culinary arts. Cookbooks account for 10 percent of all publishing sales, and the Internet hosts more than eight million food sites. According to the 2003 *Forbes* "Top 100 Celebrities," celebrity chef Wolfgang Puck is as popular as NBA stars Alonzo Mourning and Juwan Howard.

Inexpensive airfares and telecommunications have increased Americans' travel abroad. In the past ten years, U.S. travel has risen by 41 percent, and dining is Americans' favorite activity when abroad. At the same time, high immigration has increased the number of restaurants here that serve cuisine from around the world. Together, these factors mean that Americans are more familiar with new and unusual foods and increasingly willing to be more adventurous. Dining out in America is no longer a meat-and-potatoes proposition.

The most dramatic reflection of Americans' new gastronomical spirit is their receptivity to previously unfamiliar types of ethnic cuisine. Even classic American restaurants like Red Lobster are introducing ethnic elements to their menus. "As Americans we have become more sophisticated. Red Lobster is fine dining for much of Middle America, so we believe in introducing our customers to these great flavors," Keith Keogh, vice president of culinary and beverage excellence for Red Lobster, told *Restaurants and Institutions* magazine. "You turn on television and the Food Network and *Good Morning America* are talking about dishes with ethnic ingredients and introducing people to the latest trends."

The numbers back up such anecdotal evidence. A 2001 National Restaurant Association Ethnic Cuisines study, for example, revealed that between 70 and 80 percent of diners are familiar with some foreign and ethnic cuisines, including: Hunan, Mandarin, and Szechuan; German, French, Greek, and Spanish; Japanese; Indian; and Cajun, Creole, soul food, and Caribbean.

In *Restaurant Business* magazine's year 2000 ratings, out of the ten fastest-growing casual dining chains in the United States, *eight* served some form of ethnic cuisine. Look at the rankings that follow, and note the impressive growth rates associated with these ethnic cuisines:

- Bahama Breeze (Caribbean cuisine, growth rate 90 percent)
- Zio's Italian Kitchen (growth rate 63.6 percent)
- Baja Fresh Mexican Grill (growth rate 62.7 percent)
- Copeland's of New Orleans (growth rate 53.6 percent)

- Buca di Beppo (Italian cuisine, growth rate 50 percent)
- Panera Bread/St. Louis Bread Company (bakery and café, growth rate 44.8 percent)
- P.F. Chang's China Bistro (growth rate 44.4 percent)
- Rubio's Baja Grill (growth rate 42.2 percent)
- Famous Dave's (barbeque, growth rate 40 percent)
- Roy's Restaurants (Asian cuisine, growth rate 40 percent)

In addition to fast growth since their inception, these restaurants have registered impressive sales volumes. Bahama Breeze reported system-wide sales of $100 million with average unit sales of $6 million. In 2000, P.F. Chang's had system-wide sales of $234 million and average unit sales of $5.9 million.

More important, the distinction between casual dining chains and independent casual restaurants is narrowing. Casual chains—like Yan Can—are more likely to position themselves as chef-driven or—like Chipotle (gourmet burritos and tacos) or Così (coffee and sandwiches)—to offer menu items that appeal to customers who like to think of themselves as more sophisticated than burger-and-pizza folks.

In addition to the explosion of new kinds of cuisine, current food trends include different cooking methods and techniques and special ingredients, like the fresh, locally grown seasonal produce and organic meats and poultry model pioneered by Chez Panisse. This is an approach that more and more moderately priced and upscale restaurants are adopting. Some restaurants mix and match trends. For example, Charles Phan adapted the Chez Panisse concept to Asian food, making San Francisco's The Slanted Door a phenomenal success.

Diet and nutritional trends, like the Atkins and South Beach diets, also shape customers' likely preferences and restaurateurs' opportunities to create new unique selling propositions.

Consider these National Restaurant Association research findings:
- Seventy percent of adults said there are more nutritious foods available now in restaurants than five years ago.
- Full service restaurant operators have noticed a shift away from entrée orders that raise nutritional concerns.
- Seafood is now more popular at fine-dining restaurants. According to the survey, 64 percent of fine-dining operators reported that customers are ordering more seafood entrees than they did two years ago. Similarly, 44 percent of family-dining operators reported increases in seafood sales over the same time period.
- Among family- and casual-dining restaurant operators, 50 percent reported an increase in sales of entrée salads compared from two years ago. The increase in entrée salads for fine-dining operators was only 38 percent.

The baby boom generation is a big driver of this health-oriented trend. Baby boomers, the largest demographic group in the nation, are not to be ignored. Boomers have the highest amount of disposable income of any age group. Not surprisingly, they are casual dining and upscale restaurants' most frequent patrons.

Rapidly moving into the age group where health becomes an increasing concern, boomers refuse to go quietly into the night; they want to look good and feel good, and their food choices reflect that. Even if Atkins, South Beach, and other similar diets fade, health and nutrition concerns will be around for years to come. To accommodate these concerns, restaurant operators will have to adjust their menus accordingly. Following this trend, restaurant concepts that cater primarily to these demographic groups are currently offering and will continue to offer smaller portions of fresh, healthful foods.

Consistent with these trends, sushi and ceviche are menu items that are growing in popularity, being seen as healthful and low in carbohydrates. Not only has sushi proliferated in high-end and casual restaurants, it is now available in supermarkets and (of all places!) 7-Eleven convenience stores. In fact, a recent National Restaurant Association survey found that between 1995 and 2000, sushi consumption in the U.S. increased by 40 percent. This trend will grow even faster when the word finally gets out that eating raw fish is actually no more risky than eating cooked chicken or pork.

No matter how health conscious they are, people still want to indulge occasionally, and well they should. So remember in your menu planning to provide them the choice to do so—perhaps a perfectly grilled cut of fish or an irresistible dessert concoction.

Of course there will always be customers for whom portion size and value are synonymous, and they will want to be "super sized." Your research will tell you if this is your market.

Future generations will grow up eating in restaurants, traveling abroad, and watching the Food Network. This is borne out by a recent poll in *Restaurant Business* magazine, which found that, at a time when primetime TV viewing was holding steady, Food Network viewing was up 8 percent among boys aged two to eleven. This trend will lead to an increasing demand for fresher, higher-quality foods with bolder, more authentic flavors. For example, in *Restaurants & Institutions* magazine, Rafi Taherian, Director of Residential Dining at Stanford University, estimates that 15 percent of the nine to ten thousand meals he serves each day is Indian food.

One of the keys to competing successfully is keeping up with the latest food trends, which can help you develop your unique selling proposition. One of the reasons that chains are so successful is that they have a pretty good idea of what their customers are looking for. To keep up with current trends, they spend thousands, if not millions, of dollars to hire research-and-development specialists, who research trade publications, study their competitors, analyze trend data, and conduct extensive focus group testing. Take the example of the hugely successful Cheesecake Factory, which shuffles its two hundred menu items *every six months* to keep up with culinary trends.

You may not have the resources to hire a culinary research-and-development team like the chains do, but you can still stay current. Eat at various types of popular restaurants, read trade journals (which, by the way, often publish chain operators' research findings), and read other popular food and wine magazines. Watch the Food Network. Read the dining and food section of your local newspaper and visit food sites on the Internet. One of my favorite things to do is to visit the cookbook section of my local bookstore and browse the new release section. Four weekly trade publications that I strongly recommend are *Nation's Restaurant News*, *Restaurant Hospitality*, *Restaurants & Institutions*, and *Restaurant Business*.

BUILDING YOUR MENU

Once your market research has revealed your target market and you have decided the type of food you will serve, the next step is to decide how big your menu will be and what items you will serve. Think of this as assembling the essential ingredients to make a perfect dish—only this time, it will be a collection of dishes!

These are the most important factors to consider in choosing the various items that will make up your menu:

- Availability and affordability of ingredients
- Required preparation time
- Availability of adequately skilled personnel
- Equipment requirements
- Kitchen layout and design
- Profitability of the menu item

If you want to open an ethnic restaurant, make sure that you can get any unusual ingredients supplied reliably and at reasonable prices. If you want your menu to rely on fresh, organic, and often locally grown and raised produce, meats, and poultry, there are several things to keep in mind. Organic foods are often more expensive, but many patrons appreciate these ingredients and come prepared to pay higher prices for them. However, fresh produce does not have to be expensive, especially if your menu changes from season to season. Meat and poultry are almost always more expensive in the late spring and summer. Luckily, this is when fruits and vegetables are cheapest and taste best.

Another factor to take into consideration is how long it will take to cook, plate, and serve each of your menu items. This is particularly important if you will be catering to meal periods with time constraints, such as breakfast and lunch, or fast food any time of the day. When we first switched our concept at Zuni to cater to pretheater customers, we had a hard time preparing dishes as fast as people wanted them. Most pretheater customers want to eat and pay for an appetizer, entrée, and dessert in an hour and a quarter. They typically arrive at 6:30 p.m. and want to leave at 7:45 p.m. in order to make an 8:00 p.m. curtain. Our chef at the time came from a fine-dining environment where the typical time for each meal was two hours. Unfortunately, he designed some of our menu items accordingly. As a result, the kitchen staff was not able to cook and plate these items fast enough for the service staff to sell all three courses. The result: we missed out on valuable sales.

In order to execute your menu successfully, you will need a well-trained kitchen staff, especially a chef who understands your concept and its labor and service requirements. We'll go more into how to build a staff in a later chapter.

You should make sure that you have any special equipment you need to make the kind of food you want to serve. And you should allow for enough kitchen space to prepare the food on your menu.

Finally, you must be sure that you can sell the items on your menu profitably. We'll go into menu pricing later on in this chapter, but the principle is simple: you must know that your target market can afford prices that will cover the cost of ingredients, preparation, and overhead and still leave room for a profit. New York celebrity chef Daniel Boulud's DB Bistro Moderne charges $99 for its double-truffle burger, which includes two layers of black truffles and is stuffed with braised short ribs and foie gras—it is in the *Guinness Book of World Records* as the world's most expensive hamburger. Nevertheless, with black truffles running $875 per pound, the restaurant's publicist says that it's practically giving away the burgers at cost. DB makes up for the thin margin through volume: its truffle burgers (including a $59 single-truffle version) are its best-selling items.

HOW BIG SHOULD YOUR MENU BE?

You've probably eaten in one of those Chinese restaurants that has a menu so big you don't even know where to start. You've also probably eaten at classic burger joints with menus that don't go much beyond burgers and fries, and maybe some chicken or fish sandwiches thrown in. Your menu most likely will land somewhere in between these two extremes. If just choosing from one of those vast Chinese menus is hard, think about what it must be like to have all of those ingredients on hand and to prepare them all right! While there's such a thing as too much choice, too little choice can be a problem, too.

Except for pizzerias and burger and hot dog joints, few restaurants can succeed with a limited menu. Unfortunately, I had to learn this lesson the hard way.

Following the soup craze started by Al's Soup Kitchen International—which the Soup Nazi popularized on the hit TV comedy series *Seinfeld*—I opened a shop called Souper Dog in New York City selling soups and gourmet chicken sausages and hot dogs. Souper Dog got good reviews in the *New York Times* and *Gourmet* magazine, but it only lasted about one year. The problem was that although my customers loved the soups and sausages, it was hard to convince them to eat them regularly enough to make it a viable business. Also, much of the pedestrian traffic passing the store was out-of-town tourists who didn't quite get the soup-and-chicken sausage thing. Many people from the Midwest were looking for something familiar or had plans for destination restaurants. On top of that, we soon learned that as a meal, soup was seasonal. People are far more likely to eat soup during the coldest months of the year, which is why Al's Soup Kitchen International is only open from November to April. The final factor was that the actual unique selling proposition behind the success of Al's Soup Kitchen International was the impact of Al's status as the *Seinfeld* Soup Nazi. His reputation for being ornery made him legendary. Tourists would come from all over the country, line up in the cold, and pay $7.50 for a twelve-ounce cup of soup, some bread, and a piece of fruit—all just to experience the thrill of being yelled at. Only in America, folks. To their disappointment, they often found that Al is actually quite nice. Sure, the soup was very good. But how was anybody else going to get customers to pay $7.50 for a bowl?

The real lesson, however, was that even in a city as densely populated as New York, a one- or two-item menu just does not offer enough options to attract the required amount of *repeat* customers to be viable. Within days of converting Souper Dog to Wrapsody, a shop selling twenty different wrap sandwiches, along with soups, salads, and sausages, the operation's sales quadrupled. The more diversified menu allowed me to appeal to a broader market and attract a larger number of customers.

If you think that you have identified an opportunity to be successful with a limited menu operation, you should make sure that: (1) your menu items are widely accepted, like hot dogs, burgers, or pizza; (2) your food is convenience oriented and easily eaten on the go; (3) your menu is very reasonably priced; (4) you are in a heavily trafficked location; (5) your food and beverage costs are 25 percent or less; and (6) your rent and other occupancy costs are low.

The bottom line is that today's customers want affordable, healthy menus offering choice, flexibility, and excitement. A recent National Restaurant Association survey found that 90 percent of adults said they like lots of choices on restaurant menus so they can decide what they want to eat.

An ideal menu has an array of entrées and appetizers that include different types of meats, seafood, poultry, starches, and vegetables. Your menu should also offer various methods of preparation—sautéed, grilled, steamed, roasted, and assembled raw.

A broad menu has the added advantage of allowing you to meet both traditional preferences and those driven by a nationwide trend toward healthier eating. For example, health-conscious consumers are more likely to prefer grilled or steamed foods to those that are fried or covered with heavy sauces.

Also bear in mind that customers may have food allergies and other dietary restrictions. For example, some people may have allergic reactions to foods that include peanuts and shellfish. Others may have religious convictions or dietary restrictions that prevent them from eating foods like pork, shellfish, or beef. Make sure your menu includes items that provide options for customers with allergies.

MENU PRICING

Now that you have a pretty good handle on the appetizers, entrées, and desserts that your menu will offer, it is time to decide what to charge for each item. The goal when pricing your menu should be to maximize sales and profits. However, this is much easier said than done! Effective menu pricing can be tricky. If your menu items are priced too high, you run the risk of pricing yourself out of the market or of driving customers away. On the other hand, if your prices are too low, you risk not only losing valuable profits, but also sending the wrong message about the quality and value of your food, beverages, ambience, and service.

What Is Important to Me As a Chef

Paul Canales of Oliveto

People are always asking me how I stay inspired, energetic, and open to new possibilities. When I begin to think of designing a menu, I think about history, tradition, authenticity, and butchery, as well as cooking techniques, creativity, collaboration, and, most important, flavor—or, more precisely, savor. Over several years, I have created an extensive repertoire that my team and I constantly update and expand.

On any given day, the menu at Oliveto changes from 25 to 75 percent and on opening day of one our special dinners series, 100 percent. For me, this is the best way to sustain my interest and to provide a creative and collaborative environment for my team. My chefs have been with me for an average of eight years, and a daily changing menu provides plenty of opportunities for each of us to generate ideas, develop them into finished dishes, and stay inspired.

As always, we give a nod to tradition, then creatively and collaboratively leap forward into the future. One of our unstated goals is that our cooking experience be as fun and challenging for us as it will be delicious and memorable for our customers. One way we fulfill this goal at Oliveto is to procure and work with either wild or sustainably and humanely raised whole animals. This includes all of our fish, poultry, rabbits, lamb, pigs, and now beef animals. We employ every possible part of an animal in the service of deliciousness. We literally take an animal from head (or snout or beak) to tail and bring all the things we know and care about together in order to create a uniquely exciting experience for our customers. In addition, we know all of the farmers who are raising our animals. We know their philosophies and practices, as well as their concerns for their animals and their farms. And they, in turn, know ours. They understand that their efforts to raise healthy, happy animals must translate positively to our customers' experience

One of the most common methods of menu pricing—used by both first-time and experienced restaurateurs—is the "follow the leader" or "monkey see, monkey do" method. Using this method, operators price their menus based primarily on what competitors are charging. This is only appropriate, though, if a restaurant must meet or beat the competitors' prices in order to survive, such as in fast-food and other convenience-oriented concepts, where price is often the deciding selection factor. Customers also select according to price in highly competitive markets and when economic times are bad.

Some restaurant owners play follow the leader because they do not know any better, or they assume that price is the main driving factor behind all dining choices. As a new restaurant owner, you should not automatically assume that higher menu prices will drive customers into your competitors' open arms. This kind of thinking can lead you into a trap: you may unintentionally define your menu items as homo-

of the food we prepare. In other words, our "so what" test to matters of food policies and politics is understood ultimately in terms of flavor, texture, juiciness, and so on.

When we start our day, we work with what is left of each animal from the day before. For example, if our two hundred plus pound pig that we get from Paul Willis comes in on Tuesday and we use the legs right away, by Thursday, we have the shoulders, loins, and bellies to work from. This continues all week with each of the animals we use. The exception, of course, is fish, which we purchase each day after learning from our friend Tom Worthington at Monterey Fish what came in that morning and what is best.

There are many benefits to this approach. First, we are always working with different parts of each animal, so we are constantly stretching ourselves creatively to design interesting and exciting offerings for our customers. This keeps our minds sharp, our palates keen, and our menus dynamic and vibrant. We also get the benefit of butchering all of our animals in-house. Not only does this keep me and my chefs grounded in artisanal practices and processes, it affords an ongoing learning environment for our cooks. The result is a dynamic, creative, and collaborative work environment with far lower turnover than typical high-end restaurants, which helps me to control my labor costs. Finally, by creatively utilizing every part of each animal in ways that produce pure profit, our overall food cost is significantly lower than like restaurants of equal caliber.

All of the above holds true for our produce as well. Almost all of the fruits and vegetables we use come from small farms that are within one hundred miles of the restaurant. Most of them are certified organic. We buy what these farmers are growing, so we adhere strictly to local growing seasons. This is why you won't see fresh tomatoes on my menus much past mid October, or peas and asparagus in February. And like the farmers who raise our animals, we know each of these growers very well and have close relationships with them. In the same way that the whole animal approach keeps us keen, sharp, and inspired, responding to what is available from our local farmers causes us to think in a dynamic and facile way.

geneous rather than differentiated, thus missing an opportunity to use your pricing structure to increase your restaurant's perceived value.

Tricky as it may seem, effective menu pricing is not guesswork. The basic idea is to know your costs. That way, you can price your menu to reflect the value of your food, decor, and service and at the same time attract enough customers to make a meaningful profit. It may take several tries before you come up with a workable plan, but the effort is worth it.

This is where the legwork you did in earlier chapters becomes absolutely crucial. Your choice of concept and target market will be key to determining your price structure. If you were to open a fast-food restaurant in a low-income neighborhood, for example, your prices would probably have to be lower than for a similar restaurant in a high-income neighborhood. In fact, it is not uncommon for McDonald's franchises to charge different prices for the same menu items in different neighborhoods. There are a couple of ways to determine pricing. The method I suggest here is best suited for a diversified menu with menu items of varying costs and prices.

PRICING BASICS

To understand menu pricing, there are two industry terms that you are going to have to become familiar with: *cost of sales* and *cost of sales percentage.*

Simply put, cost of sales is the cost of the ingredients, that is the groceries in your freezer and on your storage shelves that you will use to make your menu items. In order to measure and compare costs to sales, costs of sales is usually expressed as a percentage of sales and is called the cost of sales percentage. The basic formula is costs/sales = cost of sales percentage. For example, let's say you sell a steak plate for $20 and it costs you $5. The steak plate's cost of sale percentage would be $5 divided by $20, or 25 percent. If the cost of sales percent for each one of your menu items were 25 percent, the overall cost of sales for your restaurant would be 25 percent. Think of it this way: with a 25 percent cost of sales percentage, out of every dollar of sales your restaurant makes, 25 cents would cover food costs—ingredients—and 75 cents would be left over to cover all of your other operating costs, such as your salary, labor, and overhead.

Two other variations of the cost of sales formula are cost/cost percentage = sales and sales x cost percentage = cost. Later, to price our menus, we are going to use the cost/cost percentage formula. For example, let's say we determined that the cost of a menu item is $3 and that our desired overall cost of sales is 30 percent, the menu item would be priced as follows $3/.30 = $10. Similarly, if we wanted to sell a menu item for, say, $15 and wanted an estimate of what its cost would have to be to achieve an overall 30 percent cost of sales percentage, the calculation would be as follows: $15 x .30 = $4.50.

No matter what your concept, the first step in successful menu pricing is to prepare a realistic budget or financial feasibility study, which you did in chapter 5. You can only come up with a profitable price structure after you have realistically projected food costs, labor and related costs, other overhead costs, and your desired profit. Once you know these costs, you will be able to determine what price level will be appropriate to cover them and give you your desired profit.

You may want to do a quick review of chapter 5 and especially table 5-1 before proceeding.

One of the most important estimates you made in your financial feasibility study was an estimate of your overall food cost percentage or a *targeted food cost percentage.* This percentage, is one of the components that we will use to price your menu. In most successful table service restaurants, the targeted food cost percentage is usually between 28 and 35 percent. With your targeted food cost established, your next step is to cost your menu's ingredients.

COSTING MENU INGREDIENTS

One of the most important steps in pricing your menu *profitably* is to determine the cost of your ingredients and the costs of preparing them. As a general rule, the more costly the ingredients and labor are, the higher you should set the price. For example, restaurants generally charge more for steaks and seafood than they do for chicken or pasta. Also, a pasta dish will cost more in a high-end restaurant than it would in a diner since high-end restaurants generally require more costly skilled labor.

The first step in menu costing is to establish recipes for each of your menu items. Later we will discuss the importance of establishing standard recipes and portions but for now let's work on how to cost your menu properly. Once you and/or your chef have established standard recipes, the next step is to determine the cost of each ingredient. The total costs of each recipe's ingredients plus a certain amount allocated for waste will be the cost of the menu item. To do this, we are going to use a Recipe Costing Sheet. In the business, we also call this exercise plate, portion, or recipe costing. To make the process easy to understand, we will cost a simple recipe and a complex recipe. Table 6-1 is an example of a Recipe Costing Sheet for a simple hamburger.

- **Ingredients:** In the ingredient column, list the ingredients that will be used to prepare your menu item. For our basic burger, the ingredients are ground beef, a hamburger bun, and mayonnaise.

- **Unit:** Unit refers to the unit of measure (pounds, ounces, dozen, gallon, quart, case, and so on) that each ingredient is purchased by. In our example, ground beef is purchased by the pound, buns are purchased by the dozen, and mayonnaise is purchased by the gallon.

- **Purchase cost per unit:** The purchase cost per unit is the current market price paid per pound, per dozen, gallon, and so on. In our example, the cost of ground beef is $2.25 per pound, buns are $4 per dozen, and mayonnaise is $10 per gallon. You can get current market prices from your most recent invoices. Prices usually vary with the seasons and other market conditions and it is not always possible to adjust menu prices with each fluctuation. Therefore, to get a more representative cost, ask vendors what the yearly highs and lows typically are for various ingredients. Once you know the highs and lows, you can use either an average, that is, the high plus the low divided by two, or the high price. For example, assume that chicken breasts range in price from $2 per pound in the spring and $3 per pound in the summer. In this case, you would use the average, ($2 + $3) ÷ 2 or $2.50, or $3 the high. Whether you use the average price or the high price will depend on your concept and the pricing environment that you are operating in.

- **Serving unit:** Serving cost unit is the unit used to measure the amount of each ingredient. For example, the size of each burger is measured in ounces, buns by the piece or each, and mayonnaise in ounces.

- **Serving cost per unit:** The serving cost per unit is the cost per measure divided by the number of units in each measure. For example, the serving cost per unit of ground beef = $2.25 ÷ 16 ounces or $.14 per ounce. Similarly, the cost of each bun is $4 ÷ 12 (one dozen) or $.33 and the unit cost of mayo is $10 ÷ 128 fluid ounces or $.075 per ounce.

- **Serving size:** Serving size is the amount of each ingredient that will go into the recipe, for example each burger will get 6 ounces of ground beef, 1 bun, and 2 ounces of mayo.

- **Serving cost:** The serving cost is the cost per unit x the portion size. For example, the portion cost of 6 ounces of ground beef is $.14 × 6 or $.84, the cost of each bun is $.33 × 1 or $.33, and the cost of mayo is $.075 × 2 or $.15.

- **Waste factor:** Once the costs of a menu item are determined, you should add an additional amount to account for the unavoidable small amounts of waste that occurs during the preparation process. Also provided for in waste are spices used during the cooking process since it is almost impossible to measure a pinch of this or a pinch of that. While some owners believe that making a provision for waste can encourage employee theft equal to the amount of the waste, I think that not making a provision for waste would result in unrealistically low food costs. There is no fixed waste factor. The amount of waste will depend on the concept, preparation methods, and the skill level of your staff. In my restaurants, I would use between 10 and 15 percent depending on the menu item. Use a percentage that will allow you to price your menu competitively and still maximize profits. Before we get to an example of costing a more complex menu item, three terms that you should become very familiar with are trim and shrinkage and yield percentage.

TRIM AND SHRINKAGE AND YIELD PERCENTAGE

To price your menus properly, you must I repeat you must understand the concept of trim and yield. Too many operators do not understand this concept and end up with menu item costs that are too low and menu prices that are not profitable. Trim is the amount of a food item that gets lost due to butchering, trimming, or cleaning during the preparation process and shrinkage is the amount that is lost due to cooking. The yield is the actual amount left after trim and shrinkage, and is expressed as a percentage. For example, a five-pound (80 ounce) New York strip steak will not yield 10 eight-ounce servings after trim and cleaning. After trim and cleaning, the usable or actual weight may only be 64 ounces because you are probably going to lose 16 ounces or 1 pound due to trimming of excess fat. Your yield in this case would be 64 ounces ÷ 80 ounces, or .80. If the original cost per pound of the New York strip was $6, the real cost or yield after trim would be $7.50 or $6 ÷ .80. In this case, instead of using $6 per pound to calculate the serving cost per unit, you would use $7.50 and

TABLE 6-1: RECIPE COSTING SHEET

Ingredients	Unit	Purchase cost / unit	Serving unit	Serving cost / unit	Serving size	Cost / serving
Ground beef	pound	$2.25	ounce	$0.14	6 oz	$0.84
Hamburger bun	dozen	4	each	0.33	1	0.33
Mayo	gallon	10	ounce	0.075	2	0.15
Sub total						1.32
Waste factor (10%)						0.13
Total menu Item cost						1.45

TABLE 6-2: RECIPE COSTING SHEET

Ingredients	Unit	Purchase cost / unit	Yield %	Actual purchase cost / unit	Serving unit	Serving cost / unit	Serving size	Cost / serving
New York strip steak	pound	$6	0.8	$7.50	ounce	$0.47	8oz	$3.76
Baked potato	case	20	n/a	n/a	each	0.25	1	0.25
Sub total								4.01
Waste factor (10%)								0.40
Total menu item cost								4.41

the serving cost per unit would be $7.50 ÷ 16 ounces or $.47 per ounce. Another way to do the calculation is as follows: 64 ounces ÷ 80 ounces = .8 × 16 ounces per pound = 12.8 ounces yield per pound. And then $6 per pound ÷ 12.8 ounces yield per pound = $.47 per ounce. If you were to simply divide $6 by 16 ounces your cost per ounce would have been $.37, and the cost of each steak would be understated by $.10 (.47 – .37). You would do the same calculation if instead of a steak the piece of meat were a roast that shrunk due to roasting. The Recipe Costing Sheet in table 6-2 shows the calculation for a steak with an 80 percent yield.

Trim does not apply only to meats it also applies to fish, poultry, and vegetables. The yield percentages of certain whole fish are very low, for example red snapper at 45 percent, black sea bass at 40 percent, and flounder at 38 percent. This means that when these fish are purchased whole, after trimming head, bones, fat and so on, less than 50 percent is usable. To illustrate, let's assume you paid $3 per pound for a whole red snapper. After trim, the actual or yield cost per pound would be $3 ÷ by .45, or $6.67 per pound. Not surprisingly then, when purchased whole, fish is a lot less expensive than when purchased filleted.

A great resource for learning about trim, shrink, and yields is *The Book of Yields* by Chef Desk, which not only gives yield percentages on almost any food item, but also has a calculator for costing and pricing menus.

TABLE 6-3: RECIPE COSTING SHEET

Ingredients	Unit	Recipe quantity	Cost / unit	Food cost
Shrimp	pound	1 pound	$8	$8
Scallops	pound	1 pound	10	10
Lobster	pound	1 pound	20	20
Sole	pound	1/2 pound	12	6
Heavy cream	quart (32 ounces)	8 ounces	4	1
Butter	pound	8 ounces	3	1.50
Egg yolks	dozen	5	1.20	0.50
Fish stock	quart (32 ounces)	8 ounces	6	1.50
Dry sherry	750 ml (25.4 ounces)	2 ounces	8	0.59

Sub total $49.10
Waste factor (10%) 4.90
Total food cost 54.00
Cost per serving ($54 ÷ 10) 5.40
Servings: 10
Serving size: 6 ounces

TABLE 6-4: RECIPE COSTING SHEET

	Salad	Salmon entrée	Total
Selling price (1)	$6.95	$17.95	$24.90
Food cost (2)	1.45	5.95	7.40
Contribution margin ÷ gross profit (1) − (2)	5.50	12.00	17.50
Food cost percentage (2) ÷ (1)	21%	33%	29.70%

COSTING A MORE COMPLEX RECIPE

In table 6-1, to make the costing process easily understandable, I used a seven-column Recipe Costing Sheet. However, if you are comfortable with the costing process, you can simplify the table and use fewer columns. Table 6-3 is an example of costing a more complex recipe for Seafood Newburg using a simplified five-column Recipe Costing Sheet.

STANDARD PORTIONS AND RECIPES

Establishing standard (specified) serving sizes for each menu item and standard ingredients to be used in each recipe will not only help to ensure consistent food quality (taste and texture) and portion sizes, but will also establish benchmarks against which future actual operational and financial results can be measured. For example, without standard recipes and portions you would not be able to develop objective expected costs for your menu items or objectively price them. With expected costs, you will be able to compare them to actual results to see if you are meeting your financial goals and objectives. Also controlling portion sizes and recipe ingredients, will allow you to directly control your food costs. Established standards will also help to promote efficiency since you would be able to assign routine tasks to less experienced and skilled kitchen staff.

CALCULATING MENU PRICES BASED ON COST AND FOOD COSTS PERCENTAGES

Now that you know how to cost your menu items, you are ready to take the next step in the pricing process. Let's use two of the menu items that we worked on. For the hamburger, we determined that the cost of its ingredients is $1.45. Your next step is to use your targeted food cost percentage to determine what a profitable price would be. Let's assume that based on your financial feasibility study, you determined that in order to be sufficiently profitable, your targeted food cost percentage had to be 30 percent or less. Using the cost/cost of sales percent formula, the targeted menu price for your burger would be calculated as follows:

Food cost $1.45
Targeted food cost percent   30 percent
Targeted menu price ($1.45 ÷ .30) = $4.83

This price would be rounded up to $4.90 or $4.95, to be in conformity with standard menu pricing practices.

Similarly, if the Seafood Newburg was offered in a formal white tablecloth operation, with a targeted food cost of 25 percent, its targeted menu price would be calculated as follows:

Food cost per serving $5.40
Targeted food cost percent   25 percent
Targeted menu price ($5.40 ÷ .25) = $ 21.60

Again, this price would be adjusted to $21.95 or $22.

PRICING TO MAXIMIZE PROFITS

In some cases, the targeted menu price will not be the final price that appears on the menu. Very often, its a preliminary price that will be adjusted up or down depending on the menu item and/or the perceived price sensitivity of the target market. For example, let's take the example of the burger that we priced. Although it's targeted menu price is $4.90, in most urban casual table service restaurants it would probably sell for $5.95 or $6.95. That's because in these types of restaurants, customers are usually willing to pay between $6 and $7 for a burger. By charging $4.90, you would be missing an opportunity to maximize profits, particularly if immediate competitors are getting more than $5 for a similar burger. This is not to say that you should gouge customers, but that you should price to make a good profit and at the same time, give your customers good overall value for their money. Chances are, there will be a greedy competitor charging $8 or $9 dollars for the same burger, and you would be perceived as giving more bang for the buck.

Similarly, the fact that the targeted price of a menu item may be higher than what you think your target customers may be willing to pay, does not mean that you should not sell it at a lower price. Obviously, you would not make as much as you would if you sold it for its targeted price, but you could still make a decent profit if you sold it at a slightly lower price. Understanding the concept of *contribution margin,* will help you to understand why.

CONTRIBUTION MARGIN

An item's contribution margin is the amount of dollars that it will "contribute" to the bottom line. Obviously then, the higher the contribution margin, the better! Put simply, a menu item's contribution margin is its cost minus its selling price. For example, an item selling for $10 and costing $5 would have a contribution margin of $5.

To illustrate the importance of contribution margin and pricing, let's assume that your restaurant's overall targeted food cost is 30 percent and that two of your menu offerings are a Caesar salad and a salmon entrée. Let's also assume that based on your market research you discovered that given your service, design, and décor elements, $6.95 was an acceptable price for the Caesar salad, but that $17.95 was the best price you could get for a salmon entrée. However, when you priced the salmon entrée using your 30 percent targeted food cost, the targeted menu price was $19.95 ($5.95 ÷ .3). Should you go ahead and sell the salmon for $17.95? The answer is yes! Table 6-4, illustrates how contribution margin works and how pricing the salmon at $17.95 could still allow you to meet your operating objectives.

From table 6-4 you can see that although the salads food cost percentage is lower than the salmon's, its contribution margin is also lower by $6.50 ($12 - $5.50). In other words, the salad's contribution to the bottom line (profits) is $6.50 less. Note also that while the salmon's food cost percentage is 3 percent higher than its targeted food cost (33 to 30 percent), that the salad's food cost percentage is 7 percent lower than its targeted food cost (30 to 21 percent) and that the overall food cost for both items is 29.7 percent or roughly 30 percent, which was the desired overall targeted food cost percentage. It should also be clear that you would be more profitable if you sold more salmon entrées than Caesar salads since despite a higher food cost percentage, each salmon entrée contributes more to the bottom line or profits.

Your goal then when pricing your menu, is to create a mix of price points and profit margins that will come together to allow you to maximize your profits and at the same time give your customers the best value for their money.

Although, your menu pricing strategy should be based first on your overall targeted food cost percentage and the actual cost of your menu ingredients, other factors that should influence your pricing decisions are:

- Your immediate or direct competition
- Price elasticity (price sensitivity) of your menu items
- Perceived value of restaurant experience: food, service, décor and atmosphere

Once you have a handle on pricing your menu items, the next step is to determine how flexible (sensitive) your target market is at accepting your prices. In other words, at what menu prices would your target customers choose your competitors. Refer back to the demographics and psychographics that you identified in your market study. Also, check out the prices and volume of business at restaurants that are similar in concept to your proposed restaurant. Don't simply follow the leader, but do know your competitors' prices and understand that they are one of the factors that customers will take into consideration. But remember, your goal is not simply to be priced competitively but to maximize your sales and profits.

This is a good opportunity to reflect on your restaurant's unique selling proposition. Think about how much more your target market might be willing to pay for what they value. You can enhance your restaurant's perceived value—and the prices you can charge—by emphasizing food quality or uniqueness, portion size, presentation, style of service, atmosphere, and decor. The values that you assign to these elements should help you to establish a range of prices that you think your target customers would accept based on their perception of quality.

Finally, ask yourself what profit margin you want to make—and can realistically expect. The expected profit margin does not have to be the same for every item. You may want to have a signature dish—like DB's truffle burgers—on which you are willing to accept a smaller profit per unit because it helps make your menu unique and/or sells a high enough volume to boost your total profit on that item.

Shortly after opening, check the effectiveness of your pricing strategy; you want to take every opportunity to maximize your sales and profits. If, for example, you determine that you are selling more of your higher-priced items, this could indicate that factors other than price are influencing your customers' spending decisions, and it presents an opportunity to increase your prices, either by rotating more higher-priced items onto the menu or by offering higher-priced specials. If, on the other hand, you determine that most of your sales are made up of lower-priced items, your target market is apparently price sensitive, and you should adjust your prices to focus more on volume sales.

MENU LAYOUT AND DESIGN

Once you have finished selecting and pricing your menu items, you should think about how your menu will look and feel. Your menu's design and layout should be consistent with your restaurant's overall design and decor. Naturally, it should take into consideration your concept, target market, and target customers. If you went to a fine-dining restaurant and they handed you a hand-written grease-covered menu, your expectations about the quality of the food and service to follow would probably drop, and it would definitely tarnish your dining experience. On the other hand, if you went to your local barbeque or other greasy spoon because you wanted a greasy spoon experience and they gave you a fancy menu written on silk paper and cloth napkins (not that this is likely to happen!), you would probably focus more on not soiling the menu and napkins and less on enjoying your messy but delicious food. In short, your menu should define your restaurant and set customer expectations.

In addition to making your menu's look, touch, and feel consistent with your restaurant's atmosphere, you should make sure that it is easy to read and understand. This raises the question of what sort of language you should use to describe your menu items. The trend toward globalized cuisine has changed not only the way Americans are eating and thinking about food, but also the vocabulary used to talk about eating. To be sure, foie gras, crème brulée, and tacos have long been familiar foods, but how long have Americans known what they were ordering when they asked for *shumai* or could tell the difference between tandoori and *biryani*? Urban self-styled sophisticates might not bat an eye at a menu including a coulis, but would a Des Moines diner know what it is? Part of your market research on food trends should include becoming familiar with this new vocabulary so you can use the appropriate language to appeal to your target audience. That being said, when naming menu items, you should describe foods in words that are familiar to your target market.

A few years ago, before the Atkins craze, I decided that Zuni should offer a vegetarian main course in response to customer requests. To do this, the chef offered a vegetable ragout, pronounced *ragu*. Customers who knew what it was ordered it and loved it. But with all the requests for a vegetarian alternative, I could not figure out why this menu item was not selling more. Then one day, one of my older pretheater customers asked me to describe the vegetable "rag out." After hearing this pronunciation, and considering that many of my pretheater guests met the same profile, I decided that I probably would not want anything that was ragged out either and placed "vegetable stew" in parentheses after "ragout," which led to a nice increase in sales of this item.

By the way, if you are not a native English speaker, be sure that your menu is understandable to Americans. Have a native English speaker look at the menu before you print it. Sometimes mistakes in English can be charming, but they also can be confusing or even downright unappetizing!

Some upscale and casual restaurant operators seem to find it necessary to use flowery language to describe their menu items and to mention every single exotic ingredient in a sauce. The best approach when describing menu items is to keep it simple: list the main protein or ingredient, the starch, the vegetable, and how each has been prepared; the type of sauce; and any special ingredient you want to highlight that will be *meaningful to your customers*.

Pick a font for your menu that is big and simple enough to be easy to read. Not to sound like a broken record, but once again: think about your concept and your target market. If your target customers are baby boomers or older, you don't want to make them have to put on reading glasses to see your menu. If your target customers are young, hip, and sophisticated, choose a font that has a sense of style about it. Whatever font you use, a good rule of thumb is to avoid using dollar signs, which tend to remind people of prices and make the menu look more expensive than it really is.

The best way to get ideas about menu layout and design is to collect menus from successful restaurants whose concepts are similar to yours, particularly those that happen to be situated in your market area. The fact that these restaurants are suc cessful means they are doing some things right, and you probably will be going after some of the same customers. As in pricing, the idea is not simply to copy the compe tition, but to look for improvements that will entice customers to your restaurant.

Eat or have drinks at competing restaurants. Ask the staff what the best-selling items are and look to see where they are positioned on the menu. Use this research, creativity, and your gut instinct when designing your menu. There are lots of soft ware programs on the market specifically designed for menu layout and design. If you are uncertain about your creative ability and if your budget permits, consult a professional menu writer and/or designer to convert your vision into reality.

You definitely ought to consider printing your menus in-house, especially if you will have a seasonal menu. There are many inexpensive laser and color printers on the market, allowing you to change your menu items and print new menus quickly and at minimal cost. For example, if you were to run a special that proved to be very popular and profitable, you would be able to easily substitute it for another not so popular and profitable item.

Your menu is one merchandising tool that all of your customers will see. Research has shown that the average customer spends at least three minutes reading a res taurant menu. These are precious minutes, and you should use them as effectively as possible to influence your guest's selections, maximize sales and profits, and promote your restaurant. The more you can influence sales toward items with high contribution margins and unit sales, the more profitable your restaurant will be. Design your menu so that these items stand out. Research shows that it is easier for eyes to focus on the right side of a menu, book, or magazine and that the prime merchandising positions in a list or column are the first, second, and third spots. One method commonly used in many family style and casual restaurants is to box these items or use clip art and colors to highlight them. With off-menu specials that the wait staff delivers verbally, consider that people remember the first couple of items they hear and then the last.

Finally, if you will offer takeout, make sure that you have a folded version of your menu easily accessible near the entrance so customers can pick one up while pass ing by or on the way out after a satisfying meal.

CHAPTER 7

FASHIONING DESIGN & AMBIENCE

Good food alone will not guarantee success, since—as I can't repeat often enough—it takes a combination of food, service, decor, price, and good management to be successful. After all, most of us have had good dining experiences in restaurants where the food was not of particular note, but where there was a certain good feeling and sense of entertainment and conviviality.

More and more restaurateurs are turning to creative design elements to differentiate themselves. They know that a well-designed concept can mean the difference between success and failure, particularly in the fine dining and upscale segments. Fine-dining customers expect good food and service; good design and ambience help to put the overall dining experience over the top.

In the competitive fast-food market, for example, McDonald's and other chains are beginning to offer softer seats and more elaborate design elements in order to attract and keep new customers. This new "quick casual" concept has been a hit for the 155-unit Chipotle Mexican Grill, which McDonald's used to own. With an emphasis on high-quality food, upscale ambience, and quick service, each store generates average sales of $1.05 million with an average check of $8. In a 2001 study, the Sandelman & Associates consulting firm surveyed 68,600 customers in sixty-two U.S. markets, and found that 54 percent of fast-food customers were willing to pay higher prices "for better food and nicer atmosphere" at quick-casual restaurants.

Certainly, there are successful restaurants for which atmosphere and decor do not play an important role. In fact, some pride themselves on their disdain for design. Big Nick's, a crowded diner on Manhattan's Upper West Side, has random newspaper clippings on the wall and hasn't been renovated since who knows when. But its scruffiness is part of its charm, combined with its reputation for inexpensive, giant burgers. You can be fairly sure that in most instances where customers are indifferent about design and decor, they are attracted by low to moderate menu prices.

YOUR TARGET MARKET

The more your customers can identify with and feel comfortable in your restaurant, the more likely they are to return. Are your target customers older and more conservative? Provincial? Family oriented? Young and hip? Hardworking and down-to-earth? Are they rural, urban, or suburban dwellers? The ambience and decor that works for a family style or casual restaurant in Washington, D.C., will probably not work well in rural Mississippi. This is not to suggest that rural dwellers don't want atmosphere or good design, but their idea of an appealing ambience is probably different from that of a city dweller. The best design in the world will be wasted if it does not resonate with your customers.

All too often, designers and first-time restaurateurs ignore their market and get carried away spending money on things that they like or think are "cool." These restaurants often fail. Did you catch that episode of *The Apprentice* where one team of Donald Trump wannabes made the mistake of decorating a neighborhood restaurant in an ultramodern, Pan-Asian theme, when it needed a homier atmosphere? Not surprisingly, one of the contenders heard the inevitable: "You're fired!"

YOUR RESTAURANT'S LOOK AND FEEL: A BRAND IMAGE

Based on your understanding of your target customers, start by developing a clear vision of how you want your restaurant to look and how you want patrons to feel while seated in the dining room, bar, or waiting area. Your restaurant's ambience will be anything that your customers see, hear, touch, smell, feel, and taste, and it will be communicated through your choice of food, decor, furnishings, lighting, acoustics, air flow, flatware, dishes, glassware, your staff's dress, and your service and management staff's overall attitude.

If you can't imagine your restaurant's style, you probably won't be able to implement it. For example, do you want customers to feel pampered? Nostalgic? Energized? Relaxed? Transported? All of your design choices will affect their mood. You should also consider what you want people to envision when they think about coming to your restaurant and what lasting impression they will take with them when they leave—one that will keep them coming back. In short, you should be thinking about establishing your own brand image.

It's often hard to translate these ideas into a design, so be realistic about how good your aesthetic judgments are. Do you receive compliments on your clothes style, or do you get comments on how your outfits don't quite work? Do your friends praise your home decor, or are they still laughing at that giant baby-blue velour sofa you can't bear to throw away? There's no right answer here. Just be honest with yourself. If you are uncertain about your ability to create the right atmosphere, then hire a design consultant to help you. Consultants can suggest inexpensive ways to create the atmosphere you want, saving you up-front costs as well as helping to generate future sales by encouraging return business to your welcoming atmosphere.

The more clearly you can define your concept, the better your designer and/or architect will be able to help you implement it. To get ideas that express your concept, look at design magazines, books, and other trade publications and visit restaurants whose styles you like. Share these ideas with your designer to help launch the design process.

WORKING WITH A DESIGNER AND/OR ARCHITECT

The first step in implementing and achieving your design objective is to find the right designer and/or architect for your project. If you're planning to build or remodel a space, you will need to work with an architect to draw up plans and submit them to the city for approval. A space planner or interior designer can help you interpret your style by planning the layout, selecting furniture and place settings, deciding on colors, choosing lighting, and so on. Many architects also function as designers or retain designers as part of their staff. Designers on the other hand are not architects, but they may hire architects to work for them. When selecting a designer or architect, you can take the following steps:

- Ask for references from other restaurant owners, particularly those with concepts similar to yours and with design elements that you like.
- Look at restaurant design books, magazines, and other trade publications. Most publish the names of the featured designers. If the designer of a particular space is not listed, you can call the publication to get contact information.
- Go to www.aia.org and www.interiors.org. These websites list names, addresses, areas of specialization, and other pertinent information of member architects and designers.

If this is your first restaurant, look for architects and designers with industry experience. In addition to knowing about code requirements, space flow, functionality and durability of materials, and project management, they will have a good understanding of the issues involved. They will be familiar with the various trades, contractors, and bureaucrats and can help you avoid costly change orders and delays, which can gobble up your budget.

When I was opening my second restaurant, which we built from scratch, we had negotiated a four-month rent-free period with our landlord. We figured that because it was a tiny space, this would be enough time to get all of the necessary permits and complete the build out. One of my partners opted not to hire an experienced architect and instead hired a less expensive, inexperienced expediter to obtain all of the required permits. Because the expediter had trouble cutting through red tape in order to obtain the permits in a timely fashion, we had to reschedule all of our tradesmen, which put us back three months. Not only did we have to pay rent for three months without generating sales, we also had to pay our staff, various insurances, and storage fees for equipment that was delivered on schedule. Real estate is too expensive in most cities to make design and construction mistakes. An inefficient design can result in lost seats, poor service, and high maintenance costs, which can end up costing you thousands of dollars in sales.

Because mistakes can be very costly, it is critical that you select knowledgeable and experienced professionals for the more technical aspects of your project. You may be able to get away with some of the design and remodeling handiwork yourself. But absolutely consider getting an architect, designer, or contractor, as appropriate, with industry experience to do the following tasks:

- Prepare, file, and monitor the required architectural and mechanical drawings with local authorities
- Ensure that all of your construction, material selection, equipment design, and installation conform with local, fire, building, and health codes
- Advise you on the right selection of seat, floor, wall, and ceiling materials based on your budget, concept, and volume estimates
- Ensure that all of your equipment is ordered with the right specifications so each piece will fit in its designated space
- Supervise the various trades to ensure that all of your gas, electric, and water outlets are located and installed to match your equipment specifications, thus avoiding costly equipment and construction change orders
- Design the flow of food and service staff to and from the kitchen, bar, and service stations so it is seamless and comfortable for your guests
- Select the proper table sizes and lay them out in a way that will maximize your seating capacity and allow for easy access to each table

If you are new to the restaurant business and have no experience with these matters, I can assure you that these professional fees will be a good investment that will pay for itself many times over.

Some equipment suppliers offer free design and architectural services if you purchase most or all of your equipment from them. But remember, few things in life are free. Compare the cost of the equipment from another dealer plus an independent designer or architect with the cost of the supplier's equipment including the free services; "free" may not be so cheap after all!

Before you make a final decision on a design professional, ask for resumes and referrals. Do your due diligence, check references and visit other projects that they have designed. Talk to owners and managers about the timeliness and quality of their work, paying particular attention to the resultant functionality and efficiency.

Design Matters

Marites Abueg and Keith Morris of Abueg Morris Architects

Betty's Laotian, once a popular neighborhood restaurant, was losing its customers. Once working class, its surrounding neighborhood was now an upscale shopping and dining area with lots of upscale eateries and retail shops. From her small loyal customer base, Betty knew that her food was good, but she knew that she had to do something to attract the affluent customers that now lived, shopped, and dined in the area. To help solve her problem, Betty called us in.

Typical of many Asian restaurants, Betty's had little in the way of design. Her dining room, with its quarry tile floor, blue walls, random art works, 1970s track lighting, and bits of grease here and there, was screaming for a makeover.

In San Francisco's East Bay, going to restaurants is no longer just a dining experience. For many foodies, dining out is a form of entertainment and temporary escape. Therefore, to help Betty's attract new customers, we decided to create a sense of theater. There was, however one little problem. Betty had a limited budget, so we had to make most of our dramatic effects come from lighting and color.

To create a sense of drama, we installed a raised seating platform with an iridescent canopy. This reorganized the large space into different levels of seating and created a sense of drama within the dining "theater." We wanted the see-and-be-seen crowd to be able to look out onto the dining room and the street. In the back, we installed dimly lit cozy booths for

Early on in your discussions, tell your consultant your budget. This will help them manage the design and construction process and choose cost-effective and functional solutions so you don't run out of funds before your project is finished. You should also discuss the type of food you plan to serve so it is reflected in your design. Last but not least, give them a copy of your market and financial feasibility study so they understand your target market and the amount of business you will need to reach your desired profit goal. These factors will influence the number of seats and other design elements in your restaurant, which will determine seat turnover and the length of the dining experience.

Select someone with a compatible personality who will listen to your ideas without preconceived notions about what your place should look like. Settle on a fee structure (fixed, hourly, percentage-of-costs fee, or a combination), and spell out what will be included in the fees, such as the number of design options and the number of meetings and hours. You should also discuss responsibility for change orders and conflict resolution. Have your attorney review the contract before you sign it. A well-written and properly executed contract will delineate the various duties and responsibilities of both parties, set the tone for a professional relationship, and help to avoid finger pointing and delays in the event that disputes should arise.

intimate romantic dining, and we installed mirrored wall niches for the side tables so that diners seated there could sneak peeks of other diners. All in all, we created an upscale dining experience with a sense of magic and escape using tricks of lighting, color, and careful placement of design elements to break up the space and frame views into and out from the room. A year later, patrons are lining up to get in the door on weekend nights once again.

Should you find yourself in Betty's situation, use the following tips to help create a pleasant dining environment inexpensively:

- Spend money on things that customers come into direct contact with, such as tables, seating, place settings, entry door handles, and bathroom fixtures.
- Use durable materials. Your restaurant will keep its luster longer and save maintenance costs.
- Do not light your space evenly! Even lighting produces a cafeteria look and a haze that makes it difficult for eyes to focus.
- Use lighting and color to create drama, to highlight features, and to hide unpleasant spots.
- To hide unsightly ceilings, use dark colored paint and down lighting.
- To create intimacy, put low voltage accent lights, candles, or table lamps on tables for menu reading, but leave the non-circulation areas around the tables in shadow.
- Point light toward accent walls or decorative areas to draw people in the door.
- Leave some mystery in the space. Use fabric or screens as entry elements to create a "slow reveal" when customers walk in the door.

COSTS

Unfortunately, one of the most talked-about stories in this business is the restaurant that doesn't open or that opens late because of budget overruns. Rule number one, therefore, is to prepare a realistic capital requirements budget and try to stick to it. If you have ever built a house or renovated your co-op or condo, you know how difficult it is to avoid those hidden costs. Any number of things can sneak up and bite you in the you-know-what! Include provisions for contingencies and overages, particularly if you have to work with or renovate an old, existing building.

Your goal should be to minimize the amount of capital investment required to meet or exceed your target customers' expectations. The way to do this is to spend your money on features that your research and your intuition suggest your target customers will value and that will set you apart from your competition. Prioritize your spending on the must-have features: heating and cooling, lighting, acoustics, seating, tables, plates, flatware, and glasses. You can spend whatever is left over on the nice-to-have features, such as fine finishes and accents.

There is a direct correlation between average check size and atmosphere. Remember Big Nick's—scruffy, but inexpensive! In its 2001 Restaurant Industry Forecast, the National Restaurant Association reported that restaurants with per-person dinner checks of $20 or less invested an average of $1,000 per seat in design and decor, and restaurants with per-person dinner checks of $50 or more invested an average of $3,000 per seat in design and decor. Obviously if your concept and feasibility study calls for an average check of $10 or less, you can be relatively sure that your customers will expect a casual atmosphere without much in the way of frills. On the other hand, if you are projecting an average check of $50 or more, you know your customers will expect comfort. In short, the nicer your atmosphere, the more you will be able to charge.

How much will it cost to design and create the right ambience for your restaurant? It all depends on what you want. There are so many variables: the quality of materials and finishes, the designer's fee, your concept (fine dining, upscale or casual, fast-food or takeout and delivery), the look and feel you want, and the size of your space. Naturally, fine materials and finishes or custom-made components are going to be expensive. That does not mean that good restaurant design and decor has to be complicated or expensive. It can be as simple as using the right combinations of light, colors, spatial relationships, wall coverings, materials, and textures. For example, when we converted our original concept to Zuni, it cost us approximately twenty thousand dollars to create a completely new ambience simply by changing floor coverings, artwork, wall and ceiling colors, and lighting fixtures. That was a relatively small investment for a dramatic effect, which received this glowing comment from *The New York Times* food critic in a 1995 review: "Southwestern motifs abound in the pleasant dining room, with its deep-blue ceiling and brick walls painted in soft yellows and oranges."

Tiger Blossom, which was located in Manhattan's trendy East Village, is another excellent example of achieving the desired atmosphere on a limited budget. For an investment of $32,000 ($533 per seat), a former children's store became a sixty-seat fine-dining Asian fusion restaurant. With simplicity as his main goal, designer Garrett Singer repeated patterns in the restaurant's decor and brought in simple artifacts that he bought in Chinatown, a couple of neighborhoods away.

Here are some tips to help you avoid costly overruns:

- One of the biggest causes of cost overruns result from the seemingly small "while you are at it" change orders. These add up quickly. Avoid this temptation; we spent about $10,000 in "surprises." And don't even *think* about major changes after starting except in the direst of circumstances.
- Before making any changes to existing equipment, such as the fire protection system or the utilities, investigate the costs of upgrading.
- Make sure that all contractors, architects, and designers are thoroughly familiar with all applicable code regulations.
- If you will be doing a renovation, make sure that your contractors find out what's behind the walls and above the ceiling tiles. Don't let them wait until demolition starts to find hidden surprises that will require costly major changes.
- Thoroughly investigate the capacity and condition of existing utilities.
- Set a realistic timetable for completion of the work.

- Don't rely exclusively on your architects and designers to educate you about the process. Talk to other restaurant owners with similar projects to find out what surprises they encountered and how they solved them.
- If a problem arises during construction, avoid the temptation to throw money at it. Insist that your contractor find a creative way to solve it, particularly if your budget is tight.

FLOW

Whether you are building your restaurant from scratch, buying, or leasing an existing restaurant, one of your primary concerns should be space flow, which was mentioned in chapter 2. Do you remember the running gag on the children's show *Sesame Street* that taught about "in" and "out"? A waiter keeps going in or out the wrong swinging doors into a restaurant kitchen and, of course, falling over and sending a huge tray of dishes every which way. If you don't plan your flow right, this could be you! Your number-one goal in layout and design is to figure out how to make the most profitable use of your space while meeting and/or exceeding your customers' needs and expectations. The concept of *flow* is central to this.

The ideal floor plan is one-directional, with no crossing flow patterns, that is, service staff and customers aren't crossing each other's paths. Unfortunately, this is virtually impossible. So your goal is to create a floor plan with as few crossing flow patterns as possible, especially avoiding them between the bathrooms and the kitchen, where servers are constantly delivering food and returning dirty dishes to the dish wash area.

The best way to illustrate the idea of flow is with an example that failed: "5 Ninth is hindered by an awkward layout.... The restaurant looks fabulous. But the kitchen is in the basement, while the main dining room is on the second floor. As a result servers are clumping up and down the stairs and often muscling their way through a tangle of bodies in the first floor bar area. The lanes of foot traffic are easily jammed. And the townhouse is so narrow that 5 Ninth, in order to maximize the space, has a few tables that barely fit two people but are used for three or four." The lesson to be learned from this critic's comments is that although the restaurant looked fabulous, proper flow and layout are very important components of a restaurant's overall atmosphere.

The dining experience starts the moment your guests walk in the door. Not only are they influenced by the way they are greeted, the visual impact of the decor, noise level, and odors, but also by the ease with which they are able to get to their tables and be seated. Your service staff should be able to quickly maneuver between their assigned tables as unobtrusively as possible, and they should also be able to move freely and easily to and from the kitchen and their service and point-of-sale (POS) stations.

Another consideration is the distance from the kitchen and service stations to the dining areas. The further away dining areas are from the kitchen and service stations, the more fatigued your servers will become during the course of a busy shift, and the less likely to provide good service. At Zuni, because of space limitations, our only coffee and bread station was located in the back of the restaurant, which seats seventy-two. Having had the experience of helping to wait on and bus tables during busy periods, I know how tiring and hard a job it is. If we had had space for one more service station, we could have had one or two fewer servers during crunch periods and would probably have been able to sell a few more desserts, since the servers would not have had to travel all the way to the back of the restaurant to get coffee. This would have meant reduced costs and extra sales for us, and more tip income for the servers. We also would have saved each server a couple hundred yards of running back and forth during busy shifts.

The ease with which your staff can accomplish their tasks will enhance the diner's experience and make your staff's jobs considerably easier. Good space flow can also reduce labor costs, since the more functional your floor plan is, the fewer servers you will need. This will be particularly evident during peak periods and in high-volume operations. We'll go more into the details of space flow and table arrangement in the next chapter.

Although there are no set guidelines for the distance servers should have to travel between tables and service stations, some experts have suggested a maximum of thirty steps and a ratio of twenty-two seats for each fully stocked service station for maximum efficiency. Obviously, in very large restaurants and in operations that have their kitchen and dining rooms located on separate floors, it is even more important for you to have strategically located, well-stocked service stations. Volume levels at peak times of business will also determine the number and size of service stations needed. For fine dining, where the meal period is typically two hours and longer, service station access and location is not critical. In fact, many fine-dining establishments locate service stations out of diners' sight in order to create a more luxurious dining environment.

In fast food and takeout operations, short straight lines that do not overlap are particularly important. The difference between success and failure could lie in well-designed flow plans.

For example, at my takeout and delivery wrap shop, while I knew that the bulk of my business was going to be during lunch, I completely underestimated the volume and did not design the proper flow between customers ordering at the order station, and those paying at the cash register station. Until I corrected this problem, there was often chaos during heavy rush periods, which resulted in frustrated customers and loss of valuable sales.

ACOUSTICS

San Francisco Chronicle restaurant critics rate restaurant ambience using bells and an exploding bomb to indicate noise levels. One bell represents pleasantly quiet (under 65 decibels); a two-bell restaurant allows patrons to talk easily (65 to 70 decibels); at three bells, talking normally gets difficult (70 to 75 decibels); at 4 bells patrons can only talk in raised voices (75 to 80 decibels); and an exploding bomb indicates that a place is too noisy for normal conversation (over 80 decibels).

Noise is a major complaint among restaurant guests. A 1997 National Restaurant Association study found that noise surpassed service, food quality, and cleanliness as the number one customer complaint. In 2001, a survey by the influential Zagat restaurant guide found that noise was guests' top complaint in major metropolitan cities. American Express's *Briefing* magazine reported the results of another recent market study, which indicated that nearly three quarters of today's consumers prefer "a quiet restaurant where it's easy to have a conversation."

Unfortunately, they're not likely to find one. A recent study of Bay Area restaurants conducted by the Audiology Division of the University of California, San Francisco, found the following noise levels at various types of restaurants on busy nights: bistros and family-style restaurants averaged between 50.5 and 71.5 decibels respectively, with family style reaching 128.2 at peak periods; restaurant and bars averaged 90.1 decibels and peaked at 142.1; while other restaurants, types not specified, averaged between 83.2 and 86 decibels with peak levels reaching 145.1. Using the *Chronicle*'s guidelines, only bistros and family-style restaurants would have been comfortable at other-than-peak periods. All other restaurant types at average decibel levels would have gotten an exploding bomb, "too noisy for normal conversation." The following decibel levels, from *Restaurant Business*, help to put these peak noise levels in perspective: rock concerts are 110 decibels, a pain threshold is 130 decibels, and a jet taking off is 140 decibels.

With all research showing that customers want less noise, why do restaurants keep getting noisier? Because most first-time independent operators don't think about noise, much less managing it. For most new owners, it's almost always an afterthought. The good news is that there are some relatively simple and inexpensive ways to help solve the problem.

Don't get me wrong; I am not suggesting that restaurants should be like libraries! After all, a certain level of noise or "buzz" enhances each restaurant experience. If your dining room is too quiet, people won't come back since they don't want others overhearing their private conversations. The idea is to create what is known as "convivial intimacy," that is, encouraging guests to feel secure in their own sense of intimacy while still being part of the crowd. I can assure you that the buzz of guests having a good time and the sight of waiters weaving in and out of tables is absolutely intoxicating. Nonetheless, noise *management* (not noise elimination) is essential to ensuring customer satisfaction and success. The question then becomes how much buzz is too much buzz?

Here comes that broken record again. It all depends on your target market and concept. For example, if your concept is upscale, plan on having conversational noise levels, since the emphasis will be more on the food and the dining experience. Why would anyone want to spend a lot of money for a nice meal and environment if they can't have a conversation? Or whisper sweet nothings into that special someone's ear? Similarly, if your target market will be mostly baby boomers, plan for lower noise levels. As we get older, our hearing capacity declines and our tolerance for noise diminishes.

The noise in your dining room or bar area can either be reflected or absorbed by everything, including walls, ceilings, floors, equipment, and furnishings. The harder the surfaces, the more the noise will be reflected and amplified. Your goal, then, is to put some decorative elements in the space that function to absorb some of the noise. Naturally, you don't want your waiters to walk around saying, "Shhh!" at your new restaurant. Remember, the idea is to manage the noise so that it becomes a pleasant buzz. Luckily, there are relatively easy ways to baffle noise, such as installing the following material:

- Carpeting and runners
- Booths, banquettes, or chairs with well-padded backs
- Window coverings and curtains
- Banners
- Decorative fabric or padding on the walls
- Padded tables
- Three-quarter-inch to one-inch painted, plain, or fabric-covered acoustical tiles on walls or ceilings
- Three-quarter-inch to one-inch fiberglass panels or baffles padded with fabric on ceilings or walls
- A good sound system with properly located speakers and an appropriate volume

You can also try the following techniques to reduce noise levels:

- Increasing spacing between tables
- Playing appropriate background music, using the right-sized amplifiers, and properly locating speakers can mask loud voices and the clatter of dishes

Of all the methods listed above, ceiling treatments are the most effective.

Sometimes, a target market and concept call for a design with high noise levels—mainly trendy see-and-be-seen cafés, restaurants, bars, and clubs that cater to a hip, urban clientele. For this demographic group and other occasion seekers, a high noise level creates action and excitement that enhances the restaurant experience.

Very often, it is possible to build in some flexibility. If you have a large enough space and can plan an efficient and functional layout, it may be possible to have two different acoustic environments: one for the bar and lounge area and another for the dining room. This will allow your restaurant to accommodate different demographic groups simultaneously. For example, boomers may want the option of having cocktails and appetizers while mingling with Gen Xers in the bar and lounge area, as spouses or empty-nester parents have a quiet dinner in a calmer environment.

MUSIC

Since the beginning of time, there have been deep psychological and emotional associations between eating and drinking and music. There are few celebratory or festive occasions for which this combination does not make for a good time. Restaurants are places we often go to eat and drink, celebrate special events, or enjoy each other's company.

Each restaurant type calls for a different level of energy, which your choice of music will directly affect. What you have to do is play to the crowd. Your own personal choice of music may not be appropriate, unless your musical tastes are similar to those of your target audience. Like other aspects of your design, your choice of music should be tailored to your target market and should also be consistent with your concept, food, and decor. Just as it would be inappropriate to play loud music at a fine-dining establishment, it would also be a mistake to play soft classical music in a trendy urban restaurant and bar.

The right background music plays an important role not only in helping to create the right overall ambience, but also in helping to relax customers and put them in a good mood or set the stage for an enjoyable restaurant experience. Some restaurateurs would go so far as to say that it's not just the food, but also the mood that keeps customers coming back. My friends and I kept going back to Calle Ocho, an upscale Latin restaurant in New York City, not only for the food, but also to experience the sultry, rhythmic background Latin music that makes us feel transported to the tropics. That, and a few mojitos!

Believe it or not, scientific studies show that music tempo can affect how long customers stay and how much they spend. For example, two studies, one in 1966 by Smith and Curnow and another in 1986 by R. E. Milliman, found that slow, relaxing music can raise tabs by as much as 40 percent. More recently, a 2003 University of Leicester study of guest psychology and restaurant traffic discovered the following:

- Restaurants that play classical background music have the highest check averages, with customers spending an average of 9 percent more
- Playing loud up-tempo music while patrons were waiting to be seated in a crowded restaurant caused them to leave before being seated since they saw their circumstance as an "avoidance condition."
- Slow music of any genre causes customers to drink and spend more.

The magic number for speeding up servers and shortening customer stays appears to be a rate of 120 beats per minute or faster. When Diner 24 first opened in New York City, people were sticking around for two hours, longer than the table turn rate the hip twenty-four-hour diner had counted on. So the restaurant switched to a more upbeat ambient sound with groups like Massive Attack, a popular British band. Tables began to turn over in an hour and a half.

This doesn't mean that you should play loud rock or rap music in an upscale restaurant if you want to encourage table turns. What you could do, however, is keep the genre of music you've selected, but change the tempo to make it more upbeat.

You can also use different tempos at different meal periods to change the mood and influence table turns and average check sizes. For example, you can play the same type of music at breakfast, lunch, and dinner, but choose more upbeat pieces and play them a little louder for breakfast and lunch when customers are more pressed for time, to help turn tables, and switch to slower, more melodic pieces at dinnertime to calm customers down and build check sizes. At Zuni, we had a slightly different twist. Between 6:00 p.m. and 10:00 p.m., when our clientele was mostly theatergoers and neighborhood residents, we played jazz standards. But after 10:00 p.m., when our clientele was mostly younger off Broadway actors and their friends, we switched to more contemporary music.

Installing a good sound system and buying and keeping your CD collection current can be quite expensive. These costs vary widely. Music services such as DMX and PlayNetwork can provide music for as little as thirty-five dollars per month and can customize music to suit your target market and meal period. A cheaper alternative is Vibetrax, which provides five to ten free genre-specific CDs every month in exchange for installing display racks of free postcards featuring their music.

You can also make music part of your unique selling proposition. Zuni attracted a crowd of regulars with its Monday-night jazz trio. Some of the city's most talented jazz musicians would often drop in for impromptu performances. Further uptown, Caffe Taci made Fridays into opera nights, where Juilliard and Manhattan School of Music students became so popular that the Italian restaurant established a pertable minimum charge and still had people waiting.

LIGHTING

More than any other design element, lighting creates mood. Good lighting can not only affect the atmosphere and mood of a room but also customers' sense of comfort and security. A well-lit room often makes people look good, which in turn can make them feel more comfortable and relaxed. Some restaurant operators have argued that people spend more when they think that they look good. Unquestionably, most of us want to be in light that flatters our appearance. Commenting on the effect of lighting and our sense of well-being, restaurant critic Marian Burros of the *New York Times* wrote in a recent review of Union Pacific: "To Mr. DiSpirito's credit he has completed a pleasing remodeling job, making what was a cold, uninviting space into something warm and welcoming with *lighting that makes everyone look good.*" (The emphasis is mine.)

The goal of any lighting system should be to make people and food look as attractive as possible. Properly selected light sources, levels, and hues can also make food look more appetizing. Lighting does not always have to be warm and fuzzy. A concept might call for high energy and action, which can be accomplished with the right lighting system, as well as with the right noise levels and music.

The more upscale your concept is, the more important your lighting systems will be in terms of creating the right mood in the bar and dining areas. Also consider that most people over forty tend to have problems reading without glasses. If your dining room is too dimly lit, baby boomer patrons (like me!) will not be able to read the menu even with glasses. Don't forget, we are the most affluent demographic group with the most spending power, particularly when it comes to dining out. So make sure to provide enough light for people to read the menus comfortably. Obviously, you don't want to ignore the under-forty crowd, which seems to find dimly lit dining rooms and bars more comfortable and/or romantic. Your goal should be to find a happy medium between too bright and too dim without being boring.

Ideally, your lighting systems and color schemes will allow for changes in mood and ambience. By changing the lighting levels and tabletop settings, you can make the same room feel cheerful for breakfast and lunch, bustling for cocktails, and romantic for dinner. Here's how Marian Burros of the *New York Times* rhapsodized about Union Pacific: "Shades of red are everywhere: plum walls, raspberry upholstery on the chairs, a wonderfully glittery red wall hanging. The room looks cheerful during the day and romantic at night."

While we could not achieve quite as dramatic an effect at Zuni, we raised the lighting levels in the dining room during lunch hours to accommodate our patrons who wanted to discuss business over lunch. They frequently brought laptop computers. During the dinner period, when most of our customers were theatergoers, we adjusted the lights to suit their preferences. After 8:00 p.m., we lowered the lights to create a more casual atmosphere.

The best way to control light levels and effect mood changes in your dining and bar areas at different times is to install a good dimming system. Dimmers are also good for cleaning up since you will be able to crank the lights up after closing to see all the bits of food and dirt on the floors. Dimmers will also come in handy if your restaurant will be large enough to have more than one dining room or section. For example, when you are not busy, you could close a section by making it dark, to avoid having your restaurant look too empty. This is very important, since many customers tend to avoid empty restaurants. Many big, boxy restaurants frequently use this tactic.

The proper use of color and light can make a room look larger, smaller, or more intimate. But be careful! Using light and colors can be very tricky, since, as we all know, the same color looks different under different light intensities. Also, light reflecting off colors in the room affects the colors' hue. I learned this the hard way when we opened Poco Loco. As the name suggests, we wanted to create a room that was a little crazy. So, stupidly, we painted each wall of the room in a different bright color. We were using indirect incandescent cove lighting on the walls, and direct downlighting from an off-white ceiling. When we turned on the lights at night, we were totally surprised. Because of the various colors' reflective properties, none of the walls looked like the color we had painted! It was more than a little crazy; it was totally crazy. After hiring a professional interior designer, we soon learned that when used properly, reflective properties along with natural light and mirrors can be very cost-effective lighting and mood-changing options. We switched to one neutral color on all of the walls, installed a large mirror, and used pink-tinted incandescent bulbs for the downlighting. This went a long way toward making our customers look good and saved us energy and money. Amazing, isn't it, what a little creativity can do.

Most lighting experts agree that because of its warm hue, incandescent lighting—that is, your typical screw-in bulb—is the best type of lighting for making people and food look good. Halogen lamps are also said to be good for this purpose. Although incandescent lamps are less expensive than fluorescent lamps, they are not very economical or efficient. A 15-watt compact florescent bulb will give almost the same amount of light as a 60-watt incandescent bulb and will last almost ten times as long. Compact fluorescent lamps are more economical, but they do not exactly enhance the appearance of people or food. Some interior designers maintain that tinted fluorescents do a better job; however, fluorescent lamps do not work with dimmers, and their lives are usually shorter when used in recessed spaces and enclosed fixtures.

Effective lighting is not only about the proper choice of lighting, but also about the proper application of direct and indirect lighting. With indirect lighting—like wall sconces or cove lighting—the light is more dispersed and covers a broad area. In effect, it washes a space in light and gives it an overall glow. When indirect lighting lamps are concealed, the light minimizes shadows and can make people look more attractive.

Direct lighting, also called downlighting, focuses light on a specific spot. A good example of direct lighting is a spot light or a chandelier. Strong downlighting highlights imperfections and therefore should not be focused directly on guests, accentuating any perceived blemishes. Also, most people will tend to feel uncomfortable if their table is more brightly lit than the immediate space surrounding them. Instead of putting people in the spotlight, surround them with softer lights.

Like table and seat selection and music, lighting can be used to encourage high turnover. The higher the light levels, the faster the turns. This explains why most fast-food establishments tend to be brightly lit, which helps to speed up the ordering and pick up process. Bright lights also discourage lingering.

Properly lighting your restaurant, whether to create the right mood or to speed customers along, can be a competitive advantage. With this in mind, and if your budget permits, you may want to allocate enough funds to hire a lighting design consultant with restaurant lighting experience. An experienced professional will be able to help you select the following elements:

- Light fixtures and their placement
- Light intensities and contrasts
- Wall, ceiling, and furniture colors
- Light direction and levels for different rooms
- A combination of fluorescent and incandescent lamps for maximum efficiency and cost effectiveness
- The best combination of direct and indirect light

New York Times restaurant critic William Grimes tells what it's like when lighting is done right. "Although long, narrow and windowless, the room feels light and airy. White marble floors and pure white walls, softly illuminated by a mysterious violet light, expand the sense of space. It's a neat bit of design work, putting the food in a seductive visual context. *A lot of thought, rather than a lot of money*, has gone into Sumile. It's smart design for smart food, all of it tied up in one very attractive package." (The emphasis is mine.)

Lighting systems can be costly to install, operate, and maintain. The cost of the electrical work alone can be expensive. On the average, lighting accounts for approximately 25 percent and 10 percent of the energy costs of most fast-food and table-service restaurants, respectively. The costs of eliminating the heat produced by lighting add another 10 percent in warmer climates where air conditioning is needed. Replacement and energy costs can be reduced by using fluorescent instead of incandescent lighting and by using higher-than-suggested wattage lamps at 50 percent capacity. If you can't get fluorescent lights to fit your atmosphere, then it is better to budget for slightly higher energy costs. Before you choose very high ceilings, consider the difficulty and costs of replacing bulbs and fixing light fixtures. All of these expenses should be included in your financial feasibility study. If you are taking over an existing restaurant, consider retrofitting it with more energy efficient and modern lighting sources.

RESTROOMS

A major decision in your restaurant's design and layout will be the location for the restrooms. Some restaurateurs like to keep them as far away from the dining room and bar as possible. Others would rather keep them well concealed, yet near the bar and dining room for easy access. There are no hard and fast rules here, but be sure to consider customer and service staff traffic flow as well as the location of the main water and sewer lines.

In many cities, local ordinances specify a minimum number of toilets or water closets and sinks or washbasins based on your projected occupancy and staff levels. For all newly constructed restaurants, federal Americans with Disabilities Act (ADA) laws require that at least one bathroom be accessible to and sized to accommodate people who are physically disabled. Restaurants that were in existence before ADA laws are usually exempt from compliance, provided there are no plans to make major modifications to the space. Restaurants that do exclusively takeout and delivery are not required to provide bathrooms.

As you might expect, the public's main concern about restaurant restrooms is cleanliness. Most restaurant restroom facilities do not make the grade. For example, two recent national public opinion surveys by Opinion Research Corporation found that restaurant restrooms ranked second only to public restrooms in terms of uncleanliness. The three problems most often cited were messy stalls, odors, and trash on the floor. Also, 77 percent of the people surveyed said they felt that an unsanitary restroom indicated management's overall attitude toward cleanliness, and 75 percent said that they were unlikely to return to restaurants with dirty or messy restrooms. Clearly, although customers spend very little time in restaurant restrooms—women average eight, and men four minutes—these short visits have an impact on overall guest experience. Your goal should be to use them to enhance the overall restaurant experience.

Unsanitary and untidy restaurant bathrooms are the result of management oversight. The three major complaints can be easily remedied by simply assigning an employee to periodically check for these sorts of things. Having been in the trenches, I can tell you that most employees hate to deal with the "messy stall" issue, whether it results from a toilet overflow, a cookie toss, or an inconsiderate customer. The easiest way to deal with this issue is to install floor drains and a pipe with a spigot for a hose connection; this way, when a mess occurs, it can be quickly washed down the drain. Floor drains also make it easy to wash and sanitize bathroom walls and floors, especially in the men's room near the urinals. Another way to deal with messy stall issues caused by inconsiderate customers (and believe me, they are out there) is to install auto-flush toilets and urinals, particularly in fast-food establishments that are subject to heavy use.

Attentive management and sanitation accessories like floor drains and proper ventilation, including exhaust fans, can take care of odor problems. You can also use air-freshening units, but they are not as effective. Most cities have local ordinances that will require bathroom ventilation. Other issues that annoy customers, yet are easily remedied, include: faulty stall doors and locks; empty paper towel, toilet paper, and toilet seat cover dispensers; empty soap dispensers; and stall doors without hooks to hang bags or jackets.

Two new bathroom fixtures that can be very effective in conveying management's concern for cleanliness are motion-activated hand towel dispensers and water faucets. Although they can be expensive to buy and install, they offer significant cost savings on water and paper towel usage. Since customers don't have to touch the dispensers or faucets, there is no need to worry about customers using them without washing their hands thoroughly.

Bathroom design and ambience also should provide a certain sense of comfort and privacy. Obviously, the more upscale the restaurant, the higher customer expectations are in terms of quality fixtures, wall and floor tiles and other materials, finishes, and accoutrements. In all cases, the materials you select should be durable and easy to clean and maintain. Nice things to have in women's restrooms are mirrors over the sinks, a small table or shelf for makeup, and full-length mirrors near the exit door. Lighting definitely should make people look good here!

A nice touch in family-oriented restaurant bathrooms (both men's and women's), when there is enough space, is diaper-changing tables. For men, rustproof privacy screens should be installed between urinals; they will have to be washed daily. Men also like mirrors over the sinks.

Typically, unisex bathrooms are found in small eateries that lack sufficient space to provide separate rooms for men and women. But recently, some trendy and upscale restaurants in large cities are opting for unisex restrooms as a way to differentiate themselves from the competition. One such restaurant that has recently caught the media's attention is Mie N Yu in Washington, D.C. Not only are the bathrooms unisex, there is also a common wash-up area. The upscale China Grill restaurants designed by famed restaurant designer Jeffrey Beers are also well-known for unisex restrooms.

Unisex restrooms can be an efficient use of space and an easy way to meet building codes, particularly when it comes to complying with ADA requirements if there is not space for an extra bathroom. Other small restaurant operators have taken the gender signs off the bathroom doors, allowing both sexes to use whichever bathroom is free as a way of alleviating long lines for the women's restroom.

Despite their successful use as a marketing tool by some trendy restaurants, unisex bathrooms are risky and may actually turn off some customers. It may not be smart to plan on them if you are not familiar with the local social mores of your target customers. Also, some cities require separate bathrooms if alcohol sales exceed more than 30 percent of total sales.

AROMAS AND OLFACTORY AMBIENCE

Few people I know can resist the smell of a fresh pot of coffee brewing, fresh bread baking, or garlic and herbs sautéing in butter or oil. Yet whenever most restaurant operators think about smells in a restaurant context, they think bleach or pine scent. They seem to somehow forget how powerfully enticing the smell of good food cooking can be. Don't take my word for it. Listen to veteran *New York Times* food writer and restaurant critic, Eric Asimov: "The scent of warm yeasty bread, of freshly cooked basmati rice, of pungent *nuoc mam* and mint in a Vietnamese place or of horseradish and lemon at an oyster bar—for starters—sharpens the appetite and opens the mind to awaiting pleasures. Yet few restaurants understand that simple equation. Instead, you are welcomed by the smell of cleanser, the receptionist's perfume or old coffee. Astounding."

An open kitchen is one of the best ways to fill your dining room with these wonderful aromas. Certain types of tableside preparations such as sizzling platters (fajitas for example), flambéed meats or desserts, or Basque style *a la plancha* (served in the same iron skillet in which the dish was prepared) also work very well. Another way to get this effect is to install aroma infusers in your dining room ventilation system. These infusers can dispense an aroma of your choice, such as fresh coffee, chocolate, or bread. An even cheaper alternative is to burn scented candles.

Just as pleasant food aromas can entice customers and sharpen their appetites, unpleasant odors such as stale bar mops, stale beer at the bar, rancid fryer oil, or day-old garbage can turn them off. So be alert to any of these avoidable mistakes.

BE FLEXIBLE

Good design and the right ambience will not guarantee success, but they can add to or detract from a good restaurant experience. They will establish your restaurant's personality and shape customer and staff expectations. Coworkers going out to celebrate a birthday or a job promotion are probably not looking for a sedate romantic atmosphere. Similarly, people who frequent cafés or other see-and-be-seen restaurants are comfortable in boisterous and highly energized atmospheres.

Whatever your basic design, however, it should be flexible enough to change with customers' differing needs at different mealtimes and on different occasions. It is entirely possible for a restaurant to have both luxurious and casual elements. In large metropolitan areas, where rents are high, many restaurants by necessity offer faster service at lunch and more relaxed formal service for dinner.

You don't have to be everything to everyone, but your design and atmosphere should say clearly what you are and provide a cohesive experience from the time your customers walk in the door to the time they pay their check and pick up their coats. Speaking of which, the more formal your restaurant is, the more seriously you should consider having a coat check. Some casual places provide hooks on the walls or on the ends of booths. Whatever you do, make sure (sorry, but here we go again) that it's what your target customers might like.

CHAPTER 8

SETTING
THE TABLE

This chapter will go into all the cost and design issues you need to consider when ordering chairs and tables and all the tableware, glassware, and flatware that goes on them.

TURNS AND TABLES

One of the concepts that you soon will obsess about is table turnover, that is, how long it takes to serve one set of customers and clear the table so another set of customers can eat there. Expected and actual table turnover rates will affect everything from your profitability to your staff needs to the way your restaurant is set up and designed—how many and what kind of chairs and tables you have and how you lay them out.

The choice between providing comfort and needing to turn tables is a constant challenge for most restaurant operators. The exception is the very expensive fine-dining establishments that figure on one or two turns per meal period. Since most of us can't add more seats, the next best way to increase volume and sales is to turn tables more frequently. The secret is to do so without making your customers feel hurried. But how do you make people feel welcome and comfortable in a convivial atmosphere without having them stay too long?

The best way to handle this issue is to know your concept well enough to anticipate the average period for each meal—breakfast, lunch, and dinner. Average dining periods are roughly two hours or more for fine dining, one and a half to two hours for casual upscale, one to one and a half hours for casual dining, and fifteen minutes to a half an hour for fast food. Include these estimates in your profit calculations. Once you have this figured out, you can establish subtle but effective ways to turn tables that will be completely invisible to your customers.

The smaller and harder you make your seats, the faster your customers will move along. Square and rectangular tables turn more frequently than round ones. By strategically placing seats in open spaces, you can also guarantee a higher rate of turnover there. In a 1999 environmental psychology study of restaurant design, Stephani K. A. Robson of Cornell University School of Hotel Administration contended that patrons at unanchored seats in open spaces (as opposed to booths along walls) are likely to feel more exposed and less in control, and therefore can be expected to leave sooner. This certainly has been my experience. Not surprisingly, Robson noted that this tactic is used effectively at T.G.I Friday's, Red Lobster, and other casual restaurants where unanchored seats turn far more rapidly than anchored seats at banquettes or at the bar.

Closely spaced tables can also help with table turns, but remember to leave enough space between tables and chairs—at least eighteen inches—for your service staff to do their jobs seamlessly and efficiently. Allow twenty-four to twenty-six inches for each chair at a table. Armchairs require twenty-eight inches.

Your concept, the shape of your dining room, and your table shapes, sizes, and layout will determine the number of seats that your dining room will be able to hold. Generally speaking, more square tables can fit in a space than round tables, but it is often possible to fit one or two more people at a round table than you can at a square table. For example, you can seat five people at a forty-two-inch-diameter round table, which is typically used to seat four.

There are no exact allocations of square feet per person in a restaurant dining room because of the many variables. For initial space planning purposes, suggested per-person square footage—including aisle and service station space—is fourteen to sixteen feet for fine dining and ten to twelve feet for casual dining. Booths and banquettes allocate space most efficiently. Guidelines are ten square feet per person for banquettes and eight square feet per person for booths. Arranging tables diagonally increases seating capacity. Fewer large tables with more seating per table increases seating capacity, but reduces flexibility. Also, with large tables, your restaurant could be full without every seat being taken. For example, four tops (tables that seat four) are often used to seat two or three people. Some years ago, one of my clients who ran a diner complained bitterly about his inability to maximize his seating capacity because he had too many booths for four that were constantly being used by parties of two.

At Zuni, we were able to seat most customers comfortably in booths for four, which averaged about six square feet per person. Also, French bistros, sidewalk cafés, and other see-and-be-seen concepts use tightly packed small tables to create the right amount of buzz, which is an integral part of the bustling European-style café experience. Before you decide on space allocation or spend a lot of money on tables and chairs or installing booths and banquettes, a smart thing to do would be to check whether your planned seating capacity is in compliance with local code requirements.

The best floor and table design, when possible and if your budget permits, is a mix of open tables, banquettes, and booths of various sizes. Not only does this selection help with seating flexibility and table turns, it also offers guests the choice of being in an intimate, private, or see-and-be-seen situation. But be careful with booths! While they are very space efficient, they encourage longer stays and can be problematic for maximizing your seating capacity during busy periods. Because they offer a sense of privacy and intimacy, people love booths. Booths also take more time to clean because you have to wash between the cracks and crevices and pull out the tables to get bits of food from underneath them. Banquettes are much better for flexible seating since two tops (tables that seat two) and four tops can be pushed together with a banquette to accommodate large parties. Open tables are good for table turns, as well as for customers with back problems who do not want to sit in booths or banquettes. Also remember that customers are reluctant to sit at tables with views of the bathrooms or the kitchen, unless the kitchen is open.

CHAIR AND TABLE CHOICES AND LAYOUT

Your design and atmosphere will include your choice of table shapes and sizes, chairs, and other types of seating such as banquettes and booths, and the way you arrange them. A mixture of different table shapes and sizes helps create visual harmony and a sense of place. Different table shapes are also great for spatial orientation and can actually make a room seem larger. Best of all, different sized tables help to create seating flexibility that will accommodate various parties of guests. A two top (that is, a table that seats two) and a four top can be combined to seat a party of five or six, or any other number of combinations.

Think about whether your restaurant will attract large or small groups of diners. If it will be family style, trendy and casual, or upscale—catering to families and large groups—you will need a selection of large tables of various shapes. On the other hand, if your restaurant will be food driven and/or romantic, you will probably need a larger selection of intimate two tops (also known as deuces), three tops and four tops.

The goal in table selection and arrangement should be to maximize seating capacity, while allowing for proper flow, functionality, and comfort. If you do not choose the right mix of tables and seating arrangements, you can potentially lose valuable seats, which can result in lost sales and profits. For example, a few years ago, I was involved as an expert witness in a lawsuit in which the owners of a busy upscale Florida restaurant sued their architect, claiming that poor space planning and table arrangement resulted in forty-two fewer seats and an estimated $14 million in lost profits over the remaining life of their lease. They also sought damages claiming that poor booth design made it difficult for customers to get in and out of their seats, which in turn resulted in the loss of return business. The case was settled for a lot less than requested, but it was still a substantial amount of money. More important, both sides agreed that there was indeed a potential loss in profits as a result of poor space planning.

CHAIR AND TABLE SELECTION

Tables, chairs, and other seating can be quite expensive. There are countless styles to choose from, and prices vary considerably depending on whether you are buying new or used or having them custom made. Typically, upholstered and custom-made chairs are the most expensive, though it is possible to get good custom pieces for less than some showroom stock pieces. The cost, naturally, will depend on your design and the materials you select. Look for pieces that are well constructed and sturdy, because if your restaurant does well, they will get an awful lot of use!

Good sources for information about restaurant furniture are local or nearby restaurant industry trade shows or other restaurant owners in your market. I strongly recommend that you attend at least one good trade show. Not only will you get to see many different types of furniture, fixtures, equipment, and supplies, you will also get a chance to comparison shop by talking to the various manufacturers or their representatives about their products and prices. Very often, you will find dealers for used and rebuilt items as well. Two websites among many on the Web that are helpful are www.restaurantfurniture.biz and www.restaurantequipment.net.

A good way to get used items on the cheap is to attend auctions from restaurants that have gone out of business. The downside to this approach is that it might be difficult to find matching pieces when you need replacements. Depending on your concept, this may not be a problem. In some operations, mishmash furniture is part of the design element and the patrons consider it to be downright chic. I am sure that you have seen many successful bistros with a mixture of tables and chairs.

Whether you buy stock or custom-made pieces, some guidelines can help. When purchasing tables and chairs, check for sturdy construction. For all types of furniture, get samples delivered to your site before you place your final order. Sit in the chairs for a week or two to see if their comfort level suits your concept. Match the chairs and tables to confirm that there are at least twelve inches between the seats and the tabletops, so your guests can get in and out of their seats easily. Also use this opportunity to check that the chairs will fit under the tables when not in use, freeing up aisle space.

CHAIRS

To ensure that your chairs not only match your concept but are also functional, comfortable, and easy and cost effective to store and maintain, keep the following guidelines in mind when selecting chairs:

- Chairs that are colored with stain or dye are easier to maintain, and the colors last longer, than those that are painted.
- The recommended incline for chair backs is a 15-degree angle.
- A chair's seat should be at least sixteen inches from the back of the chair to the edge.
- The height from the top of a chair to the floor should not be more than thirty-four inches. Higher chairs can impede service.
- The distance from a chair's seat to the floor should be sixteen to eighteen inches.
- If your concept calls for high volume, consider getting stackable chairs. They are easy to store, and it makes cleaning floors easy.
- Chairs that are easy to clean and move save labor.

TABLES

Like chairs, tables should also be functional, comfortable, and easy and cost effectively cleaned and maintained. Keep the following guidelines in mind when selecting tables:

- Standard table heights are twenty-six to thirty inches.
- Self-leveling table legs or bases allow you to adjust for uneven floors and wobbles. The table base should be large enough to support the weight and distribution of all the platters and plates that will be placed on it without tipping over.
- Tabletops can be wood, marble, stone, ceramic, Formica, or Corian, all of which can be stain resistant. If you plan to use tablecloths, tabletop appearance is not critical. If you will not be using tablecloths, you should select a tabletop that is consistent with your concept and overall design, that is durable, and that is—very important—easy to clean. Stone tops are very durable and attractive, but they stain easily.
- Tabletops should be waterproof.
- Table bases should have ample legroom. The best choices are the four-pronged spider base or the cylindrical mushroom pedestal base. Pedestal bases do not get in the way of chairs when they are pushed under tables, or in the way of guests' legs when they are seated.
- Square two tops, known as deuces, can be either 24 by 24 or 24 by 30 inches. A typical place setting is twenty-four inches square; a more formal setting will require a 24-by-30-inch table. Your concept, style of service, and the amount of flatware, glassware, and plates you will use to set the table will determine the size of your tabletops. In family-style operations and Chinese restaurants, tabletops should be large enough to hold platters that allow for sharing. The

more upscale the concept, the more space per person you will need at each table.

- Tables that seat three or four people, known as four tops, are available in 36-by-36-inch square, 30-by-48-inch rectangular, 36-inch-diameter round, or 42-inch-diameter round sizes. Remember, in a squeeze you can fit an additional person at a round table.
- Combining a two top and a four top or using a 48-inch-diameter or 54-inch-diameter round table can accommodate five or six people.
- Combining two four tops can accommodate seven or eight people.
- Cocktail lounge tables can either be 20 by 20 inches square or 20 inches round.
- Tables with swing-up wings of various sizes can convert a square table into a round one, conserving space and increasing flexibility.

UPHOLSTERY

Upholstered seating offers an opportunity to mix and match colors and textures with your overall design and decor. It also helps with noise control. However, make sure that cushioning for banquettes and booths does not sink so low that guests will find it difficult to get in and out of their seats. The amount of space between the booth seat and the table edge is very important, since booths cannot be pushed back to accommodate large people.

When choosing upholstery, your primary concern should be maintenance. Always use commercial-grade upholstery that has been treated with stain-resistant chemicals to maximize its useful life. Commercial-grade vinyl comes in many colors, patterns, and textures and is durable and easy to clean. Some of the higher grades are indistinguishable from leather and could easily be used for upscale dining. Leather, which is also durable and easy to clean, is more expensive.

TABLETOP DESIGN

Items typically used to set a tabletop are dinnerware (plates); glassware; flatware (knives and forks); condiment holders for sugar, salt, and pepper, tablecloths; and napkins. The three terms that you should be familiar with for tabletop design are:

- Place setting, which is a set of plates, glasses, knives, and forks for one person
- Table setting, which is a place setting plus a tablecloth and a napkin
- Tabletop, which is a table setting plus condiment holders and any other items on the table, such as candle holders, bud vases, and additional wine glasses

Table settings vary according to concept, style of service, cuisine type, and target market. There are many acceptable alternatives between very formal and very basic, but as a rule, the more formal and upscale the restaurant, the more guests will expect in terms of tabletop design. For example, while patrons of a formal French restaurant will anticipate white tablecloths, intricately folded napkins, and myriad place settings, customers at the local family-style diner would feel quite at home with disposable paper napkins, basic water glasses, and no tablecloths.

If your concept will be fine dining or high-end casual, you can use tabletop design elements such as candles, flowers, fine china, glassware and flatware, additional glasses, and various color tablecloths and napkins to enhance your ambience. The more customers are prepared to spend for a restaurant experience, the more they will expect table settings that are not only visually appealing, but also pleasant to the touch and comfortable to hold.

The three most important considerations when buying tableware (plates, glasses, and flatware) are:

- Cost
- Availability
- Durability

Tableware varies in style, design, and costs. Depending on your choices, your initial investment can be quite substantial. Before making your final purchase, a good way to avoid costly errors is to get samples of all of your place settings and take them to your restaurant. Once there, set your various tabletops (the different shapes and sizes) to make sure that all the items complement each other, fit properly, and look the way you want them to, not just on the tabletops, but in the context of the room itself. Check that the flatware will sit well on the plates without slipping into the base when resting on the plate's edge.

Noncommercial tableware is not designed to withstand the rigors of constant use and cleaning found in a busy restaurant environment. So don't plan on using those beautiful place settings you saw in your local department store or the ones that Grandma gave you to open your new café. Cooking methods will also be important in selecting dinnerware. If some of your plates will have to be placed under a broiler (with cheese nachos, for example) or sit on ice for long periods of time, you must choose pieces that will withstand these temperature extremes.

Unfortunately, after your initial investment, your replacement costs are likely to continue at a fairly high rate. It is estimated that 20 percent of tableware has to be replaced every year due to breakage and theft. In high-volume operations, the estimate can be as high as 80 percent. A common joke in the business is that your tableware replacement costs will drop after each of your staff has a five-piece table setting at home. So before choosing tableware, particularly if you have a high-end concept in mind, make sure that your projected volumes and check averages will support your investment.

With all of your table settings, it is important to make sure that replacements will be readily available. Ask your prospective vendors or suppliers about delivery lead times. Will it take three days, a week, or three months between the time you place an order and the time it is delivered? This is particularly important if your concept will be high-end and you use custom-designed tableware, which can take as much as three months or more to fulfill an order.

Your ability to store tableware properly and securely is also important. Obviously, the greater the variety of place settings you choose, the more storage you will need. The amount of lead time necessary to replace tableware is another important storage consideration. If you will be using custom-designed pieces with long replacement lead times, you will need to stock and store more of each item. In short, the less storage you have, the more important it will be to choose items that will be readily available.

Determining the right amount of opening tableware inventory can be tricky. If you order too many pieces, you tie up badly needed working capital, a common first-timer mistake. But if you order too little, you may provide slow service and overwork your dishwashers, increasing breakage and losing badly needed business. For advice on how much to buy, ask other operators with similar restaurant sizes and concepts. Also, some tableware manufacturers and suppliers—Oneida Foodservice and Libbey, for example—offer charts to help you decide how many of each piece of table setting to order. Combine these suggested quantities with your own realistic volume projections, good judgment, and common sense.

For example, if your seating capacity is fifty and dinner will be your peak period, during which you expect to turn your tables three times (that is, seat 150 customers), you will probably need at least 125 dinner, salad, dessert, and bread plates, or 2.5 times (two and a half times the amount of seats) your rush-hour demand. This should be enough to allow for extras to replace broken and stolen pieces, in addition to allowing time to bus, scrape, wash, dry, and reuse each plate a few times. You won't necessarily have to order 150 of each item, since with fifty seats, you won't be seating all 150 people at the same time. If your volumes are higher with the same seating capacity, you probably will need higher inventory levels since the more often glasses and plates are used, the more likely they are to be broken.

If, on the other hand, you will be running an expensive, fine-dining establishment with fifty seats and expect to have only one seating for dinner, which will be your peak period, you will probably only need about seventy-five pieces of each place setting. Here, you will only be seating fifty people, and will not have to wash and replace each piece during the course of dinner. The extra twenty-five pieces should be enough to make provisions for breakage and theft.

One final word: avoid buying tableware from catalogs unless you can get samples to touch, see, and examine personally.

DINNERWARE

Of all of your place settings, your dinnerware (dinner, dessert, bread, salad, and soup plates), which is usually sold by the dozen per piece, will probably be the most costly. In a family-style restaurant, you will not need fancy and elegant china, but instead can buy something that is simple, pleasant to look at, and gives the best impression of your portion sizes. For upscale dining, your chef will probably want plates that can be used as a canvas on which to paint his or her food presentations. In these cases, some shade of white is usually the best color choice.

If your concept calls for a colorful plate, check to see that it complements rather than detracts from the look of your food. A good way to avoid mistakes with plate colors, patterns, and food presentation is to present some of your menu items on sample plates before placing a final order.

Plate size has important portion size and control implications from both the guest and kitchen staff perspective. When kitchen staff is not properly supervised and trained, they are usually inclined to serve too much on large plates and too little on small plates. At Zuni, for example, when we switched from 10½- to 12-inch dinner plates, our food costs increased by about 3 percent in the first month after the switch since some members of the kitchen staff felt that they had to put more on the larger plates.

Form the guests' perspective, large plates can make portions look skimpy while small plates can give an impression of abundance. At Zuni, when we finally got the portion size on the new 12-inch plates under control, in addition to getting compliments on the plate presentation, some of our regulars started asking if we had reduced our portion sizes.

Some useful questions to ponder before buying dinnerware include the following:

- What are the prices of dinnerware styles and patterns that are suitable for my concept?
- How will dinnerware styles and patterns work with my atmosphere and decor?
- What shapes and sizes of plates will be appropriate for my menu items and portion sizes?
- What are the shapes and sizes of the tables in my dining room?
- What do my target customers expect in terms of dinnerware?
- How durable will my plates have to be? For example, will they have to be placed under salamanders (broilers) or sit on ice for long periods of time?
- How many meals will I have to serve at peak periods?
- What is my dishwasher's capacity?
- How and where will I store my dishes? Where will they sit during the washing and drying process? Note: roughly 75 to 80 percent of broken plates happen in the dish wash area.

GLASSWARE

Many of the same criteria used to select dinnerware—such as concept, target market; overall ambience, design, and decor; availability; and storage—will apply to selecting glassware. You target clientele and the types of cocktails you plan to serve will be the most important factors in determining the types of glasses to buy.

There are three types of glassware: tumblers, footed ware, and stemware. Tumblers are cylindrical and flat-bottomed; they are commonly used for drinks served on the rocks (over ice cubes), highballs, beer (a pint), and shots. Footed glasses can have curved or cylindrical bowls, a short or no stem, and a base, or foot. Any type of drink can be served in the right size footed glass, such as a brandy snifter. Footed glasses are also used to serve drinks straight up. A stemware glass has a long stem between the bowl and the base. As you might expect, this is the most fragile type of glassware. Wine, martini, and champagne glasses are stemware.

Glasses enhance the presentation of drinks. In trendy restaurants and bars, visually appealing large, frosted beer mugs, oversized frozen margarita glasses, and whimsical martini glasses can increase the drinks' perceived value and help to increase sales. Certain types of martini glasses can also be used to serve and display appetizers and desserts like shrimp cocktail, ceviche, ice cream, and sorbet.

Restaurants offering table service only will usually not carry a full liquor license, being licensed to sell only wine and beer. These establishments need only water, wine, and beer glasses, not the myriad of cocktail glasses typically found in a restaurant and bar with a hard liquor license. The more upscale your concept and the more extensive your wine list, the larger the variety of wine glasses you will need, since matching wines with the proper glasses is part of a restaurant's overall ambience. To wine connoisseurs—who hold that swirling wine in the properly shaped glass helps to release its various fruit, oak, and other flavors into the nostrils—the olfactory pleasure of savoring a wine's aromas enhances the drinking and dining experience.

Serving wine does not always require the use of stemware. Some casual, family-style Italian and Greek restaurants create a rustic dining experience by serving table wine by the pitcher with basic water tumblers. In fact, some industry experts argue that people would drink more wine if stemware etiquette weren't so formal and pretentious. Your concept and the demographics and psychographics of your target market will dictate the quality of wines to serve and how formal or informal your wine service should be.

Certain types of cocktails will require specific glasses. For example, can you imagine serving a martini in anything other than a martini glass?

Most spirits and beverage glasses are not supposed to be filled to the brim, and knowing the right portion sizes for various types of glassware is critical for controlling beverage costs. For example, although the standard wine glass has an eight- or nine-ounce bowl, the standard pour when selling wine by the glass is usually five to six ounces, which allows customers to swirl their wine. Think of the amount of profit that would be lost if each glass were filled to the brim! Another good example is a brandy snifter, which is available in sizes ranging from 5½ to 34 ounces, but is never meant to serve more than one or two ounces of brandy. One way to avoid over-portioning is to use portion-specific glasses. For example, instead of using a tall draft beer glass that holds more than 12 ounces, you can use a squat, large diameter glass that holds only 12 ounces. For more on this discussion, see chapter 9.

Because glassware is fragile, stemware in particular, buy only the sturdiest. The strongest glassware is made of fully tempered glass. The majority of stemware is usually fully tempered, but some types of glassware such as tumblers and mugs may have only tempered rims. The most durable glasses are those with curved or barrel shaped bowls, rolled edged rims, and swirled or ribbed patterns. Cylindrical or straight-sided glasses are less durable. Avoid glassware that requires special handling, such as flared rimmed glasses. These tend to break easily.

Glasses break either from thermal shock (sudden temperature change) or from direct impact with other glasses or objects. But as we say in the business, "Glasses don't just break; people break them." While you may not be able to eliminate breakage completely, the following handling practices will reduce the incidence considerably:

- Do not load glasses and other tableware into the same bus tubs. Use separate bus tubs and racks made specifically for glasses.
- To avoid thermal shock, always have enough glasses on hand so you won't have to serve cold drinks in hot, wet glasses right out of the dishwasher.
- Do not use glasses to scoop ice. Use plastic scoops, not metal scoops, which can chip rims.
- Avoid stacking glasses one inside the other or picking up multiple glasses at the same time.

To determine the number of glasses to buy for each type of drink you will be serving, use the same approach that you would when buying dinnerware. As would be expected, the key determinants will be seating and bar capacity, projected volume levels at peak periods, and your budget. Since glasses are a lot more fragile than plates, you may have to order slightly higher quantities.

For a restaurant with table service only, buy twice as many glasses as the number of each type of drink you expect to serve during your peak period. For a restaurant with a bar, you may want to get four times as many. Don't forget to factor in availability and load times.

FLATWARE

Flatware is handled more than any other tableware item, so your goal should be to find pieces that are comfortable to hold. Before you make your final decision on what to buy, get samples and heft them. If they feel light and flimsy to you, chances are, they are going to feel the same to your customers. Don't forget the steak test—a knife and fork need to be able to cut up a steak.

The standard flatware pattern includes eight items, many of which are not used in casual dining: teaspoon, dessertspoon, soupspoon, iced tea spoon, dinner fork, salad fork, cocktail fork, and dinner knife. Some patterns have as many as twenty items, including round-tipped butter knives, fish knives and forks, and steak knives. Others are limited to a basic setting, such as dinner fork, knife, teaspoon, and tablespoon. Generally, your concept and menu will determine your flatware needs. Again, the more upscale the concept, the greater the likelihood that you will need different knives, forks, and spoons for different courses—although the Conran restaurants, a high-end restaurant group in England owned by the world renowned designer Terrance Conran have pioneered a current trend toward an uncomplicated and informal use of cutlery in upscale restaurants, using the same type of knife and fork for savory courses and the same type of spoon for desserts and soups.

Except for exceedingly high-end fine-dining restaurants, which use silver-plated flatware, a stainless steel blend of flatware commonly referred to as "18/8" is the best choice for most casual and upscale restaurants. This stainless steel blend is usually composed of 74 percent steel, 18 percent chrome, and 8 percent nickel. It is very resistant to food acids and cleaning chemicals, and it stands up to the rigors of constant usage and cleaning without losing its luster. A more expensive option is the 18/10 blend, which contains 2 percent more nickel. These blends are also very sturdy and are usually nicely weighted.

When choosing flatware, look for forks with smooth, rounded edges and slightly concave handles. Forks with thin shanks are usually difficult to hold and bend easily. Select single-piece knives with smooth, rounded edges. If you choose knives with hollow handles, check to see that the handles are securely welded to the blades. Spoons should have bowls with smooth edges and slightly concave handles. Better quality flatware is shaped so the stress points (the necks) are slightly thicker. Generally, the more ornate the design, the fewer scratches will show. For optimum sanitation, flatware should be air-dried before it is polished.

Flatware can be expensive and has a way of disappearing into the garbage. To avoid loosing flatware in the garbage when plates are being scraped, have service staff place them in special flatware holders when tables are bused. Also, if you will be operating in an environment with high pilferage by customers, such as a college town, it may be wise to use generic low-cost flatware.

TABLECLOTHS AND NAPKINS

One of the most effective ways to change a restaurant's overall ambience is to dress or undress its tabletops with tablecloths and cloth napkins. For example, when I converted Poco Loco, a kitschy casual Mexican bar and restaurant, to Zuni, which was more upscale, we started dressing the tables with white tablecloths and white cloth napkins. That design element most changed the public's perception of our new establishment. Immediately, neighborhood residents started associating the restaurant more with food and dining and less with being a bar. Not surprisingly, when celebrity chefs and restaurateurs in New York City were looking to make fine dining less formal, the first thing they did was to undress their tabletops. The trend is becoming so popular in New York City that it prompted *New York Times* food writer Amanda Hesser to pen an article entitled "No Tablecloth? This Is Fine Dining?" detailing the many celebrity chefs—including Jean-Georges Vongerichten, Daniel Boulud, and Marcus Samuelsson—who have made the switch. While some restaurateurs are opting for completely bare tabletops, others are using paper to top their tables, which is wrapped up and discarded when the tables are bussed.

Despite the trend by prominent restaurateurs in some major cities toward making fine dining less formal by removing tablecloths, they are still widely used in many fine dining and casual restaurants. In fact, many restaurants use different color napkins and tablecloths at different times of the day and meal periods to change the atmosphere and energy level in their dining rooms. For breakfast and lunch, some use soft pink to create a more restful feeling, and white is used at dinner to enhance a more formal, energetic feeling.

To maintain their high-end image, fine-dining restaurants tend to use white linen napery (tablecloths and napkins), which have the feel that fine dining clientele expect. In addition to being soft to the touch, cotton cloths are more absorbent than blends and are better suited for wiping hands and mopping up spills. Also, when starched, cotton napkins are ideal for making decorative folds. The problem with cotton napkins and tablecloths is that while they are available in a wide array of colors, they are not colorfast.

Many lobster and seafood and Italian, Greek, and Mexican family-style restaurants use checkered plastic tablecloths. Typically, however, tablecloths and napkins are either made of cotton, polyester, or a cotton-polyester blend. Many casual restaurants use all-polyester cloths and napkins, which is available in more colors and is much more stain-resistant and colorfast than cotton. The downside with pure polyester is that it is neither soft to the touch nor absorbent and is therefore not good for cleaning up spills and wiping hands. It also does not fold well and consequently is not good for decorative folds.

An alternative to all cotton or all polyester is a cotton-polyester blend, which offers some of the benefits of both cotton and polyester. The composition of the fabric determines its softness and ability to hold folds. The more cotton, the softer the fabric and the better it will be for holding folds and vice versa. Many restaurants straddle between fine dining and upscale by using all-cotton napkins, and cotton-polyester blend tablecloths.

For most independent restaurant operators, the best and most cost-effective way to get table linens is to rent them. Companies in most cities specialize in providing clean linens on a regularly scheduled basis. An alternative is to buy and launder your own, but the expense of paying for space, labor, utilities, detergent, water, and laundry equipment maintenance is usually not cost effective. Not that renting table linens is cheap! In New York City, using a clean tablecloth and napkin with every table turn adds $1.10 to the cost of every meal sold. In 2003, the annual laundry bill at one of New York's most prominent restaurants was almost $150,000.

Fortunately, there are ways of getting around using a fresh tablecloth with every table turn. To protect tablecloths and get multiple uses, many casual and upscale restaurants cover them with butcher paper, which is removed and replaced with each table turn. Another method is to cover tablecloths with a piece of clear glass or plastic cut to fit the tabletop. After each table turn, the glass or plastic is wiped down and reset with clean place settings.

CHAPTER 9

RAISING THE BAR

There is nothing like the sense of conviviality at an attractive busy bar to draw customers in the door. Not surprisingly, then, most restaurants in busy urban areas situate their bars so passers-by can see them easily. After all, if you can entice people in for a drink, you increase the probability that they will stay or come back another day for lunch or dinner.

A bar also provides an ideal opportunity to sell cocktails and high-margin appetizers while customers are waiting to be seated. When a waitress walks by with an enticing appetizer, heads turn and people ask for menus. Also, as dining out becomes more popular, and with the ban on smoking in restaurants in some states, bars once seen as places mostly for drinking are becoming increasingly popular as places for dining for both male and female single diners. Reflecting this, Zagat surveys now include sections for "best dining at the bar" and "best places to meet for a drink." Interestingly, most of the establishments named in these categories are restaurants—not bars. At Zuni, we had quite a few customers who ate dinner regularly at the bar. Many newcomers to the neighborhood met new friends at our bar. Never doubt this old saw for a minute: "It is more fun to eat in a bar than to drink in a restaurant."

This is great news for restaurants, because bar dining can be more profitable than standard dining. Not only do people tend to spend more when they drink, but bar stools turn a lot faster than tables do. The big bonus, however, is that profit margins on the sale of alcoholic beverages in restaurants are substantially higher than they are on the sale of food. While the cost of sales on food in a well-managed table service restaurant runs 28–35 percent of food revenues, the average overall cost of sales also known as pour costs on alcoholic beverages can average 16–20 percent, 16–28 percent, and 16–33 percent for liquor, beer, and wine respectively.

If you can get the economics and the concept right, a bar can contribute substantially to your success and future profits. Not only can a bar be a good stand-alone profit center, it can also be integrated with your restaurant financial planning to allow you to provide a better unique selling proposition for your customers. Bill McCormick and Doug Schmick—co-owners of McCormick & Schmick's Seafood Restaurants, a group of full-service seafood restaurants known for their high-quality bars—explained the synergies between their bar and dining room to *Total Food Service* magazine: "We have always felt that the strength of our bar sales helps subsidize the price point in the dining room. If you look at a product in the dining room for which we charge $18 or $19, that same product in a facility where we didn't have a strong bar program would be around $21."

In short, a well-managed bar can very often mean the difference between success and failure, or between marginally profitable, profitable, and very profitable for a restaurant. Good food may keep customers coming back, but the booze will help ensure that you make a profit.

YOUR TARGET MARKET

The key to deciding on whether and what kind of bar to have, as always, is to understand your market and to formulate the right concept based on the demographics of your location. First, let's look at overall demographics related to bars. According to *Beverage Digest* magazine, which tracks beverage consumption in the United States, alcoholic beverage consumption declined steadily from an average of 2 gallons per person per year in the 1970s to an average of 1.2 to 1.3 gallons per person per year in 1992, when it leveled off and remained steady until 2001. During the decline years, people drank "less but better," preferring to drink premium wines and spirits.

Today, not only are people drinking "better," they are also beginning to drink more. Consider the following:

- According to the Distilled Spirits Council, Americans drank more spirits overall including premium spirits in 2002 than they did in 2001. The council also reported an overall increase in spirits consumption of 4.5 percent in 2003 over 2002.
- A July 2004 Gallup survey found that since 1992, "The percentage of Americans reporting that they had at least one drink in the past week rose from 48% to 68%."
- According to the Wine Institute, wine consumption in the United States increased by 5.9 percent in 2002 over 2001 consumption to 250 million cases. With this increase, "America is currently the third largest wine-consuming

nation in the world and will almost certainly become the largest by the end of the decade." The institute also reported that U.S. wine consumption increased another 5 percent in 2003.

- A recent study conducted by the Brown-Forman Group found that not only did wine sales in restaurants increase by 8 percent over 2002 sales to $9.9 billion in 2003, but wine drinkers visit restaurants more frequently, leave more satisfied, and spend 10 percent more than other customers.

With this overall positive trend in mind, your job is to figure out how it applies to your target customers. What is their disposable income? How old are they? How often do they go to restaurants or bars? What kind of ambience do they like?

Look for areas with lots of childless married couples and or married couples with adult children at home. Not surprisingly, these groups spend the most on alcohol in restaurants and bars.

The size of the bar and its placement within your restaurant will depend on your restaurant's location and concept. The importance of selling alcoholic beverages to your projected overall profitability should play a big part in how much space you allocate to the bar.

If, for example, your concept is fine dining focusing exclusively on food and wine and the fine-dining experience, your bar typically will be a small, service bar. A service bar has few if any bar stools or tables for dining in the bar area. The bartender's primary function is to mix and pour alcoholic drinks for patrons seated in the dining room. In addition to fine-dining establishments, service bars are also common in diners and small casual restaurants where there is not enough room for a full bar.

That said, some of the most successful fine-dining restaurants in the country have very successful full bars. Examples are The Four Seasons in New York City, Boulevard in San Francisco, and Café Atlantico in Washington, D.C.

The decision to sell liquor or to include a bar in your restaurant has many start-up, design, and layout implications, some of which will be discussed in the following sections.

ALCOHOL AND OVERALL PROFITABILITY

Because the profit margins on alcohol are much higher than on food, alcoholic beverage sales can be so much more profitable than food sales, the greater the percentage of your total sales is from alcohol, the better it will be for your bottom line. The ideal ratio of food to beverage sales is 60 percent to 40 percent. I was surprised to read that some operations actually do better than this. Chicago's Bin 36 does 50 percent of its sales in alcoholic beverages, three-quarters of which come from wine by the glass—a particularly profitable beverage. However, most well-run restaurants and bars can do very well averaging 25-35 percent in beverage sales.

When the bar is mainly a waiting area for diners, it usually does not play as prominent a role in a restaurant's overall profitability as when it is an integral part of the business.

After you have decided how important bar sales will be to your overall profitability, you will be able to determine whether you have enough space for the type of bar you have in mind to accommodate required volume levels. You would have done this in your financial feasibility study.

LIQUOR LIABILITY INSURANCE

In most if not all states, restaurants and bars are required to carry liquor liability insurance to protect themselves from law suits brought by victims of automobile accidents caused by drivers who may have gotten drunk on their premises. Liquor liability insurance varies from state to state and is usually included as part of an umbrella insurance policy. In some states, insurance carriers offer reduced premiums to restaurants and bars that have trained their servers (waiters and bartenders) on how to handle intoxicated customers through an insurer-approved program. In New York City, the cost of liquor liability insurance did not add substantially to our umbrella policy. Most if not all restaurant insurance brokers can advise you on the appropriate amount of coverage you will need. Your local restaurant association is a good source for finding brokers, and then shop around for a broker who will work to get you a less expensive policy.

LICENSES

In order to sell alcoholic beverages, you need a state license. Many states offer two types of licenses: one to sell spirits, wine, and beer—called a "full" liquor license—and another to sell only beer and wine called—you guessed it—a "beer and wine" license. Full licenses typically require a lot more red tape and usually take longer to obtain. In some states, like Oregon, you must sell food as well if you want to sell spirits or "hard" liquor. This requires submitting a menu, a seating floor plan, and a schedule of when your cooks will be in the restaurant. None of these requirements are necessary for a beer and wine license.

There are two types of states: control states and license states. The licensing requirements in control and license states can differ significantly, so it is important to know which type of state your restaurant will be in. You can do this at the National Alcohol Beverage Control Association's website (www.nabca.org), which lists all the control states and the names, addresses, and telephone numbers of the state and local licensing authorities and provides a link to license states.

In some control states, state-owned and controlled outlets sell alcoholic beverages to customers, bars, and restaurants. In other states, liquor suppliers are privately owned but must buy alcoholic beverages from the state. Control states publish a monthly list of all of the state-owned stores and their addresses along with available brands and prices.

In license states, privately owned and operated wholesale liquor distributors, which state authorities strictly regulate, sell alcoholic beverages to state-licensed restaurants and bars. Most of the license states publish a monthly list of all of the wholesalers in the state along with their product lines and prices.

The sale of alcoholic beverages is highly regulated in every state through myriad rules, including if, when, and where you can operate, what hours you will be allowed to do business, and from whom you can buy your inventory. Regulations vary from the ridiculous to the sublime:

- Arkansas does not allow the purchase of alcohol with a credit card.
- In Alabama, alcohol cannot be purchased by phone, fax, or over the Internet.
- Servers in Utah cannot offer guests a wine list; the guest must ask for it.
- In New York, supermarkets are allowed to sell beer but not wine.
- New York City does not allow the sale of alcohol within two hundred feet of schools, churches, or other houses of worship.

You may also have to comply with local regulations. Don't assume that because you meet state regulations you will be able to sell alcohol. Most states have local option laws, which allow residents of local communities to determine whether or not to allow the sale of alcohol. Regulations often vary even within the same town. Areas that allow the sale of alcohol are called "wet" areas, and those that don't are called "dry." It is not uncommon for certain local authorities to require applicants to be fingerprinted, post notices on their premises and in local newspapers, and appear before the city council.

Needless to say, obtaining a license can be a lengthy and complex process that often requires hiring attorneys or other professionals who specialize in dealing with the state liquor authority and local community boards to file and expedite the required application forms. The best way to find a liquor license professional is to ask other restaurant owners or your state or local restaurant association for referrals.

In states like New Jersey, Massachusetts, and Illinois, where only a limited number of licenses are available, the cost of buying a license from a current holder can be in the tens, hundreds of thousands, or even millions of dollars. For example, a recent issue of *Nation's Restaurant News* reported that licenses go for between $200,000 to $300,000 in Boston and $1 million to $2 million in New Jersey. In other states, such as California, licenses can either be bought from the state when they are available or on the open market from former restaurateurs or brokers; in California, these costs run approximately $12,000 and $17,000, respectively. Currently, in New York State, the cost of a three-year full liquor license, which can only be bought from the state, is $5,300.

Thus, before signing a lease or making other significant capital commitments based on your ability to sell liquor, it is crucial that you thoroughly investigate your state and local laws and ordinances. You should also find out what the actual cost of obtaining the license will be. Over the years, I have heard numerous stories about people who built bars in restaurants only to find out later that for some obscure reason they or their location did not qualify.

Fortunately, most of the required information is available online. To get licensing information, visit the website of your state or local restaurant association for links to your state's liquor authority. Two other excellent sources are the Distilled Spirits Council of the United States (www.discus.org) and the National Alcohol Beverage Control Association (www.nabca.org).

BAR SIZE AND LAYOUT

Will you have space for a bar and for beer, wine, and liquor inventories? Will you serve food at the bar? If so, is there enough space? If space is not available for a full bar, will you have room for a service bar? The answers to these questions will affect the size of and the design and layout of your bar. You don't want your bar to be too big or too small. Knowing volume levels will also help you to design an efficient and work-friendly space. That said, bars in table-service restaurants do not have to be particularly large to be successful.

The best way to get a good understanding about the proper layout and design for a bar is to visit other restaurants with bars of different shapes and sizes. Sit at the bars and observe the ease with which the bartender can move around and access beverages, ice, equipment, tools, and condiments. Don't be afraid to take along pen and paper to make notes. Not only did I visit bars and take notes, I also asked the owner/manager of my favorite restaurant and bar if he would give me a tour of his bar during off hours. There are also numerous books about bar design and layout. Pick one up and study some of the many diagrams to get more ideas.

As mentioned in chapter 7, space design is an art. If you are not good with spatial relationships, then hire an architect or contractor with restaurant and bar design experience to create a bar layout with the right amount of bar stools, standing room, and tables to meet your desired volume and profit levels. Also, if you plan to serve food in the bar or lounge area, make sure that you will have room for appropriate-sized tables. If you do not want to encourage eating, you may want to plan for small tables.

To set up your bar for maximum profitability and efficiency, make sure that all of the necessary equipment, glassware, and bar tools are properly sized and arranged for quick and easy access. Ingredients such as beverages, ice, garnishes, and mixers should also be easily accessible. To design an efficient bartender station, use the one-step rule, which requires that a bartender should not have to take more than one step in order to make 90 percent of his or her drink requests.

If you want a bar that is visible to the public, locate it where the dining room does not block it visually or physically. For example at Zuni, which is a long, narrow restaurant, the bar is located at the front, street entrance. As a result, when the bar was crowded, passers-by often assumed that the entire restaurant was full since they could not see the dining room to prove otherwise. Needless to say, there were days when we lost a lot of dinner business because of this. Guests with reservations also had difficulty wading through crowds to get to the dining room on busy bar nights.

But you can't have everything. We did, after all, deliberately put the bar up front to attract business. Also, given the shape of the space, there was no better place.

If there will be a strong emphasis on pairing wines with your menu, you will probably have to carry a wide wine selection, which will require additional storage space. To keep wine at the right temperature, you may need to install wine cellars that maintain different temperatures for reds and whites. You may also want to do more wine merchandising at the bar with visual displays, which may require additional storage space behind the bar, and other wine displays in the dining room.

If at all possible, locate the bar near plumbing lines to avoid additional plumbing costs. The farther plumbers have to run water and waste lines, the more expensive your plumbing costs will be. Bars also require numerous electrical outlets for refrigeration, point-of-sale systems, blenders, slush machines, back- and under-bar lighting, and glass washers. In New York City, health codes dictate that slush and frozen margarita machines must be within a certain distance from a hand wash sink. Health, Americans with Disabilities Act (ADA), and fire code requirements also affect layout and design considerations, especially aisle space. Licensing requirements in some states and localities may influence bar location. For example, some states prohibit bars that are visible to the public. To learn more about federal ADA requirements for restaurant bars, go to www.ada.gov and click on "Small Business." Local ADA requirements are sometimes more stringent than federal laws, so be sure to check with your local authorities.

Once you have the logistics figured out, an alternative to building your own bar is to buy and install a modular bar. Modular bars, though expensive, have advantages. They are built to your specifications, come already outfitted for plumbing and electrical needs, and are easy to maintain, upgrade, or remodel if necessary. Visit the Glastender Inc. website (www.glastender.com) for examples.

BAR CONFIGURATION

A bar is made up of a front bar, a back bar, and an under bar. The *front bar* is where customers sit, eat, and drink. You should allow at least twenty-four inches of space for each bar stool. The width of a front bar varies, but most are at least twenty-four inches wide. In the back of some front bars, there is a recessed area about four inches wide called the glass or drip rail. Bartenders may use this area to mix drinks. The wall of the front bar, which separates the bartender from the customers, is called the bar die and is usually forty-two inches high. (In fact, most if not all bar equipment is designed to fit behind or beneath a bar that is forty-two inches high.) A footrest usually runs along the full length of the bar die about a foot off the ground.

The *back bar* is comprised of shelves behind the bar for storing glasses and displaying various types of liquors. Wherever glasses are stored, health codes mandate that the shelves must either be ridged or covered with a heavy plastic netting to allow air to circulate through the glasses to prevent bacteria growth. Some bars place glass-fronted refrigerators in the back bar to display and merchandise white wines and bottle beers. A back bar's width varies with the type of bar and the amount of space allocated for the bar. In most bars it is about twenty-four inches. There are usually mirrors with shelves, which are also used to display and merchandise shiny bottles of booze, above the back bar's storage area. At Zuni, because of lack of space, our back bar shelf was about twelve inches wide. In order to compensate for lack of space, we used stepped shelves.

The *under bar* is the area under the bar on the bartender's side of the bar. This is where you will typically find refrigeration, speed rails, hand-washing sinks (a health code requirement), glass-washing sinks, glass washers, drain boards, soda guns (dispensers), ice bins, blenders, and so on. The working or aisle space between the front bar and the back bar is usually thirty-six inches, but it may vary with code requirements.

SMOKING

In many states, smoking is not permitted in bars and restaurants. That said, if smoking is allowed in your state and you want to accommodate smokers and non-smokers in your bar or restaurant, you will need to install proper smoke filtration systems. When smoking was still permitted in restaurants in New York, we tried two systems that were suspended from the ceiling. Neither was very helpful when there was heavy smoking at the bar. Most HVAC engineers will tell you that suspended systems are not very effective. The most efficient systems are installed as part of your HVAC system. These systems vary in price and are almost always very expensive.

BAR SUPPLIES

To ensure that your bar runs efficiently and profitably, make sure that your bartenders or "mixologists" will have properly sized glasses and the right beverages and tools. The main supplies you will need to stock at your bar are glassware, ice, and bar tools.

GLASSWARE

Determining the amount of each type of glass to buy will be similar to deciding on the amount of dinnerware, glassware, and flatware for your dining room. Many factors will affect this decision: concept, target market, projected volume, storage capacity, and product availability. As with dinnerware, the easier it is to get replacements for glassware, the less you will have to stock. Also stemware, such as martini, wine, and champagne glasses, tends to break a lot more easily than highball and rocks glasses, so you may want to have more extra stemware. And since wine, martinis, and drinks served in highball glasses tend to be more popular and less expensive than single malts and sherries, you will probably need more highball glasses than you would brandy snifters. For popular drinks, you probably will need around two to two and a half times as many glasses as the number of drinks you expect to serve on a very busy night. For other drinks, get one to one and a half times as many.

When ordering glasses, keep in mind that different types of glasses come in varying sizes. For example, martini glasses can range anywhere from six to ten ounces. Before deciding on the size of glassware, choose a standard pour size for each of your drinks. Will the standard pour of whisky be one, one and a half, or two ounces? Glasses that are not properly sized can create the wrong impression about drinks. For example, a drink served on the rocks may look measly if the glass is either too big or too small. Similarly, a straight-up cocktail can look too small in a glass that is too large. Also consider glass shapes. Drinks tend to look bigger in stemmed and footed glasses than they do in tumblers of the same capacity. Also, ice fits into rounded glasses differently than it does in other types of glasses and causes the liquids to look different.

Initially, you may want to limit the types and sizes of glasses you use. For example, instead of buying a different glass for every type of drink, you may want to use the same type and size of glass for old-fashioneds, rocks drinks, highballs, and so on. Limiting glass selection will reduce the amount of storage space you need behind the bar. Don't always count on using hanging racks, since some local health codes do not allow hanging stemware above a bar. A smaller selection of glasses will also make it easier for staff to pour consistent drinks.

Glass cleaning is also critical to a well-run operation. Bar staff can clean glasses manually or with an automatic dishwasher, or send them to the kitchen to be put in the dishwasher. Be aware that some localities prohibit hand washing of glasses. At a minimum, for hand washing, you will need a five-foot-three-inch compartment sink with two drain boards and three sinks. Each of the three sinks, one for washing, a second for rinsing, and a third for sanitizing, is ten inches long, and the two drain boards are twelve inches each. Not only does manual glass cleaning take up a lot of under bar space, but in a very busy bar you will need an extra employee—a barback—to do the washing.

A glass washer can best be described as a small dishwasher. Most glass washers are chemical sanitizing machines that require a water temperature of only 120 degrees. They are compact and can fit neatly under the back bar or the under bar. A small glass washer will require four to five feet of bar length, two feet for the washer itself and another one or two feet for soiled and clean glasses. Small washers can clean up to five hundred glasses in an hour. To minimize breakage from thermal shock and make sure that your glasses are ready to use right when the wash is done, get a machine that uses cold water for the final rinse.

When space is limited, sending soiled glasses back to the kitchen dishwasher may be the best choice. We used this method at Zuni because we had limited space. The downside was that when the dining room and the bar were busy at the same time, it took a little longer to get clean glasses back from the kitchen. This problem was further compounded because we used a high-temperature dishwasher, which meant that to avoid thermal shock and breakage, we had to allow the glasses to cool for a few minutes before reuse. It also meant that we had to stock extra glasses for busy nights.

ICE

Mixing cocktails requires a steady source of readily available and easily accessible ice, so you will need an ice machine on your premises. Ice machines come in various sizes and capacities. To determine the right size ice maker, first estimate average daily volume in the dining room and in the bar. A good rule of thumb is to figure 2.5 to 3 pounds of ice per person per day, and then add an extra 20–25 percent for use by staff and the kitchen and to allow for future growth of your business. For example, if you estimate an average volume of 100 customers on your busiest days, the calculation would be as follows: 100 x 3.0 x 1.25 (100 customers x 3 pounds of ice per day x 25 percent extra for staff and kitchen), which would indicate a need for a machine capable of producing at least 375 pounds of ice per day.

In addition to figuring out daily capacity needs, you will have to decide on a cube size. For a bar, the best is a medium-sized cube. Small ice cubes tend to melt quickly and may water down the drinks. Large cubes may not fit into all of your glasses. If you plan on making lots of blender drinks such as frozen margaritas or daiquiris, large cubes will make the blender blades work harder, affect the consistency of the drinks, and burn out the motor faster.

Storing ice accessibly at each bartender station requires insulated ice bins. Bins are usually twenty-four or thirty-six inches long and can hold 100 and 150 pounds of ice respectively. Including melting, one pound of ice usually makes about three drinks.

BAR TOOLS

To run the bar profitably and efficiently, your bartenders will need all of the right bar tools. There are all types of fancy gadgets on the market that you may be enticed to buy, but keep it simple. Most of these gadgets are self-explanatory. To see what they look like, what they are used for, and how much they cost, go to any one of the following websites: co-rectproducts.com, ebarsupply.com, tabletools.com, or bevmo.com. Examples include the following:

- Bar spillage mats
- Can and bottle openers
- Clean towels
- Cocktail strainers
- Fruit paring knife and cutting board
- Long-stemmed bar spoon
- Measuring jiggers
- Mixing glasses
- Serving trays
- Muddler
- Pourers
- Plastic ice scoop
- Wine corkscrews
- Blenders

- Fruit juicer
- Funnel
- Condiment trays
- Zester for making drinks with a twist of lemon or lime

BEVERAGES

Your well and call brands are the drinks that you will order most frequently and that you should locate for the bartender's easy access. At Zuni, between 50 and 60 percent of the spirits we sold were well and call brands, so we attached the speed rack (a storage rack that holds several of the most commonly used liquor bottles) to the back of the ice bin. Typically, well brands (usually the least expensive brands that are poured when the customer does not ask for a particular brand), also known as your house brands, are located in a speed rack in the under bar and close to the ice bin. Call (popular) brands should be located in the back bar within one step of the bartender and on display shelves where customers can easily see them. For proper merchandising, locate premium and super premium brands, which are not as frequently ordered, on highly visible shelves in the back bar.

Your objectives in selecting an opening beverages inventory should be to meet your target market's needs and to maximize profits. To achieve these goals you must not only decide what types and brands of beverages to buy, but also how much of each. If you have a full-service bar selling spirits as well as wine and beer, the decision of what to inventory will be fairly complex.

VARIETY OF BRANDS

In addition to wine and beer, the basic spirits that most full-service restaurant bars carry are whiskey, vodka, rum, brandy, gin, scotch, bourbon, and tequila. You will need to decide the variety of brands to carry and the quality of each brand to select. For example, there are several different brands of vodka—such as Smirnoff, Absolut, and Shakers Rye Vodka—each of a different quality and each priced differently. Sometimes one brand—Absolut, for example—will have many different labels and quality levels, each priced differently. To get an idea of what I am talking about, visit your local popular restaurant bar and take a look at the number of different labels on the back bar. Don't be surprised if you see at least a hundred or more different bottles of liquors and liqueurs, since that is the industry average for most full-service bars.

While profit margins are high on most alcoholic beverages, many premium brands are very expensive, so your budget will play an important role in what brand and how many bottles of each brand you will be able to carry. Obviously the more high-end your concept, the higher the quality and the wider the variety of products you will have to carry. Also, if your restaurant will be themed, for example Caribbean, you should carry a wide variety of rums or other appropriate beverages. The greater the role alcoholic beverages will play in your overall profitability, the greater the variety of brands you will need in order to attract a wide range of clientele.

When visiting local restaurant bars that will be your closest competition, talk to bartenders to find out which brands are the best sellers. If your budget permits, you may want to consider hiring an experienced bartender to consult with you on selecting your opening brands. Liquor, wine, and beer salesmen are also good sources; they will tell you which of their brands are moving in your market. But be careful! Do not rely entirely on them to tell you what to buy, since their job is to sell the brands they represent. Listen to them and compare what they say with what their competitors are saying.

You should also subscribe to trade periodicals such as *MarketWatch* for national trends. For example, the most popular spirit in the United States in 2002 was vodka, with almost forty million cases consumed annually. Second was rum, with around twenty million cases.

If the sale of alcoholic beverages will not play a major role in your business's overall profitability, you may want to develop a printed drink menu featuring a limited number of beverages. The idea would be to encourage customers to order from the menu of listed drinks. For instance, if you create a menu based on cheaper spirits, such as vodkas and rums that mix well with other flavors, you may not have to stock as wide a variety of spirits. It would still be wise to carry a small amount of beverages for popular standard cocktails such as martinis, highballs, wines, and beers.

Other advantages of this approach are that you will need less storage space, less equipment, and fewer skilled bartenders. Reportedly, a national chain of Mexican restaurants was able to reduce its inventory down to thirty-five liquors, nine mixes, four wines, and four beers using this method. The key as always is to know your target market and its drink preferences. Simple drink menus tend to work well in theme restaurants and in demographic areas that are less affluent and diverse.

In the final analysis, stocking your bar will come down to good old-fashioned common sense. Use your research to stock the brands that your target customers will expect and want to drink. The quality of drink you pour should be consistent with your concept and the image you want to project. Avoid buying products that you are not sure will move. While a well-stocked bar may look impressive, liquor that does not sell or sells slowly will be a waste of your precious working capital. Learning what sells may take a few weeks or months, but once you get it figured out, get rid of dead or slow-moving brands and replace them with faster moving and more profitable brands. You can get rid of slow-moving brands quickly by creating inexpensive specials or by offering them as comps or at reduced prices to regulars as a thank you. A good rule is not to add a new brand or label unless it will replace one that you discontinued.

QUANTITY OF EACH BRAND

After making brand selections, your next step will be to decide how many bottles of each brand to buy and stock. One of the biggest mistakes many first time and veteran restaurant and bar owners make is to carry too much inventory. Not only does it tie up badly needed working capital, it also can create security and storage problems. The more inventory you carry, the more storage space you will need and the more headaches you will have safeguarding and keeping track of it. Unfortunately, liquor shrinkage (loss) through spillage, breakage, and employee theft is a big problem in the restaurant and bar business. Reportedly, unsupervised and poorly managed bars can lose as much as 20 percent of their inventory through shrinkage.

As a rule of thumb, limit the amount of inventory you keep in stock of any brand to not more than 150 percent of your estimated weekly usage. So, for example, if your average weekly sales of Absolut vodka are two bottles, you should stock 2.0 times 1.5, or three bottles. In addition to an opened bottle at the bar, you should have three others in stock. This is called maintaining a par inventory; your par for Absolut vodka would be three bottles. To assist in maintaining pars, establish a list that details the quantities of each brand of spirit, wine, and beer that should be at the bar at the beginning of every shift. This will ensure that the bar is not under- or overstocked. Bartenders and bar managers should use this list to restock the bar at the end of every shift.

Since your business will be new, estimate what a busy week's usage will be. If, for example, you estimate that initial weekly well gin sales will be two bottles, your first order would be 2 plus (2.0 times 1.5), or five bottles. In addition to the two bottles you estimate using during your first week, you would have three in storage, in case the demand is higher than anticipated or your replacement order is late. Now let's assume that after you have been up and running for a few weeks, you determine that weekly usage of well gin is four bottles; the new par inventory would then be 4 times 1.5, or six bottles.

In all probability, the majority of liquor sales, perhaps as much as 50 percent or more, will be well (house) and call (popular) brands, so make sure you are adequately stocked with these brands using the 150 percent rule. For all other brands, use your judgment and err on the side of just enough as opposed to too much. For necessary but slow-moving brands, you can reorder when you are down to half a bottle. Some tightly run operations are able to carry only one week's par inventory. If you carry a nice array of popular brands and can offer a customer a good alternative to his or her first choice, chances are you won't lose a sale or a customer.

STORAGE SPACE, DELIVERY SCHEDULES, AND DISCOUNTS

Other factors that will influence beverages inventory decisions are storage capacity, delivery schedules, minimum orders, cash flow, and volume discounts. The less frequent your deliveries, the more storage you will need. Frequency of deliveries will depend on your geographic location and on your vendors' delivery schedules. Some vendors schedule specific delivery days for specific areas during the week. Customers who do not order in time to meet those scheduled delivery dates have to wait until the following week to get a delivery.

Most wholesalers sell by the case, broken case, or bottle. A case usually contains twelve bottles of one type. A broken case contains twelve bottles of different spirits or brands. Some distributors insist on a minimum dollar order. Most house wine and all bottle beer are sold by the case. Typically, only expensive wines are sold by the broken case or by the bottle, or piece.

Your available cash flow and your payment and credit terms imposed by state regulations or liquor purveyors will also have an impact on how much inventory you carry. In some states, regulations do not allow the purchase of alcoholic beverages on credit; other states require payments weekly, semimonthly, or monthly. In New York, for example, monthly payments are required. Late payments are reported to the State Liquor Authority, which typically will impose fines or suspend licenses.

In the early weeks and months of business, most vendors, including liquor purveyors, will insist on immediate payment by check or cash until you establish a track record with them. Some may require that you personally guarantee all shipments.

Being able to receive product on credit is important; if you do not have available cash when some of your well and call drinks are on special, you will not be able to take advantage of discounts being offered, and some discounts can be quite substantial. At Zuni, we often took advantage of specials to reduce the cost per bottle on some of our house wines from six dollars to four dollars by buying ten-case lots.

In control states, prices are fixed by law and do not vary. The state-owned outlets do offer quantity and special product discounts from time to time. License states allow wholesalers to offer specials and discounts. The price differences among distributors, however, never very substantially since state laws are designed to discourage price wars. Manufacturers and distributors must offer the same prices to all wholesalers. This usually results in fairly homogenous prices. In some instances suppliers are free to set their own specials, markups, and discounts. Look for these specials and discounts; shop around and take advantage of them when cash flow and storage capacity allow it.

BAR SHRINKAGE

As mentioned earlier, many bars lose as much as 20 percent of their liquor through shrinkage (loss). Shrinkage usually results from employee theft, pouring errors, returns, spillage, or broken bottles by accident. Most shrinkage occurs because of employee error due to poor training and employee pilferage. Like any other business, a certain amount of shrinkage is unavoidable. For example, periodically a drink will be returned either because of an honest error in mixing or because a customer does not like it. Some spillage is inevitable when drinks are being mixed. In the process of receiving and storing beverages, staff drop and break bottles from time to time. Occasionally, equipment malfunctions, causing product such as tap beer to get foamy. These represent ordinary costs of doing business and should be planned for and included in your pricing structure. Other forms of shrinkage, however, can be controlled and significantly reduced through solid management control policies and proper employee training, neither of which is particularly difficult.

REDUCE PILFERAGE WITH SOLID MANAGEMENT

Unfortunately, bartender theft is fairly common. That said, most restaurateurs would agree that the majority of bartenders are honest. Perhaps the primary reason theft is common is the fact that in unsupervised conditions, it can be easy to steal.

The easier it is to steal, the more likely it is that people will do so. Also, for some people, handling a steady stream of cash can be very tempting. What probably makes theft the most tempting, however, is a person's ability to control both ends of the sales transaction: bartenders dispense the liquor and they collect the cash. Because bartenders work for tips, it can be tempting to try to please customers by overpouring or giving drinks away. When confronted with overpouring, one bartender who worked for me said she actually thought that overpouring and unauthorized comps were good for my business since it encouraged repeat customers. Some bartenders see it as a sort of mutual back scratching; they get more tips and owners get loyal customers. The question is, loyal customers at what cost? Unlike owners, bartenders do not have the overhead of running a business.

In addition to overpouring and giving drinks away to get larger tips, the most common forms of pilferage are giving free drinks to friends, drinking after work hours and not paying for the drinks, selling drinks and keeping the money (this is accomplished by leaving the cash drawer open after ringing a drink), and selling a call (popular) or premium drink and ringing it up as a well (house brand) sale.

Not every overpour or comp is an act of theft. Giving comps to good and loyal customers is an integral and recommended part of the hospitality business. Very

Creating a Basic but Good Wine Program

Oscar Val Verde, sommelier and wine consultant

One of the most crucial aspects of a successful wine program is well trained and informed servers. Bad service is memorable and will be associated with your restaurant even if your food is good. A server is responsible for guiding guests through their meal, and when he or she is not well trained and informed, the dining experience can be tainted and may very well determine if you will have repeat customers. Training and educating your employees about wine service is not that difficult, and the time and effort you put into it will more than pay for itself with happy customers and higher check averages.

If you cannot afford a sommelier to train your staff, talk to your wine representatives; they will be more than willing to train your staff to sell their wines. In addition to teaching your staff about his or her particular brands, a good representative will also be able to teach them the proper etiquette for showing and pouring wines. Once you have a good basic training program in place, hold monthly wine tastings for your staff. During these tastings, describe the regions where the wines come from then give tastes of chardonnay, for example, from several regions and ask your staff to describe their properties and characteristics. This type of training will help them to answer questions

often, being a good host means buying a customer a drink. Regular customers like to be recognized and rewarded. At Zuni, for example, our policy was to give regulars every fourth drink on the house. One very successful restaurateur I know gives his chef a budget of fifty dollars per day to prepare special appetizers and treats for his bar customers.

What we did not do, but what you should do, is to insist that every comp be recorded and accounted for. When staff knows that you are not tracking comps, they will get overly generous. More important, not knowing how much has been comped will make it difficult for you to hold staff accountable when liquor inventories cannot be accounted for. Not tracking comps also makes it difficult to account for potential loss of profits.

The best way to prevent and discourage dishonest behavior is to institute preventive measures, such as cash controls and frequent inventory counts and checks. Sometimes frequent inventory checks are enough to control if not prevent pilferage entirely. The more often you check your stock, the more likely you will be able to detect and catch the perpetrators. Also, when thieves know they are likely to be caught, they are less apt to attempt theft. Even if there is no theft, frequent counts will let you know if any inventory is missing, how serious the loss is, and what is

like "what are the differences between this syrah from the Rhône and this one from Paso Robles?" Another good training technique that will equip them to be able to describe your wines knowledgeably and with confidence, is to periodically conduct blind tastings with three mystery wines that have a common thread, such as a riesling from Germany, Australia, and California and ask your staff to describe their properties and characteristics.

The Internet is also a great resource, since most wineries have websites with fact sheets of grape varietals and blends, oak or non-oak, and barrel time. The better educated your service staff is about your wine program, the more they will be able to up sell which will be good for your bottom line.

When putting together your wine list, try to have an interesting selection with an array of familiar names including smaller or local producers if you are in a wine growing region. Get different grape varietals in various styles and price ranges. Above all, select wine that will pair well with your cuisine.

If your concept is casual to upscale, discourage customers from bringing their own wine with a corkage fee. Pricing from wholesale should be between two and a half to three times your costs. More important, some food critics, especially those from prestigious publications, are very knowledgeable about the retail price of wine, and may react unfavorably, if they think that you are overcharging. Also, to discourage employee theft and to help keep track of your profit margins, make sure that every bottle is accounted for from the time it arrives in your restaurant. Most restaurant POS systems are equipped with software to help log bottle counts.

responsible for it. Unfortunately, most restaurant operators don't check their stock very often, or they check only after inventory is reported missing, by which time it is too late to recover their losses.

Be sure to institute proper cash controls such as the following:

- Make it mandatory that all drinks be rung into the register before they are poured. This way bartenders will not forget to ring in a drink either conveniently or by accident. It's not just a matter of trust; it does get busy at times, and people can forget to ring things up later. Remember, theft is a reality, and in a busy bar, bartenders handle a lot of cash. A computerized point-of-sale system makes this quite simple. If you won't have a computer, insist that bartenders record each drink on a guest check before pouring it.

- Insist that bartenders keep tips in a separate jar, not in the cash register. This eliminates the possibility that overages will be assumed to be tips.

- Randomly take summary readings and reconcile cash sales with cash in the drawer. This will prevent staff from taking cash without ringing up a sale.

- Institute a policy of having all comps (for both customers and staff) and spillage rung into the register. This will tell you exactly how much alcohol is being given away and will discourage excessive comps and staff drinking. It will also help you to account for missing inventory.

- Insist that the register must be closed after each drink transaction is rung up.

- Install video cameras above the bar. Most employees won't like this, but it is a great deterrent to theft. Besides, most restaurant bars are wide open during off hours, making it easy for staff and even outside repair people to steal inventory. With a camera, you will know who the perpetrator is.

REDUCE WASTE WITH STAFF TRAINING

Bartenders do not always overpour because they are dishonest, since as I noted earlier, most are honest. A lot of overpouring occurs because of lack of proper training and poor management oversight. Well-trained bartenders are less likely to overpour, and they mix more consistent drinks. Drink consistency is very important, particularly for regulars and drink connoisseurs who want their drinks to taste the same every time. A good way to ensure drink consistency and reduce over- or underpouring is to establish drink recipes. Using jiggers to measure beverages is an excellent way to get recipes right each time.

For well, call, and mixed drinks, the best way to pour accurate and consistent drinks is to use measured pourers. Measured pourers are pour devices that dispense a specific amount of liquor with each pour. Some bartenders don't like them, but so what! It's your bar. Pourers come in various sizes, such as 1 ounce, $1/2$ ounce, and 2 ounces, and they are inserted into the tops of liquor bottles. For premium (sold by wholesalers for ten dollars or more) and super premium (sold by wholesalers for twenty-five dollars or more) liquors—aged liquors, single malts, and other aperitifs—test your bartenders regularly for pouring accuracy.

Teach your bar staff how to pour draft beer properly to ensure a consistent head. Have one of your vendors come in and give a demonstration on how to pour beer with a perfect head without throwing half of the beer down the drain. Also, keep your tap system well maintained at the proper temperature to prevent wastage due to excess froth. Industry wide, it is estimated that 20 percent of draft beer is lost to waste, spoilage, spillage, and theft. This amounts to one in every five barrels. If you plan on carrying lots of draft beer, consider investing in a draft beer control system. They vary in price depending on the manufacturer. Your local beer distributor can refer you to several dealers. These systems can precisely track the amounts of each brand dispensed and can provide cost percentages for each brand. Your bar staff should also rotate refrigerated bottled beer in the bar to prevent it from getting old and becoming rancid.

To prevent over- or underpouring of wines by the glass, teach your staff exactly how many pours they should get from a wine bottle. One way to assist in this process, which is particularly helpful for new bartenders, is to mark wine glasses with masking tape at the level you want poured, and then put them discretely where staff can see them to check their pour accuracy. For opened bottles of wine that will be sold by the glass, a number of suction devices can replace the air in the bottle with inert nitrogen or an argon gas mix, which does not alter the wine's flavor or bouquet. Your wine distributor can give you leads on where to find these devices.

ACCOUNTABILITY AND PROFITABILITY

Pricing beverages menus profitably requires essentially the same steps as pricing food menus. Just like pricing your food menu, the first step is to determine the cost of each of the ingredients that will be used to mix or "pour" your various beverages, and, as you may recall from chapter 6, the starting point will be your recipes. Once you know the cost of each ingredient, you will then total them to get what is known as the pour cost, or put simply, the cost to pour each drink. Similarly to pricing food menus, you will then add a waste factor, to come up with your total pour cost. In bar operations, a waste factor is included in pricing to compensate for spills, overpours comps and so on. Once you know your pour cost, you will then divide it by your targeted beverage cost percentage from your pro forma operating budget to get your targeted menu price. At this point, you may want to go back and review the menu pricing section of chapter 6, since we are going to use the same menu pricing terms and methods.

Table 9-1 is an example of how you would go about costing the recipe for a house gin martini with an olive. Recipe is 2 ounces house gin, ½ ounce dry vermouth, and 1 olive.

In table 9-1, the serving cost per unit equals the purchase cost per unit ($7.00), divided the purchase unit (33.8 ounces), and the cost per serving unit equals serving cost per unit multiplied by the serving size.

TABLE 9-1: GIN MARTINI COSTING

Ingredients	Purchase unit	Purchase cost per unit	Serving unit	Serving cost per unit	Serving size	Cost per serving
Gin	1 liter (33.8 ounces)	$7.00	ounce	$0.21	2 ounces	0.42
Dry vermouth	1 liter (33.8 ounces)	4.00	ounce	0.12	½ ounce	0.06
Olive	1 quart (80 olives)	3.00	each	0.04	1	0.04
Sub total						0.52
Waste factor (10%)						0.05
Total menu item cost						0.57

Once you have calculated the cost of the martini's ingredients, the next step is to calculate its targeted menu price. Again using the same methodology from chapter 6, we would calculate the targeted menu price as follows:

Pour cost: $.57
Targeted (pour) Beverage cost percentage: 20 percent
Targeted menu price ($.57 ÷ .20): $2.85

Your targeted price would then be rounded up to $3.

All of the same factors that influence food pricing—demographics, concept design, décor, and service—should influence your beverage pricing decisions. For example, in a more rural bar and restaurant, the $3 price we calculated may be appropriate. However, I can assure you that the same drink in bars and restaurants in most small and large urban cities would sell for at least $5. Currently, in most of the casual to upscale bars and restaurants in the San Francisco Bay Area, the same martini would sell for between $6 and $7, and in some of the more high-end establishments as much as $9 or $10.

This brings us back to the high profitability on the sale of alcoholic beverages. At a price of $5, $6, and $7 respectively the pour (liquor) cost percentages would be $.57 ÷ $5, or 11 percent; $.57 ÷ $6, or 9.5 percent; and $.57 ÷ $7, or 8 percent. Not only are the profit margins huge, but so too are the contribution margins or the sales price minus the cost. (See chapter 6 for a definition and discussion of contribution margins.) Just imagine being able to sell a drink that costs less than one dollar for $5, $6, and $7! At $5, $6, and $7 the contribution margins would be $4.43, $5.43, and $6.43. Now imagine what they would be in a high-end restaurant or bar! To get an idea of how much more profitable alcohol is than food, go back and look at the profit and contribution margins on food in the text and tables of chapter 6. Liquor (spirits) profit margins can also be higher when poured straight-up, on the rocks, with water, or sodas such as Coke, 7UP, or tonic.

TABLE 9-2: POUR COST PERCENTAGES

Brand	Bottle size	Bottle cost	Cost per ounce	Pour cost	Sales price	Pour cost %
House gin	1 liter (33.8 ounces)	$7	$.21	$0.31	$5	6.2%
House scotch	1 liter (33.8 ounces)	8	0.24	0.36	5.50	6.5%
Bourbon	1 liter (33.8 ounces)	10	0.30	0.45	6	6.4%
Johnnie Walker Black	1 liter (33.8 ounces)	40	1.18	1.77	8	22%
Johnnie Walker Red	1 liter (33.8 ounces)	29	0.86	1.29	7.50	17%

Taking frequent and accurate inventory counts, instituting cash controls, and properly training staff will help to dramatically reduce pilferage and shrinkage. But to determine whether these procedures and controls are truly working you will have to periodically recalculate your pour costs (the cost of each drink divided by its selling price), using the changing costs of beverages, and then implement effective inventory control systems.

Table 9-2 demonstrates how to calculate pour cost percentages using current bottle costs and sales prices. In each case, the assumed pour or portion size is 1½ ounces. This table could also be used for wine by the glass and tap beer, which is purchased by the keg. You would simply change the bottle size and the pour size.

Cost per ounce equals bottle cost divided by bottle size. For example, house gin is $7 ÷ 33.8 ounces. Pour cost equals the assumed pour amount (1½ ounces) multiplied by cost per ounce. Sales price is the assumed selling price, and the pour cost percentage equals pour cost divided by sales price.

Use the conversion chart below to do calculations for bottle sizes other than 1 liter and for pricing tap beer. For tap beer, if your pour will be 1 pint (16 ounces) and the cost per keg is $100. The pour cost would be calculated as follows: $100 ÷ 1,984 ounces × 16 ounces and the result would be $.80 (or $100 ÷ 1,984 × 16 = $.80). Assuming that your selling price is $5 per pint, your pour cost percent would be $.80 ÷ $5, or 16 percent.

By taking regular inventories, you will know how much inventory you generally have on hand—the number of bottles, their cost, how quickly brands are turning, which liquors are selling and which aren't, and where various bottles are. Taking regular inventories and periodically reviewing pour costs will not only allow you to check how profitable your bar operation is each month, it will also tell you how profitable it should have been. The sooner you know pour cost percentages and profit margins, the sooner you will be able to identify problems and respond quickly to fix them.

Metric size	U.S. fluid ounces
1.75 liter	59.2
1.0 liter	33.8
750 milliliters	25.4
500 milliliters	16.9
200 milliliters	6.8
50 milliliters	1.7
Beer keg	1,984

As complex as this might sound, it is really not that difficult. For example, beverages like bottled beer and wine, which are bought and sold by the unit, are easy to keep track of by simply counting the number of empty bottles each day, by brand, and then comparing that number to your daily sales record.

If you know how many bottles you had at the beginning of the day or week, how many were purchased, and how many were sold, you can determine how many bottles you should have at the end of the day or week. For example, assume that at the start of the day or week you had 500 bottles, then 400 were purchased, and 600 were sold. At the end of the day or week, you should have 500 (beginning) + 400 (purchased) − 600 (sold) = 300. Had you not been checking, you would not have known that you had 500 bottles at the beginning of the day or week and 300 hundred at the end.

You should also count and record the number of empty spirits bottles, and then use that figure to maintain your par inventory (not more than 150 percent of your estimated weekly usage) by replenishing your par for every empty bottle. By doing this, you will know exactly how many bottles of each brand was sold each week. You can then compare this number with your sales records to see if there are any discrepancies.

To ensure the integrity of your bar inventory counts, do not let bar staff manage inventory counts or inventory controls. This is asking the rat to guard the cheese. Do it yourself or have a manager or someone else independent from bar operations do it.

The best way to make inventorying easy is to keep low par inventories. The less inventory you stock, the less you will have to track and count and the easier it will be to notice missing items.

To properly safeguard bar inventory, limit access to stored alcohol. Only a few people should have a key to the liquor closet, such as an owner, a manager, and maybe your chef. This reduces access and increases accountability. You should also keep food and liquor storage separate. Finally, check all deliveries to make sure you get what you ordered.

BEVERAGE TRENDS

Just as you should keep up with current food trends, you should also keep up with beverage trends. Much the same as diners, bar patrons like to try new drinks and experiment with new flavors or brands, and they won't always know what they want when they walk into your bar. Not to mention, a good drink can often encourage a customer who just popped in for a drink to stay for a meal. New cocktails can help to keep your concept fresh. For example, any restaurant operator in the know offers some variety of the Cosmopolitan. Another current trend worth watching is that classic drinks such as martinis, Manhattans, and collins's are beginning to come back. Believe it or not, the now-ubiquitous mojito is actually a revival of an old classic. At Tablespoon in San Francisco, they're even making a white wine mojito. Keeping up could create an opportunity to up sell customers on new cocktails made with premium brands, which could increase your margins by as much a one or two dollars.

Given the rapid growth of wine consumption in the United States, combined with the fact that wine drinkers tend to visit restaurants more frequently, leave more satisfied, and spend 10 percent more than other customers, keeping up with wine trends is particularly important. Two websites that I find particularly useful are about.com and greatwinemadesimple.com. The food section in Wednesday's *New York Times* and the wine reviews in Friday's *Wall Street Journal* are usually good for recommendations on what wines to carry. Major business magazines also carry regular wine reviews.

Most wine and liquor distributors conduct tasting seminars regularly, and some will even come to your restaurant to do tastings for your staff. Take these opportunities to experiment with new products and to get new ideas. For example, instead of using pre-made mixes, they can use fresh fruit purées to make exotic new drinks. Your bartender can also team up with your chef or pastry chef to capitalize on the dining public's current interest in fresh ingredients to create new cocktails.

CHAPTER 10

DESIGNING
THE KITCHEN

Too many first-timer restaurateurs focus almost exclusively on the aesthetics of the front of the house (FOH), that is, the dining room and bar areas. They make the big mistake of leaving the details of the back of the house (BOH)—receiving, storage, production, and the kitchen—to later, almost an afterthought. This oversight results in poorly designed kitchens and storage areas, which ultimately lead to poor service. Don't let this happen to you! Your goal should be to design and lay out both the back and the front of the house to create a seamless operational flow from receiving to preparation to production and service. If you have a limited budget, most of it should be spent in the back, not the front, of the house.

Think of the back of the house as a factory where kitchen staff will receive, store, and process raw materials (meat, fish, poultry, vegetables, and so on). As in any other manufacturing operation, the better you can streamline your operation, the more productive, efficient, and cost effective it will be. When designing your kitchen, you'll want to consider: your kitchen's size and location; the flow of product preparation within the kitchen and the flow of staff in and out of the kitchen from and to the delivery, storage, and service areas; the layout of storage and refrigeration areas; waste management; cooking equipment and placement; cleaning stations, including sinks, drains, and dishwashing equipment; miscellaneous equipment and smallware; and major equipment, including whether to buy or lease new or used equipment and how to maintain equipment.

SIZE AND LOCATION

The first thing to consider when designing your kitchen is where it will be located within the restaurant and how big it will be. These two factors can affect product flow, kitchen and dining room traffic flow, utility costs, labor costs, dining room ambience, and even operating hours. At Zuni, all of the main dry storage and long-term cold storage areas (also known as walk-in boxes) are located in the basement under the dining room and bar, which are located at the front of the restaurant. The kitchen is located at the back of the restaurant without direct stairwell access to the basement. Because the only access from the kitchen to storage and vice versa is through the dining room, we had to schedule all major deliveries precisely so that we could get everything that was needed into the kitchen before service started.

On top of that, running electric, gas, water, and waste lines all the way from the street to the kitchen was not cheap. Ideally, to avoid excessive plumbing and electrical costs, the kitchen should be placed close to water, sewer, and power lines. But being close to these lines may not be ideal for your restaurant's overall design and decor. At Zuni, our priority was for the bar and dining room to be easily seen from the street. Despite the headaches that we had to face, placing our kitchen as we did was the best way to maximize the use and profit potential of our space. You too will have to make tough decisions and compromises.

Once you've found a home for your kitchen, you need to decide how to divide your available space between the front and back of the house. Keep in mind your budget, concept, menu, frequency of deliveries, and real estate cost. Conventional wisdom used to set guidelines for laying out a restaurant. Some restaurant design textbooks recommend that anywhere from 30-50 percent of total restaurant space be allocated to the back of the house. Others recommend that the average table service restaurant allocate an average of six square feet per seat for kitchen space and eleven square feet per seat to the back of the house. Still others recommend that the kitchen alone be a third of the size of the dining room. These space allocations work in ideal situations. But how often, given today's soaring real estate costs, do any of us find ourselves in an ideal situation?

In the real world, restaurant operators frequently make compromises to maximize their seating capacity. More often than not, these decisions reduce the size of the back of the house. If we had used recommended estimates at Zuni, which has seventy-one seats and a large bar, we would have had to allocate 426 square feet to the kitchen and 355 for receiving and storage, for a total back of the house size of 781 square feet. The actual allocation is 225 square feet for the kitchen, including dishwashing and pot washing, plus another 330 square feet in the basement for receiving and storage, for total back of the house square footage of 555. That additional recommended 226 square feet for the back of the house would have cost us twenty seats in an environment with high rent and stiff competition.

Many restaurants manage to offer varied menus and do high volumes out of tight spaces. At Jo Jo, an extremely popular New York City restaurant that seats eighty-six, chef Didier Virot designed a simple, quality menu that could be prepared efficiently and compactly. With a six-burner stove, small convection ovens, one grill, and two regular ovens, the restaurant can handle 180 covers.

Fortunately, tremendous advances in cooking equipment technology, smarter and better trained chefs and kitchen staff, and the availability of frequent deliveries (which minimize storage needs) make it increasingly possible to operate out of small spaces. The bottom line is that if a location doesn't have enough floor space to generate your desired profit and leave room for a workable kitchen—even under "creative" conditions—then consider another place.

Not every restaurant can or should work out of tight spaces, particularly fine-dining restaurants with lots of kitchen staff hands and the specialty production and storage equipment required to perfectly prepare and present each meal. That said, a tight, well-designed kitchen can be less tiring and a lot more efficient than a large, poorly designed kitchen.

Go to restaurants with open kitchens and ask for a seat at their kitchen counter. You will be able to observe the equipment layout in each work section and work station and see staff movements as they perform their culinary ballet while cooking your meal. My favorite perch is the counter at Boulevard in San Francisco.

LAYOUT AND FLOW

Flow patterns are just as important in the kitchen as they are in the dining room. There are two types of flow in the back of the house: product flow and traffic (staff) flow. In the typical table-service restaurant, food and materials arrive in the back of the house, where they are stored, prepped, and prepared before going to the front of the house to be served to guests, after which leftovers are sent back to the kitchen as waste—in short, product flows from back to front to back. Traffic flow is the various paths and steps that chefs, cooks, and dishwashers take to do their jobs.

Your restaurant type will determine your kitchen's layout and flow patterns. The faster the service will be, the more important it will be to have flow lines that do not cross. In a fast-service environment, for example, flow patterns should be short and straight. The fewer steps each cook or counter person has to take the better. The next time you go to McDonald's or Burger King, note how well they have minimized the number of steps needed to complete the cooking, bagging, and sales process.

Where possible, separate the preparation and production areas so all types of work in the kitchen can continue simultaneously while your restaurant is open. This is not always possible in kitchens with limited space. For example, at Zuni, because of space limitations, we could not do prep work during busy service periods because the entire kitchen was needed to get food out to the guests.

The objective of a smart kitchen layout is to be efficient, cost effective, and capable of producing your menu at your expected volume. This includes specifying where each workstation and each piece of equipment will be.

A workstation is the area where a single worker performs a specific set of tasks. It consists of the floor space, counter space, production equipment (ranges, fryers, and broilers), and storage equipment that the staff person will use to perform their job, like sautéing, broiling or grilling, frying, and so on. A group of workstations is called a work section: for example, the hot food line or the pantry.

Self-contained workstations are the most cost-effective way to control kitchen labor costs. A well-designed workstation gives each employee easily accessible work and storage space. If a particular piece of equipment is not located in the proper work section, the extra steps needed to get to it can waste time and, ultimately, money. In the hot food section, consider how far each chef or cook has to go to reach refrigerated storage, sauté pans, or holding equipment such as a steam table. A range with refrigerated storage drawers or a lowboy worktop refrigeration system with drawers instead of doors make it easier for cooks to reach refrigerated storage. Overhead utensil racks above the hot line and pantry stations put pots, pans, tongs, ladles, whips, and spoons within easy reach.

Few jobs are as physically demanding and strenuous as working in a busy restaurant kitchen. So think about including elements that will make it less physically demanding on your kitchen staff. Celebrity chef Mario Batali, for example, has his plating counters built eight inches higher than normal to prevent lower back pain caused by leaning over low pieces of equipment. Similarly, a great way to make cleaning underneath and behind kitchen equipment easier on your cleaning crew is to put all of your equipment on wheels or casters.

In laying out your equipment, be sure to measure correctly. A one-inch error can be extremely costly. For example, I recently heard about an operator who purchased a ten thousand-dollar custom-built range only to discover that it was *one inch* too wide for the intended space. Don't forget to factor in adequate aisle space for staff movement and the opening of refrigerator and oven doors. Both Zuni and Wrapsody operated quite efficiently with thirty-six-inch and forty-two-inch aisles in the pantry and hot line sections, respectively. In some cities, aisle widths are code regulated, so be sure to check with your local building department.

RECEIVING AREAS

The first step in the restaurant production process is accepting deliveries of food, beverages, cleaning, and other service supplies. Whenever possible, place receiving and storage areas close to and easily accessible to each other, for obvious efficiency reasons. Even better is to have the preparation and kitchen production areas easily accessible to receiving and storage. For example, deliveries could be received through a back door that leads into storage, which in turn is adjacent to the kitchen preparation and production areas.

Of course, these types of layouts are not always doable. In large cities, especially, it is not always possible to gain access to storage and production through a back door. Instead, it is not uncommon to see chefs standing on the sidewalk, checking and accepting deliveries above a trap door located in the sidewalk. In these instances, smart restaurant operators locate their storage and prep areas in the basement. In some cases, storage and preparation areas are located beneath the kitchen, with easy access through a stairwell. Basement space can be a plus since it is usually a lot less expensive than street-level space.

You will need an accurate scale. For most small- and medium-sized operations, a fifty- to one hundred-pound scale will be adequate. The standard weight of a case of potatoes or a bag of carrots, for example, is fifty pounds. It is unusual for even a medium-sized restaurant to get a single delivery of meat, poultry, or fish that exceeds one hundred pounds. A large operation will probably require a fifty- to two hundred-pound scale. Scales can be spring operated or digital and vary in price. Electronic digital scales are extremely accurate and easy to read, but they are also more expensive. Whichever you choose, get a sturdy heavy-duty commercial scale that will stand up to constant use. A good source for researching scales is www.edlundco.com.

Make sure that your receiving area is well lit so staff can see products and check invoices. For indoor receiving areas, use fluorescent lighting, which is bright and efficient. In these areas, health code requirements will require lights with protective shields to protect workers and food from falling glass in the event a bulb breaks.

A hand truck or a dolly will make moving things from receiving to storage a lot faster, easier, and, as a result, more cost effective.

STORAGE AREAS

Once you have everything in hand, the next step is to make sure you have places to put goods where they will be easily accessible. Storage is perhaps one of the most overlooked aspects of restaurant operations. If you are a collector, look around your house or apartment and see how much stuff you have piled up. Now multiply that fifty times over for a restaurant business, and you will get the idea of what can happen. Organized storage takes up at least one-fifth to one-quarter of the back of the house. Imagine what could happen if you are not organized. In short, to quote President George W. Bush, don't "mis-underestimate" your storage needs.

Storage is generally broken down into three categories: dry, refrigerated, and frozen. The amount of each type of storage you will need will depend on your concept, the frequency of deliveries, your menu's size and composition, and the number of meals you will serve. Menus relying heavily on frozen and canned goods will require lots of freezer and dry goods storage. If you are planning on a fast food or takeout and delivery operation, don't forget storage for disposables and paper goods. Also, most health departments will require you to store cleaning supplies and any chemicals separate from dry and paper goods to prevent contamination.

To plan your storage, determine the types and amounts of inventory items you will need and when you will need them. You'll get a good idea of these when you estimate your average daily and weekly customer counts in your financial feasibility study.

The next step is to identify what food and beverage items you will need. To do this, use your preliminary food menus to identify and make a detailed list of the ingredients needed to prepare all of your menu items. Do the same with your beverage and bar menus. Next, decide how much of your perishables (meat, fish, poultry, and vegetables) will be ordered fresh or frozen and what percentage of your menu items will be made using canned goods. This process will help you decide how to allocate food between dry, refrigerated, and frozen storage. Don't forget to factor in delivery times when calculating how much you will need on hand. Find out whether you can get deliveries every day without minimum orders; this will further reduce your storage needs and help to keep the food that you serve fresh.

The key to efficient storage, particularly in tight spaces, is proper shelving. The right selection of shelf widths, lengths, and heights will allow you to maximize your storage capacity. There are basically two types of shelving: open-grid wire shelving and solid flat shelving. Both come in different materials, including stainless steel, plastic, vinyl-coated steel, or anodized aluminum, and in varying price ranges. The Eagle Group makes shelving that comes with antimicrobial protection. For perishables, particularly in refrigerated areas, use slatted or wire shelving to allow maximum air circulation. The more air that circulates around stored products the harder it is for harmful bacteria to grow. Air circulation also helps the energy efficiency of refrigeration systems. Wire shelving offers good visibility and does not collect dust. However, these shelves may not be suitable for storing items that can leak and contaminate anything stored beneath them. A good way to prevent contamination when using wire shelving is to store items that can contaminate others in sturdy closed containers. An alternative is to use solid metal shelving, which has the major drawback of not allowing air circulation, but it is easy to wipe down and clean.

Two other important shelving considerations are flexibility and durability. As you might expect, the stronger the shelf, the more expensive it will be. Check the spec sheet or ask the vendor to determine the weight-loading capacity of shelves. Similarly, more durable finishing materials are more expensive. Stainless steel, polymer, vinyl, and epoxy-coated shelves, which are noncorrosive, are usually more expensive than chrome-plated shelves. Noncorrosive materials are ideal for refrigerated and frozen storage. You can always mix and match your shelving, using less expensive chrome-plated shelves for dry storage and corrosion-resistant ones for refrigerated and frozen items.

To maximize your storage space capacity, look for height adjustability. Posts that let you adjust shelf height in one-inch intervals along the shelf's entire length are invaluable for storing items of different heights. This great feature also makes it easy to accommodate health code regulations, which stipulate that all storage must be at least six inches above the floor. Don't forget to leave at least three feet between shelves for aisle space.

If your storage space is high and narrow, use as much of the room's height as possible. One manufacturer, Metro, makes shelving with posts heights ranging from 14½ to 86⅝ inches. If your space is wide and low, maximize storage by using wide shelves. Most shelves come in fourteen-, eighteen-, twenty-one-, and twenty-four-inch widths. Be careful about overly wide shelves because employees tend to use items at the front of the shelf. Also, when taking inventory, it's easy to overlook items at the back of wide shelves, particularly small cans. If you use wide shelves, be sure to rotate inventory regularly to keep products fresh and to prevent over buying. Shelves come in lengths ranging from twenty-four to seventy-two inches. Use lengths that allow for the most efficient and maximum use of your storage space. Also remember that longer shelves will have less load-bearing capacity than shorter ones. A good source for researching shelving options is www.shelvingworld.com.

You will need storage space in the kitchen itself for pots, pans, plates, dry spices, condiments, and smallware such as serving spoons and tongs. Several of the shelves described above can be used for these purposes. Wall-mounted units can be strategically placed above under-the-counter and worktop refrigerators. Ranges can be ordered with cabinets and storage bases and with shelves attached to the backsplash or flue. Overhead pot and utensil racks are also very useful. Various other types of over shelves, under shelves, and cabinets are also available, including security units for storing alcoholic beverages.

REFRIGERATION STORAGE EQUIPMENT

Proper refrigeration helps to reduce food spoilage. In most operations, there are usually three types of refrigerated storage: walk-in, reach-in, and under the counter.

As its name implies, a walk-in is a refrigerator or freezer that is large enough to be walked into. These units are used for extended-term bulk storage and short-term storage of perishables prepared in large batches. Large quantities of perishable fruits, dairy products, vegetables, or meats are usually moved as quickly as possible from the receiving area to a walk-in box to keep them fresh. Similarly, when items are prepared in large batches—like soups and stocks—they usually are stored in walk-in boxes after they have been cooled down. As with other storage considerations, your walk-in storage needs will be determined largely by the frequency of deliveries, your menu's size and composition, and the number of meals you serve. Many restaurant operators make the mistake of getting too much or too little walk-in storage. Remember, space (and the energy needed to maintain refrigeration) can be very expensive, so don't take this aspect of your storage planning lightly.

Walk-ins are made of insulated wall, ceiling, and floor panels. The panels are available in various sizes and can be quickly assembled on site. Prices vary according to finish, with stainless steel being the most expensive. Other choices are vinyl and aluminum. You will also need a compressor; select the size to accommodate your refrigeration unit. Compressors can either be installed close to the walk-in or up to twenty-five feet away. If possible, locate your compressor away from the kitchen or other work areas since they give off a lot of heat. Most of the shelving options discussed above will work in walk-in refrigerators.

The ideal location for walk-in storage is somewhere central between the receiving, preparation, and kitchen areas. As we know, this is not always possible. At Zuni, the walk-in box is located in the basement next to the receiving and storage areas; the kitchen and preparation area are upstairs. When on-premise space is limited, walk-ins can be installed outdoors. Alternately, many small restaurants rely on reach-in and under-the-counter refrigerated storage.

The other types of refrigerated storage—reach-in and under-the-counter, also called worktop or lowboy units—are an integral part of workstation design. A reach-in is basically the same as the standard home refrigerator except that it is usually larger and designed for heavy-duty commercial use. An under-the-counter refrigerator is a refrigerator that is designed to fit under a work counter. They are found all around the kitchen—in the hot food section and hot line, the pantry and cold food section, and the dessert section. In small kitchens, the pantry and dessert stations are usually one and the same. In the hot food section, commonly called "the line," choose refrigeration that can maintain the correct temperatures despite the unit's proximity to ovens and ranges.

Reach-ins and lowboys are generally used for short-term holding of meats, seafood, and poultry products that have been cleaned and readied for cooking, as well as for dairy products and prepared condiments, such as roasted garlic, diced onions, peppers, or tomatoes that are needed cook each meal to order (*mise en place*).

Reach-ins are typically placed within easy access of work spaces. Under-the-counter refrigeration units, which come with a countertop, are perfect for maximizing space in small kitchens, since they provide not only refrigerated storage but also a quick and easily accessible work counter for slicing and dicing. This type of equipment allows chefs and cooks to prep, wrap, and refrigerate quickly and efficiently.

Under-the-counter refrigerators offer an array of features such as half or full doors. Half doors conserve energy since you can elect to open only half of the refrigerator. The doors may be see-through or solid. This is important because excessive opening of refrigerator doors or adding too much heat to a refrigerated space (from a boiling pot of stock, for instance) will cause the refrigeration to function poorly and result in spoiled food. Reach-ins with see-through doors also conserve energy since kitchen staff won't have to open them to see what's inside.

Many under-the-counter models can be ordered with drawers instead of doors. Units also can be ordered with interior or exterior thermometers. Like walk-in boxes, the compressors can either be remote or self-contained and are included in the purchase price. To find out more about the types of refrigerated storage that may be suitable for your needs, go to www.truemfg.com. The choices are truly amazing.

Most reach-in and under-the-counter refrigeration can be custom made to suit your specifications. Prices vary according to finish, special features, and manufacturer. Look for these features in a refrigerator:

- All-metal welded construction
- Seamless interior compartments
- Self-defrosting capability
- Polyurethane cellular plastic insulation
- Self-closing doors
- A minimum five-year warranty on the compressor and motor

WASTE STORAGE

Finally, do not forget to plan for storage of waste. One of the "blessings" of being busy is that you will generate large amounts of garbage. If you don't take care of it, your success won't smell too rosy. One often-overlooked aspect of space planning in the back of the house, the kitchen in particular, is providing space for large garbage bins. In each section, hot food and cold food, and at every station, particularly where prep will be done, kitchen staff will generate large amounts of vegetable peels and trimmings from various types of meat, seafood, and poultry. (This is wet garbage.) Having large bins handy will make the entire prep process easy and efficient.

While waiting to dispose of them, you will need to store the byproducts of food preparation, production, and service, including leftover scraps from customers, cardboard boxes, used cans from canned goods, and empty beverage bottles. In rural and suburban areas, disposal companies are paid to provide Dumpsters to meet these needs, but you will still have to choose a location for the Dumpster. In large cities, where garbage pickups are available six or seven nights a week, storage can be more manageable. Nonetheless, depending on your business's size or volume, storing garbage can be a problem, especially in hot climates or seasons. Certain parts of New York City that have high densities of restaurants can smell pretty foul on sweltering hot summer nights during the hours just before garbage pickup. If you have the space, consider installing refrigerated storage for wet garbage.

A good way to reduce the volume of wet garbage is to install commercial food waste disposals. Much like residential kitchen disposal systems, you can connect them to waste lines. They come in various sizes and are priced according to motor size. Many towns and cities encourage garbage disposals, which are environmentally friendly, because they cut down on landfill use. However, they are not suitable for all sewer systems and require code approval before installation.

COOKING EQUIPMENT AND PLACEMENT

A common mistake many restaurant operators make—believe it or not—is to buy equipment simply because they think that it will fit nicely into a particular space in their kitchen. When equipping your new restaurant, it is important to select the types of equipment that are best suited to your menu items. When selecting a range, for example, you should know whether it would be more practical and efficient to have open burners, a flat top, or a griddle top. The best way to find out about the various types of equipment that are available is to attend a restaurant trade show. The National Restaurant Association and the National Association of Foodservice Equipment Manufacturers (NAFEM) organize two of the biggest shows.

In restaurants, there are two types of cooking: cooking with dry heat (sautéing, frying, roasting, grilling, and broiling) and cooking with moist heat (steaming, braising, and boiling). In large, high-volume restaurants, most of the volume cooking is done in a separate hot food section, which is usually located at the back of the kitchen. High-volume moist cooking equipment that is typically found grouped or "batteried" together in this section includes tilting braising pans, steam-jacketed kettles, and deck ovens. The other hot food section, commonly known as "the line," is where all of the high-heat, cook-to-order cooking is done. The line usually is at the front of the kitchen. Dry heat, quick-cooking equipment typically found in this section includes ranges, griddles, broilers, ovens, fryers, and short-term holding equipment such as steam tables.

In most localities, both types of cooking must be vented or placed under an exhaust hood and surrounded by various fire-suppression nozzles. Not only are heat and grease extraction and fire-suppression systems highly regulated, they can be very expensive to install. In New York City, for example, the cost alone to install outside ductwork runs $4,500 to $5,000 *per floor* of an entire building. This means that if you choose a street-level site in a ten-story building, you will be looking at roughly $50,000 to run ductwork from the ground floor to the roof. You will have to submit detailed architectural and engineering drawings, specifying the types of equipment that will be used under the exhaust hood, along with a set of fire-suppression drawings to local fire and buildings departments for approval. Most architects and contractors specializing in restaurant construction will be able to refer you to a couple of fire-suppression contractors from whom you can solicit bids. In most states, licensed fire-suppression experts must inspect fire-suppression systems every six months. Without these inspections, you will not be able to get an insurance policy to cover your business, and local fire departments will issue fines for violations, which could lead to your restaurant being closed.

For the purposes of this book, I will limit my discussion to restaurants with only dry heat cooking equipment, which is probably representative of most independent casual restaurants. You can do moist cooking with only a dry heat line, since most of the volume cooking can be done on a range top during slow periods or when the restaurant is closed to the public. Smaller stockpot ranges and flat-top (piano) ranges can also be used for this purpose. Of course, you should have two cooking sections if you can afford the additional space and equipment and if your anticipated volume is such that having them will be vital to your operation. Most first-timer owners, however, don't usually do the volume that would warrant such an investment.

GAS RANGES

The most used piece of equipment in the sauté station section is a range. This is basically the same piece of equipment as the stove in your home: a set of burners and an oven. Unlike your stove, which you would typically use to make one or two meals a day, a restaurant range is going from the minute the restaurant opens until it closes. It will be used to sauté, boil, bake, roast, and occasionally fry. Not surprisingly, the range is usually referred to as the workhorse or the backbone of a kitchen.

In deciding on the type and size range to use, consider how many of your menu items will be prepared in advance and reheated, held hot (for example, in a steam table and then plated as needed), or served à la carte. Generally, the more à la carte

Making Small Kitchens Work

Christine Mullen of Cav Wine Bar and Kitchen

In fall of 2005, when we opened Cav Wine Bar and Kitchen in San Francisco, we knew that in order to achieve our profit goals we would have to compromise on the size of our kitchen. Out of 1,500 square feet of space, we wanted to have a spacious wine bar and a dining room that would seat fifty comfortably. We also wanted to have two bathrooms. After the space was efficiently laid out to allow for proper flow of guests and servers in the bar and dining areas and to and from the bathrooms, I was left with 150 square feet for my kitchen and production areas.

Since our goal at Cav was to make drinking less pretentious and more open and accessible, my challenge was to create a diverse and creative menu that would pair well with our global selection of over three hundred wines. To accomplish this goal, my menu had to offer savory and sweet dishes with different taste and texture profiles, using a combination of preparation methods, such as sautéed, baked, grilled, roasted, braised, fried, and served naturally. With these goals in mind, I knew that my equipment selection had to include a range, an oven, a char grill, and a deep fat fryer.

Given space limitations, and the complexity of my menu, my first challenge was to select equipment that would fit into a tight space and facilitate speedy preparation. My "workhorse," therefore, had to be a six-burner range with a convection oven. As you can imagine, after fitting my cooking equipment—a six-burner range, a 2-foot grill, a two-basket fryer, two 5-foot worktops, low-boy refrigerators, and a three-compartment dishwasher—into 150 square feet, there was not much room left to accommodate staff. My entire kitchen staff, therefore, consists of my sous chef, a prep cook, and me.

I am often asked, "How do you prepare such a complex menu in a restaurant your size with such limited space and staff?" The answer is simple: planning and timely preparation. In order to start service at 5 p.m. on busy days, my staff and I start to work at around 12 p.m. This gives us enough time to check our reservations and get to work doing the necessary *mise en place* (preparation) so that when orders come into the kitchen, we can cook and plate them to order attractively and quickly.

Working out of a tight space forces me to be creative in ways other than menu creation, too. For example, with limited space and staff, we also have to time our preparation very precisely since very often we have to use our single oven or range top to prepare slow roasted savory dishes as well as desserts.

Timely deliveries of very fresh ingredients, my speed rack, and a well-trained and loyal staff, who I respect and appreciate, also goes a long way toward helping us to accomplish our goals.

items your kitchen staff will prepare, the more quick-cooking, high heat equip
ment like ranges and conventional and convection ovens you will require. Similarly,
more steam-table type menu items need less range and oven space. That is, for more
reheating, you will need more oven space and less range-top space. Additional important considerations are the number of meals that will be served during peak periods
and the other types of cooking equipment (broilers, fryers, and so on) that will be
part of your hot food line.

Restaurant (also called café) ranges are smaller and less sturdy than heavy-duty
ranges and are usually half as expensive. At Zuni, due to our kitchen size, number of
seats, and volume, we were able to use a restaurant range quite successfully. Heavy-
duty ranges, as you might expect, are constructed of heavier materials and are a
lot more rugged and sturdy. Averaging 30,000 BTUs per hour for each burner, they
also cook a lot faster than restaurant ranges. The typical restaurant range averages
20,000 BTUs per hour per burner, although some are capable of 27,000 BTUs per
hour. So the higher the volume you plan, the more seriously you should consider
heavy-duty ranges.

Finding a range to meet your specific needs should not be difficult, since most of
the top manufacturers can custom build ranges to suit almost any type of operation.
In gas ranges, the flue riser (unique to gas ranges) provides shelf space, diverts gas
vapors to the exhaust hood, and acts as a backsplash to prevent grease spills from
getting on the wall behind the range. Typically, cooktops are configured in twelve-
inch increments, which allows you to create a combination of ovens, open burners,
hot tops, broilers, and griddles. Since most major manufacturers have a myriad of
standard configurations in stock, you may not have to get custom units to maximize efficiency in your space. For example, just a few years ago, it was possible to
get a standard five-foot, all-in-one restaurant range with six burners, a broiler, two
ovens, a griddle, and a stainless steel flue riser with one shelf—for a very reasonable
price. With the ability to have three different stations—sauté, broil, and griddle—all
in one piece of equipment, a small operation can get an amazing amount of production out of a single piece of equipment.

It may be more cost effective and efficient over the long run to get custom-built
pieces of equipment that will meet your specific menus, and therefore your production, needs. You'll be happy to know that except for custom-built refrigeration
components, most custom-designed ranges are not substantially more expensive
than standard units.

Depending on your needs, you can order ranges with or without ovens. Most
manufacturers offer a choice of one, two, or no ovens. Oven sizes are usually based
on the size of the standard baking sheet, or eighteen by twenty-four inches. A range
oven is the least expensive oven on the market. Some manufacturers offer a con-
vection-oven base, which is considerably more expensive than the standard oven
base but cooks much faster. A convection oven base is usually large enough for an
eighteen- by twenty-six-inch baking pan and is only fourteen inches high. Ranges
with convection bases are also larger than standard ranges. (We'll talk more about
convection ovens in a bit.)

While it is convenient to have an oven underneath the range, there are circumstances when a stand-alone oven may be more efficient and effective. Also, the cavities of ovens located under ranges tend to be smaller than those in stand-alone ovens. If you decide to use a stand-alone oven but will need some additional storage space, ranges with storage bases are also available. Typically, storage bases are used to store sauté pans and other smaller pieces of kitchen equipment.

If you will not need an oven or storage base, you can mount your range on a specially constructed stand or a refrigerator or freezer base. If you will be working out of a tight space and you can afford it, consider getting a range with built-in refrigerated drawers. Refrigerated bases with drawers are great for reducing steps and making your kitchen more efficient. Also, you can order stand-alone refrigerated bases with drawers or with doors. This type of refrigeration equipment is specifically designed for high heat environments and is no less energy efficient than other types of refrigeration. In tight areas, this set-up is very space efficient, stacking equipment and thus creating a pivot-and-turn workspace for chefs and cooks. Being able to pivot and turn reduces the number of steps a chef or cook will have to take to cook and plate any menu item. It's very similar to the one-step rule for setting up a bar in that a cook would only have to take one step to prepare and plate a dish.

If you are planning a high-end operation with an open kitchen, you may want to consider a Euro style island range, such as a Waldorf range. With island ranges, chefs and cooks can work next to and directly across from each other, which allows them to easily pass food items back and forth, saving multiple steps. These ranges have been popular in Europe for decades and are beginning to gain popularity in the United States in high-volume upscale kitchens, especially those in open view of guests. They are good for putting on a show for the guests, but they are considerably more expensive than traditional ranges.

ELECTRIC RANGES

Because natural gas is less expensive than electricity in most parts of the country, it is the most common source of energy in restaurant kitchens. Some chefs prefer natural gas because of its ability to transfer heat instantly; unlike electric sources, no warm-up time is required when cooking with natural gas.

In some locations, however, electricity and bottled gas are the only heat sources available. If you are unable to get gas or electricity and must use bottled gas, be sure to tell your equipment dealer so your range burners can be modified for propane. More important, bottled gas puts out 25 percent less heat than natural gas, which means that food will take longer to cook. If you are planning on doing high-volume cooking with bottled gas, you will need additional burners and range-top space.

In spaces that do not have gas access or are too small to install the heat-protection systems that gas heat requires, electric cooking has its advantages. By using equipment such as induction range tops, convection ovens, and FlashBake ovens, chefs and first-time restaurateurs are able to open limited-menu, shoe-box size restaurants all over the country. One such operation in New York City is The Tasting Room, with only 750 square feet, which reportedly grosses sales of over eighteen thousand dollars per week using primarily convection ovens and induction ranges.

Getting electric ranges in situations where natural gas is not available will not be a problem. Many of the same ranges powered by natural gas can also be powered by electric energy. If you are going to use electric cookers, be sure to let your electrical contractor know *way* ahead of time. Most electric ranges and ovens require at least 208- to 240-volt single-phase or triple-phase outlets. This is a very important detail, because rewiring your kitchen or having the equipment returned for modifications can be expensive. I learned this the hard way, at Souperdog. We purchased and had delivered a five thousand-dollar hydraulic sausage stuffer, only to later find out that it required a 220-volt double-phase outlet, which we did not have. We had to have our electrician put in a new breaker box to handle the load. It was quite expensive.

A benefit of using electric power is that in some localities electric-powered cooking equipment requires less fire suppression and ventilation than gas-powered equipment. Check with local ordinances before installing heat extraction, fire suppression, and hood systems. A drawback with electric equipment is that it is generally more expensive to repair and harder to maintain than gas equipment.

In addition to standard electric ranges, smaller pieces of electric cooking equipment, like rectangular hot plates and French hot plates, can be used in small spaces or on countertops. An electric-powered range that is growing in popularity is the induction range top. Induction ranges use electromagnetic fields created by friction between cooking surfaces to create heat. Induction ranges are cheaper to operate than both gas and standard electric ranges. For example, the cost of induction heat is $.06 to $.08 per hour, compared to $1.75 per hour or more for gas. Other benefits of induction range tops include the following:

- They transfer heat as fast as gas.
- They create less ambient heat, than either gas or standard electric ranges, which ensures cooler, more comfortable working conditions.
- In some localities, they require less fire suppression, ventilation, and ducting systems than gas or standard electric ranges
- They are safer than ranges with burners since there are no flames.
- They have the same variable heat control as gas heat without the dangers of open flames.

The downside of induction range tops is that they are expensive and require the use of specialty cookware. They are also not as durable as cast-iron open or flat-top burners, and they must be handled with care. As of this writing, induction ranges are being used mostly in very small operations, for cooking demonstrations, in tight spaces, and for buffets and catering. To find out more about induction ranges, go to www.cooktek.com or call (888) COOKTEK.

COOKTOPS AND BURNERS

For both standard gas and electric ranges, the most common types of burners are: open burners, hot tops (flat tops), and griddle tops. Each of these burner types can either be purchased as part of a range or as a separate stand-alone unit.

The most commonly used burner for both gas and electric ranges is the open burner, which is the same type of burner generally used with a home stove. The big difference is that restaurant ranges are far sturdier and have much higher BTU ratings. For example, the typical commercial burner is about twelve inches wide, with metal grates weighing at least forty pounds each and BTU ratings from 20,000 to 35,000. The BTU rating of the standard home stove is about 10,000.

In addition to the standard twelve-inch burners used for sauté and other à la carte cooking, commercial ranges have eighteen-inch stockpot burners that are used for large-scale production of soups and stocks. Specialty ranges, like taco ranges, are designed specifically for use in Mexican restaurants, and Chinese or wok ranges, capable of producing as much as 80,000 BTUs, are designed specifically for stir-frying. Smaller tabletop ranges for use in very tight spaces also are available.

Both gas and electric open burners heat up very rapidly. However, pots and pans must be placed directly over electric burners, which means that kitchen staff cannot use the entire surface area of the top of the range to cook.

As the name suggests, the entire surface area of a hot-top, or flat-top range is flat and can be used for cooking. There are two types of hot tops. The sectional hot top has individual controls for each section. The graduated hot top, or ring top or French burner, has rings that can be removed to bring sauté pans closer to the flames, making it possible to sauté in the middle of the range where it is very hot and simmer or warm foods around the edges of the cooktop. Both types of hot-top burners make it easy to use a combination of sauté pans and pots simultaneously and to move heavy pots across the range's surface. For this reason, French chefs call the graduated hot top "the piano." With open burners, this would not be possible. The downside is that it takes a few minutes for these burners to heat up, which means that they must stay turned up to cooking temperature during the entire meal period. This wastes more energy than open gas burners.

GRIDDLES

Not every hot food section has a griddle station. At Zuni, because we did not serve breakfast, we opted for a charbroiler to grill burgers, steaks, fish, chicken, and vegetables. Your selection will depend on your menu and your cooking methods used. That said, a griddle is a versatile piece of equipment to have on the hot line. Depending on the type of operation, griddles can be used for burgers, hotdogs, pancakes, omelets, and more. Not surprisingly, it is the burner of choice in most diners. Griddles are similar to hot-top burners except they are made of a thicker steel plate. Like hot tops, they must stay in the hot standby mode all day long and are therefore not very energy efficient. Unlike on hot tops, food can be cooked directly on the top of griddles.

A griddle can be integrated into a range, sit atop a griddle stand with storage underneath, be mounted on a refrigerated base with drawers or doors, or be a counter model. The typical griddle top is three-quarters of an inch thick. If you plan to cook lots of frozen food, get one that is one-inch thick. It will retain more heat and recover faster than the three-quarter-inch top. Larger griddles come with temperature controls for every two feet of length. This makes it possible to have different temperatures at different spots in the griddle. With this control, you can cook eggs in one spot and burgers in another. At Wrapsody, we used a five-foot griddle to make all of our hot wrap sandwiches. A big advantage of griddles over hot tops is that they typically come with a grease trough and a drip pan, making it easy to remove surface grease. They also come with splatter guards on three sides.

OVENS

A range oven, which usually comes with the standard range, is the most widely used type of oven for line cooking. It is the least expensive oven on the market, and when properly calibrated it is an invaluable piece of equipment in any restaurant kitchen. A stand-alone oven can be more cost effective and efficient than a range oven, either because of limited space, menu range, or volume and speed requirements. Because the oven cavities of most stand-alone ovens are larger than range ovens, it may be more practical to use them in high-volume operations. For ease of use, stand-alone ovens may be more practical since chefs and cooks won't have to bend over close to the open flames when they need to reach into the oven. Stand-alone ovens can be gas or electric powered; many can be ordered as counter models. Counter models are particularly useful in small operations and in tight spaces.

The most popular stand-alone oven used in restaurant kitchens is the convection oven. They take up less space, hold larger volumes, and cook 25–35 percent faster than conventional range ovens. For this reason, cooking times may have to be adjusted for some recipes. Convection cooking also minimizes shrinkage and maximizes yield per pound. The typical convection oven is six feet tall, three feet wide, and three to four feet deep. There are also half sizes and countertop models. Double oven models with two separate cavities are also available. These models are similar in size to the single-cavity models and use roughly the same amount of energy.

Two types of stand-alone electric ovens that are particularly suited for use in small operations and tight spaces are Turbochef and FlashBake ovens. TurboChef units can take up as little as three square feet and are great for browning and crisping foods. FlashBake ovens are slightly larger, measuring about six square feet and are capable of cooking foods extremely quickly. Reportedly, a FlashBake oven can cook a boneless chicken breast and french fries in two minutes and one minute, respectively. Using a broiler or a fryer, the chicken would take seven minutes and the fries would require ten to thirteen minutes.

One of the most versatile and flexible pieces of cooking equipment to be introduced to restaurant kitchens in recent years is the combination oven and steamer, or combi-oven. According to chefs who use them, these combi-ovens are capable of doing the same things as a steamer or convection oven, but better. This single piece of equipment can be used to roast, bake, steam, braise, cook, defrost, and warm. In the dual oven and steamer mode, the combi-oven produces moist heat that helps to reduce shrinkage in meats. A combi-oven is also space efficient since it takes up half as much space as a separate stand-alone oven and steamer combined.

Combination ovens are electric powered and are available in various sizes, ranging from small countertop models to large freestanding units capable of handling very large volumes. Combination ovens are suitable for almost every type of operation from fine dining to trendy high-volume upscale operations to small limited-service operations and snack bars. Also, in some localities, combination ovens may not have to be vented, which could result in considerable savings in energy and exhaust hood space. These ovens generally have fairly sophisticated electronic controls and should be located away from high heat, grease, and steam.

Commercial microwave ovens are also available for use in restaurant operations and are mostly used to defrost and reheat food items. (Not surprisingly, residential models will burn out quickly in busy restaurant kitchens.) Other types of specialty ovens are pizza ovens and rotisserie ovens.

BROILERS

In most cases, the broiler station is part of the battery of equipment that makes up the hot food section. Where it appears depends on the number of menu items that will be broiled and the other menu items that will accompany broiled items. If a baked potato will accompany a steak, you may want it placed near the source of the baked potato. There are four types of broilers: top fired or heavy duty, charbroilers, salamanders, and cheese melters. All come with adjustable racks, removable drip pans, and individually controlled burners.

The typical heavy-duty broiler comes with an oven base and a shelf or warming compartment above the broiler unit. Heavy-duty broilers can be gas or electric powered. Gas burners have a capacity of between 65,000 and 100,000 BTUs per hour. Heavy-duty broilers using infrared heat can reduce cooking time by as much as 50 percent. Other advantages of infrared gas burners over radiant heat burners are that they heat up a lot faster, in as little as ninety seconds, and therefore do not need to be kept in the standby mode, thus saving energy. Also, because infrared heats only the food, not the surrounding air space, it makes for a much cooler kitchen.

Because of the extremely high BTU output, a heavy-duty broiler is the workhorse in most steak houses. It is an ideal piece of equipment to have in your kitchen if you will be offering primarily steaks, burgers, and other grilled or broiled meats.

Unlike top-fired heavy-duty broilers, charbroilers are under-fired broilers, meaning the heat source comes from underneath the food. Gas, electricity, wood, or charcoals can heat charbroilers. Obviously, the fuel source will influence the amount of flavor imparted to the food being cooked.

Gas accompanied by lava rocks for flavor is the heat source most frequently used with charbroilers. Good charbroilers will generally have better heat controls than top-fired broilers, and as a result, they allow for more precise cooking. A charbroiler is a very versatile piece of equipment and is great for imparting a nice smoky or charcoal flavor to food. Charbroilers come in various models and sizes ranging from fifteen to seventy-two inches in length. The number of burners varies with the length, with each burner offering between 15,000 and 45,000 BTUs-per-hour input. Electric models can require up to 10 kilowatts of power per hour and require 208- to 240-volt outlets. These models can be mounted on a stainless-steel stand, integrated into a cabinet base, or mounted on a stainless-steel counter. The downside is that charbroilers create a lot of smoke and grease, and they typically have much higher exhaust requirements than heavy-duty broilers.

The other two types of broilers, salamanders and cheese melters, are miniature versions of the heavy-duty broiler. They are similar in that all three are top fired. A nice feature of both types of broilers is that they are usually mounted off the ground, above other pieces of equipment, and so are great for saving floor space.

The salamander got its name because, just like its lizard namesake, it can easily fit into its environment. More often than not, they are integrated into a range and mounted above open burners, flat tops, or spreader plates. They can also be purchased as stand-alone or electric countertop units, and they are fairly compact, ranging in size from ten to thirteen inches deep and twenty-three to twenty-eight inches wide. In either case they must be installed under the exhaust hood and fitted with fire-suppression nozzles. A salamander is less powerful than a heavy-duty broiler and more powerful than a cheese melter. It could be a good substitute for a heavy-duty broiler if your menu will require medium- to low-volume broiling. In this context, it can also be used to warm food and as a plate warmer.

Gas-powered salamanders can have from one to six burners with BTU-per-hour input requirements ranging from 30,000 to 66,000. Electric models vary in kilowatt usage per hour and will generally require either 208- to 240-volt outlets. If you can afford it, get gas infrared models, which preheat a lot faster, in ninety seconds compared to their radiant counterparts, which take about fifteen minutes. Because of their rapid heat-up speed, they can be turned off during slow periods, which keeps the kitchen cooler and reduces energy costs. At Zuni, our salamander did not have infrared burners, and unfortunately it made working conditions in the kitchen during hot steamy summer days very unpleasant.

Cheese melters are similar to salamanders but are less powerful and consequently are less useful as a broiler. As the name implies, they are ideal for finishing cheese or crumb-topped dishes, warming plated food (making sure that it will be delivered to guests at the proper serving temperature), or as a plate warmer. They are available in various lengths, and they can be radiant or infrared heated or powered by electricity. Units are also available that heat up only when food is placed under the heating elements.

FRYERS

Second only to a range, a fryer is probably the most common piece of equipment found in cook-to-order kitchens. It's a great piece of equipment because as you well know, when done properly, fried food can be light, crispy, and unsurpassed in texture and flavor.

The fryer's location will depend on the number of menu items that will be fried or accompanied by fried items. The less fry-intensive the menu, the smaller the fryer, and the further away it will be from the action. If the fryer will be next to any piece of equipment with open flames, it must either be at least sixteen inches away or be separated by a stainless-steel plate high enough to prevent flames from jumping from the range into the fryer fat. Fryers must also be placed under an exhaust hood and protected by fire-suppression nozzles.

Fryers can either be powered by gas or electricity, and they come in varying sizes. The energy requirement for the standard fifteen-pound countertop fryer is about 25,000 BTUs per hour. There are two types of gas fryers, radiant heat and infrared. Infrared burners fry food a lot faster, and therefore require a lot less energy. In fact, they are 45 to 80 percent more energy efficient than their standard gas or electric counterparts. Infrared fryers also have much faster heat recovery times between batches and cook at lower temperatures. Heat recovery time—the time it takes for hot oil to get back to its ideal cooking temperature of 325 to 350 degrees in between batches—is a very important consideration with fryers because the longer it takes to recover, the more oil the food will absorb, becoming soggy.

Electric fryers take about six minutes for the oil to reach an ideal fry temperature, which for most foods is 350 degrees. The power requirements for electric fryers vary with size. Energy requirements range from 5.7 to 36 kilowatts per hour and require between 208- and 240-volt outlets.

Fryers are sized according to the number of pounds of oil they will hold. A more important measure, however, is the number of pounds of food a fryer can fry in one hour. For purposes of rating fryers, most manufacturers use a pound of french fries as the standard food item. As a general rule, a fryer will fry food weighing one and a half to two times its oil capacity in pounds in one hour. For example, a twenty-eight-pound freestanding fryer will fry between forty-two and fifty pounds of french fries in an hour.

If your menu will offer more than one fried item, consider getting two small or medium fryers instead of one large one. The benefits of two fryers are the ability to do the following:

- Fry two different products simultaneously
- Filter the oil more frequently by alternating fryers
- Prevent the flavors of different foods from leaching into each other
- Save energy by shutting down one fryer during slow periods

Don't forget to filter your oil regularly. The more frequently it is filtered, the better your fried foods will taste and the longer your oil will last. If you cannot afford a fryer with a built-in filtering system, consider getting a portable oil filter. The least expensive but less effective method is to use a disposable paper filter, a funnel, and a large clean receptacle such as a stockpot. But wait for the oil to cool down to less than 90 degrees first.

Finally, to avoid costly downtime due to equipment failure and high repair and maintenance costs, look for the following features when buying your cooking equipment:

- Easy to remove and clean drip pans under the burners
- Controls that are easily accessible and protected from spills
- All-metal welded construction. (Equipment that is riveted together is a lot less sturdy. Screwed-together equipment should be avoided if possible.)
- Ranges with electronic spark ignition instead of standing pilot lights (this can save gas consumption)

CLEANING STATIONS

Properly designed and equipped cleaning stations will be important to the success of your restaurant. Without properly equipped and designed cleaning stations, preparation and cooking will not be very efficient and therefore costly. More important, health code regulations in most if not all cities will not only mandate certain construction requirements such as drains, but will require specific types of cleaning equipment and will specify their location. The following section discusses cleaning equipment requirements and their design and layout.

SINKS

Planning the number of and layout of sinks is a critical aspect of kitchen design. Not only must kitchen staff wash their hands several times each day to prevent cross contamination, but most food items must be washed and cleaned before any prep starts. Few, if any, items that pass through a kitchen will not require a visit to the sink. All health departments have strict code regulations regarding the number and types of sinks that must be in every kitchen. Most health departments will also require NSF sinks (that is, sinks with rounded corners). As a rule of thumb, figure on having a sink every ten to fifteen feet.

In the kitchen and food prep areas, figure on having at least one pot and dish washing sink and a two-compartment prep and pantry sink, plus a utility and slop sink in the dry storage and receiving areas, for washing mops and cleaning floors. In most cities, pot washing requires a three-compartment sink: one sink for washing, one for sanitizing, and a third for rinsing. In really tight spaces, when not being used for pot washing, this sink can also be used for prep, as was the case at Wrapsody. At Zuni, since we used our dish machine to sanitize and rinse our pots and pans, we were able to meet code requirements with a two-compartment sink in the dish and pot-washing area. Pot washing and prep sinks can also be used as chill tanks. For example, large stockpots full of stocks, soups, and stews can be placed in these sinks and surrounded by ice to cool them down before being refrigerated.

If your budget permits, a garbage disposal unit at the prep sink for vegetable peels, meat and fish trimmings, and other suitable waste can save tremendously on the amount of garbage your kitchen staff will have to bag, store, and throw out.

In selecting sinks, particularly pot washing and prep sinks, look for recessed inner rims. This feature makes it easier to decant large pots of hot liquids, which in turn comes in handy when blanching vegetables. Pot sinks should have swivel faucets that can reach all three compartments.

If you are planning a high-volume operation and your space and budget permit, consider getting a Metcraft power-soak pot sink, which uses water jets and agitation to clean. They are about four inches bigger than standard pot-wash sinks, but they can save labor by diverting the cost of pot washing to prep. With a power-soak sink, your pot washer will only have to rinse and sanitize.

DRAINS

In addition to the drains and drainpipes that will be connected to all of your various sinks, you should plan on having a few floor drains. As you might imagine, wherever there are sinks and lots of washing, there is going to be a lot of water spillage. Not surprisingly, floor drains are just as essential as sinks. It is critical to plan the amount of and location of drains early on, since they are permanently dug into the floor and are hard to add or change after installation. In many localities, drain systems are code regulated, so be sure to check your local health code requirements.

As a minimum, plan on having a floor drain near the pot washing and dishwashing stations to catch spills and prevent standing water. Not only do floor drains prevent slips and falls, they also are indispensable when it comes to cleaning and sanitizing equipment, walls, exhaust hoods, and floors. With adequate floor drains, you can use a high-pressure hose to wash down your walls periodically and your floors regularly. Regularly washing walls and floors helps to prevent grease buildup. Floor drains also come in handy in prep and storage areas and under an ice machine to catch condensation.

In most towns and localities, building codes require that certain kitchen sinks and drains be connected to a grease trap to prevent grease from leaving the restaurant and clogging up the local sewer system. Grease traps come in various sizes. Plumbers familiar with restaurant operations can select the right size trap for your operation. Also, in order to prevent contamination from backflow and sewer gases, health codes mandate that there must be an air gap (a space between the sink and the drain pipe) for all sinks used for dishwashing, pot washing, and food preparation.

Last but not least, plan on having your drains regularly maintained, with a cleaning and snaking, at least once every four to six months. There is nothing worse than a backed-up drain during the middle of a rush.

DISHWASHING EQUIPMENT

Dishwashing can be either manual or by machine or a combination, but if you are planning an operation with any kind of volume, a dishwashing machine will be a must. They are fast, efficient, and cost effective. A small, low-temperature under-the-counter dishwashing machine uses less than two gallons of water per cycle, uses under two kilowatts of power, can complete a wash cycle in one and a half to two and a half minutes, and washes as many as forty racks per hour one at a time. With a properly functioning machine, you will be able to recycle dishes, flatware, and glassware quickly, which allows you to carry lower inventories of each of these items.

Health code regulations will dictate your required setup for dishwashing. If there won't be a dishwashing machine, a three-compartment sink will be required. With a dishwashing machine, the requirements will be different since the machine washes, sanitizes, and rinses. For best results, and to save on detergent use, make sure that dishes are pre-scraped and prewashed before placing them in the machine. To facilitate this process, situate a one- or two-compartment sink with a high-pressure swivel faucet in the dishwashing area. Local health codes will also stipulate required water temperatures, so be sure to install a water heater that will be capable of generating a constant supply of water heated to the minimum required temperature of 120 degrees.

There are basically two types of dishwashing machines: high-temperature (HT) machines, which heat water to 180 degrees to rinse and sanitize dishes, and 120-degree low-temperature (LT) machines, which require chlorine and/or other chemicals at the end of the rinse cycle to kill remaining bacteria. With high-temperature machines, dishes dry a lot quicker, since water evaporates a lot faster off of hot surfaces, but utility costs are higher and venting may be required because of the extra heat generated.

The more grease and starch in your menu items and the faster your need to recycle dishes, the greater the likelihood that you will need a high-temperature machine. If you will be running a coffee-shop type of operation, chances are that you won't need a high-temperature machine since your menu will probably not consist of items that are high in starch or grease. Your choice of temperature need not be permanent, since most low-temperatures machines can be converted to high temperature simply by installing a booster heater. In some cases, a booster heater may not be needed since many single-tank dishwashing machines are field convertible; that is, they can be converted from high to low temperature and vice versa.

Other factors to consider when buying a dishwashing machine are the wash cycle, dish (or rack) count, and energy usage. The wash cycle is the amount of time it will take for the machine to wash, sanitize, and rinse a load of dishes. Heavy-grease environments will usually require longer wash cycles. The dish count refers to the number of racks the machine will wash in an hour. The higher your operation's volume requirements, the higher your required rack count will be. The standard single-tank door-style machine can handle at least sixty racks per hour. Each dish rack is about eighteen by eighteen inches square and can hold sixteen ten-inch plates. Glass racks are the same size and hold between twenty and twenty-five glasses depending on their size. In high-volume, high-energy cost environments, infrared gas-powered machines can be very cost effective. They can cost 15-20 percent more but are very energy efficient and can produce significant cost savings over the long run. They also generate a lot less heat. One way to conserve energy with both gas infrared and standard electric machines is to run only fully loaded racks through the machine during off-peak hours. An adequate power supply will also be required: 120 volts for under-the counter machines, and 208–240 volts for single tank door-style machines.

Most first timers make the mistake of getting either too much or too little dishwashing capacity. If your machine is too big, it will take up valuable space in your kitchen and be underutilized. If it is too small, it will not meet your volume requirements and can slow down your operation. Generally, if you are planning on a small operation serving fifty or fewer meals per hour, you will be able to manage with a compact twenty-four-inch square counter or under-the counter machine.

At Zuni, our entire dishwashing and pot-washing area took up about forty-six square feet and included a two foot by two foot-square single-tank low-temperature door-style machine with a load handling capacity of over sixty racks per hour, a two-compartment sink with a swivel hose, a stainless-steel table that served as a landing area for soiled dishes, a large garbage pail for plate scraping, and over shelves for clean dishes. We used this machine to wash dishes and also to sanitize and rinse pots and pans during off-peak hours.

To get ideas about the right size and type of machine for your operation, talk to other restaurateurs with operations similar in size and volume to the one you have in mind. Ask them about their machines and how effective they are at handling their dishwashing requirements. A good source for researching the various types of machines and related costs is www.ecolab.com.

Take flow patterns into consideration when selecting a location for the dishwashing area in your kitchen. Wait and bus staff should not have to go too far into the kitchen, where their paths will cross with those of the kitchen staff, to drop off dirty dishes. The best location for the dishwashing area is out of view of the dining room, but close enough to it that it will be easily accessible yet far enough that the noise and clatter of dishwashing will not be easily heard from the dining room. Insulated walls separating the kitchen and the dining room and acoustic tiles over the dishwashing area will help to reduce noise levels.

If you are planning on a fast-food or takeout and delivery operation, you probably won't need a dishwashing machine, since most of your eating and drinking utensils will be disposables.

MISCELLANEOUS EQUIPMENT AND SMALLWARE

You will need numerous other pieces of small equipment, hand tools, knives, measuring tools, scales, pots and pans, baking pans and bowls, and serving and holding containers to measure, mix, cook, and store food. The numbers and varieties of these tools are myriad, and your needs will depend on the size of your operation, your cuisine type, and your menu. For example, if you will be running a burger or sandwich joint, chances are you won't need various types of pots, pans, whips, scoops, serving spoons, and so on. On the other hand, if you are planning a table-service French or Italian operation, you will likely require all those items and more.

Don't skimp on the quality of your small equipment and smallware. Research each type carefully and buy the best quality you can afford. Cookware–pots and pans in particular—is very important. The type of metal you select can make a big difference in price, durability, and heat conductivity. Each metal has its advantages and disadvantages. While aluminum pans are light and great for heat conductivity, they are not as durable as other metals like carbon steel, steel, stainless steel, cladded copper, and stainless steel.

It's important to give your kitchen staff the right tools to prepare food that will meet your target market's expectations. Don't forget, you will be feeding a very fickle public. Very often, the right tools will make cooking easier, more precise, and cost effective. The right portion control or recipe scale, for example, will help not only with recipe consistency, but also with food cost. Similarly, the right food processor can save hours of slicing, dicing, and mixing time.

When preparing your equipment budget, do not underestimate the cost of small equipment and smallware. While these pieces may be small in size, you will need lots of them, and the costs will add up quickly. For example, at Zuni, we had a ten-burner stove. At any given time during the rush, each one of those burners would have a sauté pan on top of it (many of which had to be washed after each use), and that was only sauté pans. Obviously, not every kitchen will be this heavy on sauté, but trust me; you will need more than one of each kitchen tool.

The following is a list of the most common types of small equipment and smallware items used in restaurant kitchens:

- Food mixers
- Food processors
- Blenders
- Food slicers
- Toasters
- Food warmers
- Serving spoons
- Hand whips
- Food turners and spatulas
- Tongs
- Kitchen forks
- Strainers and colanders
- Kitchen knives: chef's knife, utility knife, paring knife, boning knife, etc.
- Knife sharpener
- Cutting boards; most health departments will not allow wooden cutting boards
- Kitchen scales
- Ladles
- Scoops
- Thermometers
- Cookware: stockpots, double boilers, saucepans, and sauté pans
- Roasting pans, baking pans, and sheet pans
- Hotel pans (plastic or stainless steel)

The scope of this book does not permit a discussion of several other types of specialty restaurant cooking equipment that are available. The list above represents the types of equipment that any first timer could use to create a diverse menu using various cooking methods such as sauté, fry, broil, grill, bake, roast, etc. At Zuni, the extent of our cooking equipment was a 10-burner range with two conventional ovens, a 24-inch charbroiler, a salamander, and a deep fat fryer. For short-term refrigerated storage and work surfaces, we also had five pieces of strategically located work top/under-counter refrigerators, a reach-in refrigerator and a small ice cream freezer. This line-up was sufficient to allow us to create and serve a complex and diverse menu and to handle fairly high volume out of a tight space.

The world of restaurant equipment is truly amazing, with hundreds of different types of equipment to suit almost any type and size restaurant. Via the Web, you can research and comparison shop to find almost any type of equipment to suit your budget. Two websites that I find particularly useful for new and used equipment are Restaurant Equipment World (www.restaurantequipment.net) and eBay; both sites offer tens of thousands of items with photos.

Websites for some of the top cooking equipment manufacturers are: www. jaderange.com, www.blodgett.com, www.vulcanhart.com, www.randell.com, www. maytagfoodservice.com, www.montaguecompany.com, www.southbendnc.com, www.wolfstoves.com, and www.garlandrange.com. Use these in conjunction with the sites listed above to shop and compare. These manufacturers all make top-of-the-line equipment that is more expensive than other brands.

Don't bust your budget getting all top-of-the-line equipment, but buy the best equipment your budget can afford. Before you buy any particular brand of equipment, research each manufacturer by getting references from other restaurateurs.

MAINTAINING EQUIPMENT

The most common cause of restaurant equipment failure is lack of proper cleaning and maintenance. Simply following the instructions in the owners' and operators' manuals. Cleaning your equipment regularly can avoid a lot of extra costs and headaches. With refrigeration, in particular, be sure to keep condenser coils free of dirt and grease. A good way to do this is to cover them with a thin layer of foam, which acts as a filter.

Read the owners' and operators' manuals before you call a service technician. This can save a lot of downtime and money. For example, when we first got started, we had to pay for a service call on the ice machine when all someone had to do was press the reset button.

CHAPTER 11

STAFFING:
Skills and Service

Once you have a concept—including service style, type of cuisine, and ambience—you're ready to put together the staff who will help you turn that concept into reality. The restaurant industry is the nation's largest private-sector employer with more than 12.2 million employees, or more than 8 percent of the labor force in the United States. This is a good reminder of how crucial your staff will be to your restaurant's success. The service sector is our economy's fastest-growing sector. There are now more than three hundred culinary schools with over fifty-five thousand students enrolled. Working in a restaurant used to be seen purely as a dead-end job. Times are changing, and chefs, managers, and wait staff at some top restaurants now make excellent salaries. Some chefs are even celebrities.

KITCHEN STAFF

As we discussed in chapter 4, preparing consistently good food will go a long way toward increasing your chances of success. So early in your concept development, it is very important that you have a clear understanding of the necessary skill sets that you will require from your kitchen staff.

Your menu, type of cuisine, and cooking style will determine your kitchen staff's required skill and experience level. For example, if you plan to open a sushi restaurant, you will probably have to hire a skilled sushi chef with a knowledge of the best types of fish to select, the skills and techniques to properly cut and prepare it, and the ability to expertly cook the sushi rice. Similarly, if you are planning a formal four-star restaurant, with complex menu items, most of the kitchen stations—such as, pastry, salad, and sauce making—will require highly trained staff with experience in various high-end cooking techniques. On the other hand, as you would imagine, if you were planning to open a local burger or hot dog joint, the required skill sets would be a lot less. The important thing is to make sure that your staff will have the necessary experience to make and deliver food that is consistent with your concept and your target customers' expectations of quality, taste, and appearance.

I am frequently asked how many cooks and other kitchen staff members a restaurant needs. Just as you might expect, there is no set answer. It all depends on your restaurant's size, type, volume at peak periods, range and complexity of menu items, cooking methods, staff knowledge and skill level, and equipment selection and layout. Generally, the more complex the menu and the higher the volume, the more hands are required. For example, it is not uncommon for fine-dining restaurants to have several people working a single station in order to perfectly cook and present each plate. But as we discussed in chapter 10, a well-trained staff in a compact well-designed and laid-out kitchen can achieve amazing results. Another key factor in many instances is the amount and quality of preparation that can be done beforehand. Given sufficient prep time, a small but well-trained kitchen staff can make cooking and presenting very sophisticated meals a cinch.

THE CHEF

Whether you will need a chef or not depends on your concept. For example, if you are planning a burger, pizza, or sandwich operation, or a neighborhood diner or similarly casual restaurant with relatively simple menu items, you will probably not require a full-time chef. In fact, many first-time owners in these types of operations start out with their own family recipes, learning the operational side of the kitchen through the proverbial school of hard knocks. That said, even if you have wonderful recipes, it might be well worth your while in terms of money, time, effort, and frustration to hire an experienced chef or consultant to help avoid some of the hard knocks. A professional can help with the following: designing and laying out your kitchen, selecting appropriate types of equipment for your concept, and hiring and training kitchen staff. When I opened Wrapsody, even though I am a pretty good cook and knew what I wanted, I hired a chef as a consultant to create and write standard recipes for my menu and to train my kitchen staff to prepare them properly. I also retained him periodically to replace slow-moving menu items. This freed me up to work on the "business" part of my business such as menu pricing, food costs, labor costs, vendor selection, and counter staffing.

If you are planning on opening an upscale concept, especially in an urban city, where competition is fierce, having a good chef can give you an edge. As the dining public's interest in food continues to grow, people will demand better quality food, and they will want to experience a wider range of flavors and textures. Several restaurant chains around the country have used chef-driven concepts to market themselves, even to casual dining markets.

How do you find the right chef? First, you must have a thorough understanding of your food concept. With this understanding, you should eat at restaurants with food that is similar to your intended concept and that you think is particularly good. While there, ask for names of chefs and sous chefs so you can contact them. Sometimes their names are written on the menus, and you won't have to ask. Very often, talented sous chefs are looking to create a name for themselves and may be willing to work with you. Even if they are not interested, they may be able to refer you to one of their colleagues who would be. You may also want to call local food critics, tell them your concept, and ask if they have any recommendations. You can run ads in local newspapers or on the many culinary Internet sites, such as www.starchef. net, www.ontherail.com, or even on the very popular www.craigslist.org. Also, some culinary schools, such as the Culinary Institute of America (CIA) and Johnson and Wales, will allow you to post your job listing on their websites.

Once you have narrowed your list of potential candidates, you should do the following:

- Taste their food, either by visiting their current place of employment or by inviting them to cook a meal for you from scratch.
- Ask for resumes in order to check previous work experience.
- Call current and past employers to verify employment, job descriptions, and responsibilities, including accountability for food and labor costs.

When checking references, inquire about a chef's ability to manage, get along with, respect, and motivate staff. Creative and technical skills are important, but they don't mean much without people skills. Abusive chefs can ruin your business. Staff will not stay long, your labor costs will suffer due to constant training of new people, and the quality and consistency of your food will suffer. Again, I learned from experience. I once hired a new chef for Zuni even after a past employer told me that although he was a very creative and talented chef, he was difficult to get along with and hard on staff. During the interview, I told the chef that I was aware of this problem and was concerned. He assured me that he was grateful for the opportunity and would change his ways. The chef's food was very good, but within a month of his employment, many of my staff who had been with me for years wanted to quit. After talking to them, I discovered that not only was he a poor teacher, he was abusive. We had to let him go and start all over again. Look for a chef who not only wants to cook but also is passionate about the business and food.

How early you should get your chef involved will depend on your food concept, the complexity of the menu items, and, last but not least, your budget. A common mistake that many inexperienced first-timer owners make is to delay hiring and involving a chef until after the restaurant is built and shortly before it's scheduled to open; they do this partly because they think that they are saving a few months' salary. This is not necessarily a good approach, and it may backfire and become a costly mistake. For example, I can't tell you the number of times that I have heard stories about a new chef who came onboard a week or two before opening only to find that the kitchen was poorly designed and the equipment was either not appropriate for the intended food concept or poorly laid out.

Conversely, involving an experienced chef in the design and layout of your kitchen could result in an efficient space, which in turn will save labor and food costs over time. More important, if you will be opening in a high-rent location, your chef may be able to help design a well-laid-out and compact kitchen, which frees up space for seating more customers, thus increasing your profit. For example, an experienced chef may be able to help choose equipment that does the following:

- Serves multiple purposes
- Best produces your menu items
- Wears well, is durable
- Offers quick cooking
- Allows for flexibility to adjust to changes in the market and thus the menu

Bear in mind that chefs, cooks, and the rest of cooking staff don't just walk into a kitchen and start cooking. Your chef will need time to develop and test recipes, not only for taste, but also for food and labor costs and timeliness, including whether or not your food concept and your required food and labor costs will be achievable and what amount of prep and cook time will be required for each menu item.

This business aspect of hiring the right chef will be critical to your success and should not be overlooked. Let's face it: there is no point in making good food if you cannot make a profit from it. When I was in public accounting, we were called in to review a fine-dining restaurant that was constantly busy because of rave reviews in the food press, but it was continuously losing money. Upon investigation, we discovered that the combined food, beverage, and labor costs were over 80 percent, eating up any possible profit margin.

WAIT STAFF

Now let's talk about the people who will be the first contact and direct link with your customers: the wait or counter staff and, if you have one, the maître d'. Your service staff are the people who make sure that you are providing excellent service to your customers, or at least they should be. The key here is to hire the right people for the job.

Whether it's in person or on the phone to take a reservation, a delivery or takeout order, or simply fielding a question about your operation, an initial contact with a customer is very important. This is the opportunity to set the stage for your customer's entire experience with your business. Train your staff not to blow it, because, as they say, "You never get a second chance to make a first impression."

HIRING

Finding the right people for the job is important because every time you hire someone, you are adding to your marketing team. Part of your restaurant's brand and identity will be reflected through your staff, not only in the way they present and conduct themselves but in their attitude. Hiring service staff with the right attitude and personalities is one of the first steps in providing proper service and avoiding chronic customer-service problems.

Before you hire and set about to train new servers, have them trail (follow during regular work hours) an experienced server for a few days or weeks, depending on the level of service they will be expected to provide. Ask the servers training a prospective employee for their opinions regarding whether or not the trainee should be hired. It is important to give them some input into selecting their coworkers. Traits you want your trainers to look for during the trailing process are the ability to work under pressure and a high tolerance for stress and frustration. A busy restaurant can be extremely hectic, and, as we all know, dealing with the public in a busy setting can be trying at times. Let's face it, we can all be in a rotten mood at times, and when we are, it can take the patience of Job to put on a smile.

When the time comes to make your final decision, always opt for attitude over skill. It is relatively easy to teach people how to set a table or the proper etiquette of serving, but it is very difficult to teach attitude. I found that it was much easier to train nice people than it is to train people to be nice. Look for friendliness, enthusiasm, patience, and compassion. Over the years, I also found that customers are usually more willing to accept mistakes from patient and polite servers. A good way to gauge a server's performance is to look at the amount of tips that he or she gets from a wide cross section of guests. For the most part, good service will routinely yield good tips.

Bear in mind that service-related complaints do not all stem from rude or impolite servers. Many are related to factors such as the following:

- Having to wait too long for service
- Not getting the right order
- Having to wait too long for food or drinks
- Not being seated comfortably and in a timely way
- Having to wait too long for the bill
- Problems resolving billing issues
- Servers lacking knowledge about food and beverages
- Not being responsive to special needs

Many of these service problems occur because of lack of proper training or because an establishment is understaffed. This is not to suggest that you should overstaff, which can lead to annoying and intrusive service. Besides, your servers wouldn't make adequate tips, the main source of their income, and so would not stay for long.

The number of tables per server and support staff such as busers and or runners will depend on your restaurant type, level of expected service, and volume of business at peak periods. For casual table service, I would recommend no more than four or five tables per waiter. Again, the best way to get insight into proper staffing levels is to ask other restauranteurs with operations that are similar to your proposed concept and size. Visit these restaurants to observe, count the number of servers per table, and talk about the level of staffing.

TRAINING

Hiring right is only the beginning; you must back it up with proper training. In order for your restaurant to succeed at providing proper service, you must first define what good service means in the context of your restaurant and your target customers. If you cannot define and establish guidelines for proper service, it will be difficult to train employees much less ask them to adhere to any particular standards.

Common questions both new and regular customers ask are: what's the best thing on the menu? What's good here? and, What would you recommend today? In upscale operations, guests frequently ask for wine recommendations to accompany their menu choices or menu recommendations for their wine choices. Another common question in today's carbohydrate- and fat-conscious climate is, what would you recommend that's tasty but light? I have also had customers ask me for descriptions of the taste of certain exotic or unfamiliar ingredients. Sometimes these types of questions are asked to break the ice between customer and server, but more often than not, it's a genuine request for service. Answers like "everything" or "we sell a lot of this or that" can send the wrong message to your customers. This is reflected by the fact that a common customer complaint regarding service is that wait staff are not knowledgeable about a restaurant's food and beverages.

Your servers won't be able to be informed or enthusiastic about much less sell your food and beverage menu items if all they know is what they have been told by the chef or manager, or sommelier if there is one. One of my friends who is a waiter at an upscale French bistro recently complained to me that her wine director constantly pressures her and the rest of the wait staff to sell wines they have never tasted.

The best way to prepare your service staff to answer customer questions with confidence and enthusiasm and to sell your menu items is to familiarize them with the actual tastes, flavors, and textures of your food and beverages. At Zuni, in order to encourage our wait staff not only to order their staff meals off the menu, but also to become thoroughly knowledgeable and familiar with our menu items, we allowed them to have free, any salad, appetizer, or sandwich with a menu price of eight dollars or less, or any entrée priced at seventeen dollars or less at a 50 percent discount. We also arranged frequent wine tastings with our major vendors who were happy to provide this service for free since they knew that the more knowledgeable our staff was about their wines, the more they would be able to sell them.

One of my friends used to reward his staff for good service by giving them fifty-dollar vouchers to come in and eat with their friends. This afforded valuable critiques of the food and the service given by new hires.

Some people would say that this is too expensive, but when you consider the difference in food and labor between preparing a staff meal (usually leftovers from the previous day's specials) and the actual cost of the menu items, the benefits of a discount policy will far outweigh the costs. Consider, for example, your actual cost of a menu item priced at $10 if the food cost is 25 percent; it equals $2.50. I can't think of a cheaper food and beverage training program! Besides, it is a nice little perk for your staff.

Accidents and mistakes *will* happen, so a very important aspect of providing good service is to train your staff to address and solve accidents and mistakes immediately. By doing so, you will be able to minimize the damage and improve your chances of retaining a loyal and satisfied customer. Although it is important to train your waiters to respond to customer concerns immediately, my experience is that most customers want either a manager or an owner to come over and address a problem situation. Hearing from someone at the top reassures a customer that management cares. Many don't even want a comp; all they want is recognition. For example, just before I left New York to move to California, one of my former employees, Gamini, took me to lunch at Isabella's on Manhattan's Upper West Side. While we were eating, the bottom of Gamini's water glass fell out, spilling water all over his lap. Up until that point, the service had been very good, that is, helpful but not intrusive. Within seconds of the incident, our waiter came to the table to apologize and clean up the water, and within a minute the manager appeared to assess the situation and take it under control. She apologized and offered our salads and desserts on the house. What could have been an unpleasant incident turned into a ringing endorsement for the restaurant. The food was good, but not outstanding, but Gamini told me that based on staff and management response, the next time he had friends in town he would bring them to Isabella's. While this incident only involved spilled water, the same policy should apply to any situation that can negatively affect a customer's dining experience.

DEFINING POLICIES AND PROCEDURES

No matter what size or type of restaurant you will be running, you should have a written document detailing your policies and procedures. Doing so will ensure that employees duties and responsibilities are not left to chance or hearsay. The document does not have to be a manual; it can be as simple as two pages. If you would prefer to have a more official handbook and don't want to hire an attorney to write one from scratch, you can go to www.restaurantville.com or www.restaurantowner.com and download templates, which you can then customize to suit your particular situation. These templates are relatively inexpensive, but you may want to have an attorney review them for accuracy and applicability.

The following is a simple policies and procedures handout that we used at Zuni:

Dress Code
- Blue shirts are required, preferably a long-sleeved Oxford style with collar and buttons. Graphics are not permitted.

- Pants must be full-length. No multi-coloring or other markings. Neatly pressed blue or black jeans are also acceptable.
- Footwear can be Oxford, dress, solid black aerobic/cross-trainer, or similar appropriate wear.
- No hats or other headgear is permitted.
- Aprons are required at all times while on shift.
- A clean, well-kept appearance is required at all times while on duty.

Set-Up Procedures—Dining Room
- Make sure that all of the tables are properly set with glassware, silverware, napkins, candles, and salt and pepper shakers.
- Obtain aprons and bar mops from the manager.
- Make sure that wait stations are adequately stocked with silverware, glassware, and bread and butter.
- Prepare coffee machines, water pitchers, and ice bins.
- Get specials of the day from the chef.

Set-Up Procedures—Bar
- Check the bar top to make sure that it is clean and set up with bar naps, candles, sip sticks, toothpicks, and so on.
- Check condiment trays to make sure that they are adequately stocked with lemon and lime wedges, olives, cherries, and so on.
- Count the cash drawer in the presence of a manager to make sure that there are sufficient bills and change.
- Make sure that ice bins are full.
- Set up each waiter's station with fruit, straws, and so on.
- Check the status of the margarita machine to make sure that there is sufficient mix. Make additional mix if necessary.
- Check liquor inventory and notify the manager of any shortages.
- Obtain aprons and bar mops from the manager.
- Check the silverware station to make sure that it is adequately stocked.
- Get the specials of the day from the chef.

While the Dining Room Is Open for Business
- While service styles are becoming less formal, they should not become less attentive.
- Greet all customers with a warm "Welcome." It starts things off right.
- Answer all phone calls with "Good morning/afternoon/evening."
- If a manager/host/hostess is unavailable, greet all customers, ask if they had a reservation, and escort them to a table directly, if it is ready.
- Fill water glasses and inquire, as soon as it is appropriate, after presenting the menu, if the customer would like something from the bar. It is critical that the customer is not left staring at the table and becoming impatient.
- Return to the table as soon as it is appropriate to present the specials and take the order.

- Check on the table at least twice during the meal for any special requests or additional drink orders.
- If for any reason a meal will be late, offer a drink on the house and inform the manager immediately.
- Anticipate the customer; that is, at the first notice of an empty glass, offer more water or another drink.
- Apologize for any mistakes or accidents immediately and inform the manager directly.
- Do not engage or argue with rude or difficult customers. Refer the matter to the manager immediately.
- Offer to remove empty glasses and plates at the first hint of a completed meal or drink.
- Always inquire whether the customer would like dessert and/or coffee before customer requests his or her check.
- Always present checks and change on tip trays.
- Thank customers personally on their way out of the restaurant.

While the Bar Is Open for Business
- Greet all customers after they are seated.
- Do not leave the bar or customers unattended at any time.
- Maintain working levels of ice, beer, wine, liquor, and mixes.
- Refuse to serve customers that you suspect are intoxicated and inform the manager.
- Request payment for drinks immediately unless the customer is a regular, having dinner or waiting for a table, or wants to run a tab and presents a valid credit card.

Closing Procedures—Dining Room
- Clear all tables, place inverted chairs on tabletops, and wipe down and restock wait stations.
- Consolidate and refill salt and pepper shakers, sugar holders, and ketchup.
- Shut down and clean coffee and espresso machines.
- Ask a manager to zero out the point-of-sale, and present all checks, cash, and credit card slips for verification.
- Deposit used aprons and bar mops in designated receptacles.
- Complete sign-in/sign-out sheets.

Closing Procedures—Bar
- Melt or burn all ice in ice bins and wash bins with a mild bleach solution.
- Present the manager with list of liquor, beer, and wine required to restock the bar.
- Wipe down and clean bar top, service station, margarita machine, speed racks and bottles, soda guns, and so on.
- Take all bar spoons, pairing knives, mixing glasses, and other washable bar equipment to the kitchen to be washed in the dishwasher.

- Refill and place condiment trays in the refrigerator.
- Invert bar stools on top of the bar.
- Take garbage bags to the disposal area.
- Ask a manager to zero out cash register and balance.

General Policies
- Drinking and smoking are not allowed while on duty.
- Staff drinks after closing are allowed only if approved by the manager on duty. No call, top shelf, or premium drinks are allowed.
- Cell phones must not ring in the dining room or at the bar.
- Staff meals cannot exceed eight dollars. Specials are available at a discount, but only if approved by the manager on duty.
- You are responsible for your own substitutes on days you are unable to work.
- Staff cannot sit in the dining room during hours of business.
- As a customer, you are allowed to eat once a month at a 50 percent discount. This discount will not apply to your guests.

SERVICE

The chef will set the tone in the kitchen, but your service and wait staff will make the biggest difference between whether or not your customers want to come back again and again.

For some time now, there has been an ongoing debate in the restaurant community over which is most important, good food or good service. On a March 22, 2005, edition of "Forum," a San Francisco Bay Area radio talk show, the question was put to three of the top local food critics. Two felt that food was more important, while the third felt that service was just as important, if not more important.

But wait a minute, that was just the opinion of three San Francisco critics; we need to hear from others, you say. OK, let's hear from William Grimes of the *New York Times* talking about Italian waiters and service: "They understand that the main goal of a restaurant is to make customers happy. If they do the job right, something mysterious happens. Diners convince themselves that a good meal was a great meal."

Some would say that's all anecdotal. But the research backs it up. A 2003 study by the School of Hotel Administration at Cornell University in New York also seems to indicate that service is most important. In the study, when a controlled group of restaurant diners was asked to describe dissatisfactory dining experiences that caused them to complain, service experience complaints outnumbered food quality complaints overwhelmingly by a margin of two to one. The study's most compelling finding was that poor service experiences often led customers to decide never to go back to the offending restaurant. Similarly, a 2002 MasterCard survey found that 23 percent of those surveyed said they would never return to a restaurant where they were dissatisfied with the service. Granted, this was not a scientific survey, but considering that MasterCard cardholders spend more in restaurants than they do in any other travel and entertainment category, this is a pretty important finding.

In most cases, serving good food consistently will get customers in the door and keep them coming back, yet good service can also help create customer loyalty and lead to repeat visits. But when was the last time you heard of an instance where customers flocked to a new restaurant of any type, high end, casual or take out because a critic raved about the service? When we upgraded Zuni's food and decor, the first really big wave of new customers came and kept coming for months only after we got an excellent food review in the *New York Times*. The service review was not noteworthy. That said, I also know that we had a core of customers who came back regularly for years even as our competition increased because we made it a point to recognize and treat them well; we also lost a number of customers due to poor service.

Not only can good service play an important role in a restaurant's success, in today's competitive environment it can give your new restaurant a competitive edge. In fact, it seems clear that, since study after study is showing that service in restaurants is coming up so short, by focusing on good service, you will be able to create a truly meaningful USP, one that your customers will recognize and value. To gauge the level of customer dissatisfaction with service, consider these 2002 comments by Tim Zagat of the *Zagat Survey of Restaurants*: "As far as our surveys are concerned, 70 percent of [customer] complaints relate to service. Food, décor, prices, noise, smoking, parking—all of those barely make up 30 percent. That's a staggering figure." That's not all. The 2002 MasterCard survey found that 80 percent of restaurant complaints are related to poor service. Besides, isn't it good to know that you might create a competitive advantage simply by focusing on the customers already sitting at your tables or counter, instead of spending money trying to steal customers from your competition across the street or just down the road?

One fine-dining restaurant group that uses a customer-service driven philosophy to create a competitive advantage is the Union Square Hospitality Group, which owns Gramercy Tavern and Union Square Café in New York City. In addition to serving great food, one reason these restaurants dominate the top ranks of the Zagat survey year after year is the organization's laser-like focus on providing excellent service.

But good customer service is not only about creating a competitive advantage or brand image. It also makes good business. Any seasoned retailer will tell you that it is easier to keep existing customers than it is to attract new ones. Did you know that it is estimated that it can be five to fifteen times more expensive to get a new customer than to get repeat business from an existing customer?

Early in my restaurant career, I was having a hard time dealing with demanding customers during our peak periods. Some of them would say things like, "This is not hot enough," or "This is not what I thought it would be; can I exchange it?" At my wits' end, I went to a good friend who ran an extremely successful casual restaurant for advice. After listening to my ranting and raving, he asked me, "How much would it have cost you to reheat the food or give the customer a complimentary drink, salad, or dessert?" To which I answered, "About $1.50 to $2." His next question was, "How much will you spend on advertising this year to get new customers?" My answer was, "about $6,000." To which he replied, "Do the math, and the next time you have a demanding customer, give her or him a little something special, and smile while you are at it. Also, don't forget, the best advertising in the world is a happy customer with a big mouth."

To put all this in greater perspective, consider the following. According to the National Restaurant Association, repeat customers account for 60 percent and 80 percent of fine dining and casual restaurant sales, respectively. Now let's assume that your casual bistro will do 36,500 covers per year or an average of 100 per day and that 80 percent of your business, or 29,200, will be from repeat customers. Now let's further assume that you lost 10 percent of your repeat customers because of poor or indifferent service. That would mean that you would lose 2,920 customers a year, or eight per day. As a restaurant operator, I could tell you that this would be a huge loss, not only in customers, but also in potential sales revenues, and depending on your average check, it might make the difference between breaking even and making a profit. What this all means is that repeat customers are the lifeblood without which most restaurants would not survive. And when you consider the cost of getting a new customer compared to keeping an existing customer, wouldn't it be worth your while to invest a little time, effort, and money into hospitality? The moral of the story is, when it comes to customer service, always remember the good old adage "a bird in the hand is worth two in the bush."

Service Dos and Don'ts

Matthew Kanter, restaurant consultant

After thirty-one years in the restaurant business, I feel like I've experienced and seen it all. From great service to poor service to what felt like no service at all! What follows are my dos and don'ts, opinions, and insights from my experience as an owner, a manager, server (although when I worked as a server I was called a waiter), cook, kitchen expeditor, bartender, buser, and of course a patron.

- Never leave the dining room unattended unless it absolutely can't be avoided, and then only for a very brief period of time
- Patrons should never see or hear staff complaining or arguing among themselves or with other patrons, even if it is in a joking manner.
- Staff should not sit at a table with guests while on duty. If invited to do so, politely explain that it is against house policy.
- Staff should not place their hands on a guest, even casually. Of course shaking hands and occasionally a hug or kiss is inevitable but should only be initiated by the guest.
- Used glassware should not be cleared from tables with fingers inside the glasses, even if the table is empty. Stemware should always be held by the stem when full, and brandy snifters should be held in the palm of the hand. It's also a nice touch to offer to warm Cognacs, Armagnacs, and certain cordials when ordered.

By now, it should be clear that not only will good service be essential for your restaurant to compete, it can also make a difference in your bottom line. Also, as Americans continue to eat out more and more, they will expect better dining experiences with each restaurant visit and will begin to focus more on service. That said, getting the level of service right for each type of restaurant and dining occasion could be tricky.

CUSTOMER EXPECTATIONS

People go to different types of restaurants for all sorts of different reasons, and the level of expectation regarding service will be different in each case. The important thing to remember when developing your service policy is that service is not a one-size-fits-all proposition, and like other aspects of your business, it should be consistent with your restaurant type, concept, and target customers' expectations. The one constant, however, regarding service is that the more people are expected to spend for a meal, the greater their expectations will be for attentive service. This does not mean that casual or quick-service restaurants should provide sloppy or rude service! But it does explain why fine-dining restaurant patrons tend to have very high service expectations. Some of the factors that can influence customer expectation of service are customer age, average income, and family size. For

- It is not proper etiquette to clear a table before guests are finished.
- When reciting specials, servers should say "today, we have" or "today, the chef has prepared"—never "today I have."
- Servers and captains should sell or up sell the menu, but should never be pushy or embarrass a guest into ordering something they may not want. That said, the importance of selling that extra salad, appetizer, dessert, or glass of wine cannot be overstated.
- A server or manager should always approach a table a minute or two after an appetizer or main course is served to ensure customer satisfaction.
- Correctly opening a bottle of wine, especially Champagne, is not done by accident. Staff should be trained and allowed to practice with house wine to perfect their skills.

If management doesn't have time to train each server individually (often the case in small operations), a trainer should be assigned from each staff group. Make sure that trainers are capable and willing and pay them a little extra. Even if experienced, a new server may need training over three shifts, and if they are greener, as many as eight or ten.

Your team will only be as strong as its weakest link. The hiring and training of your staff is extremely important. Trust me, the wrong buser or dishwasher can cost you a lot of money in breakage. Similarly, the wrong host or bartender can turn off customers and hurt your business. Thankfully, the converse is also true: skilled, motivated, and happy employees can help your bottom line immensely.

example, results of a chain-restaurant customer loyalty research study conducted by *Restaurants and Institutions* in 2003 found the following: baby boomers were more likely to have service complaints than either matures (ages fifty-seven and older) and post-boomers (ages eighteen to thirty-seven); and families with children and people who ate out more than four times a week had high service expectations. My experience while managing at Zuni corroborated the research findings regarding age and service. For example, I found that generally speaking, boomers and older customers were a lot more service conscious than post-boomers. While working the counter at my takeout shop, Wrapsody, I learned that for fast- and quick-service customers, speed and convenience were more important than friendly service. This is not to suggest that your staff should be rude or impolite, but a warm welcome and thank-you should be the extent of the conversation when twenty to thirty people are lined up waiting to be served.

The key to developing an effective service policy is to thoroughly understand and be in tune with your target customers' service expectations. The more you understand this, the better you will be able to educate and train your servers. Ask yourself if your restaurant's customers are there just to eat or to dine; do they just need some protein in their stomach to get through the day, or do they want a complete dining experience.

WHEN SERVICE IS A PROBLEM

Everybody knows that service is important. Yet, at the risk of sounding like a broken record, study after study shows that service in most restaurants continues to be a problem. Why, you ask? The two major reasons are: overall public perception of the service profession and poor management.

Even management can have a poor perception of the service profession. Since waiters are tipped instead of receiving a full-scale wage, many restaurant owners do not look at them as professionals and so do not put enough effort into training wait staff, or even treating them decently, which results in attitudes that cannot help but be apparent to customers. Contrary to popular perception, being a waiter is not a dead-end job. Many owners and managers in the nation's top independent and chain restaurants got their start as counter workers and servers. Also, waiters at some of the top restaurants in major cities earn incomes of fifty thousand dollars or more per year. Not so long ago, being a chef or cook in a restaurant was looked down at. Today, being a chef is a highly regarded profession. Not only are chefs well compensated, some have become millionaire celebrities. My hope is that as Americans continue to dine out more and more, and as our economy continues to shift from a manufacturing base to a service base, the perception of the waiter profession will change and become more positive, as has long been the case in Europe.

The second reason for poor service, poor management, stems from three problems: inexperienced owners and managers, bad hiring practices, and poor training. Remember, the restaurant business attracts a lot of people who get into it for all the wrong reasons. Many owners are ill equipped to handle the day-to-day pressures of running a business, much less to hire, train, and manage staff. I can't tell you the countless stories that I have heard from some of my better wait staff about working for ill-prepared, disrespectful, and ill-tempered owners and managers. It's hard to be a good server when working in these types of environments. Providing good service must be an inherent owner and management philosophy. To coin a phrase, many people "talk the talk, but they do not walk the walk."

The service business is a people business, and knowing how to manage and treat people respectfully goes a long way toward providing proper service. It's really quite simple: happy staff make for happy guests. Take cake of your staff and reward them for good work and service, either by compliments, gift certificates, or whatever rewards you can afford. They in turn will respect you and reward you with good, long loyal service. For example, after a particularly hectic rush, in addition to thanking my service staff, I would always make it a point to go back to the kitchen and thank everyone, from the dishwasher to the chef. I always saw appreciation in their faces. As a result, I had both kitchen and service staff that stayed with us for years.

Another important benefit of being respectful to your staff is that your reputation as an employer can affect your ability to hire. In Zuni's neighborhood, the lousy bosses were well-known and had a hard time hiring and keeping employees. That said, while you are being respectful and fair, you should also be firm. Lead your staff by example, and remember: "What you permit, you promote."

CHAPTER 12

GETTING THE MONEY TO MAKE IT A REALITY

So you've set your goals, done your research, and prepared a market feasibility study and your pro forma operating budget/financial forecast, break-even analysis and capital budget are ready to go. Now all you need is the cash to make it happen, and if you are like most first-time entrepreneurs, you will probably have to raise some or all of it.

Remember the ninety percent fail rate myth mentioned at the beginning of this book? Well, your potential investors will have heard it, too, which won't make it any easier to raise money. But if you've done your homework and legwork, all you need now is to dig in and be prepared to sell yourself and your concept. Many have done it, and so can you! So let's talk about sources of capital.

Like most first-timer restaurateurs, you will probably have to rely on a patchwork of sources. After your own savings and investments, your best bet for raising money will be from people in your immediate circle of family, friends, acquaintances, and associates. Reportedly, Thomas Keller raised the capital to open his world-famous restaurant, The French Laundry, from fifty different investors, with investment amounts ranging from as little as two thousand dollars up to fifty thousand dollars. Before approaching investors, including your family and friends, try to come up with some of your own seed capital. Putting some of your own capital at risk will help to instill confidence in investors, particularly those outside your immediate circle. Investors will want to know that you are prepared to put your money where your mouth is, and that in addition to investing sweat equity you will be taking some of the financial risk with them. Also, as we shall see later, you will have a much better chance of getting funded, particularly through the Small Business Administration, if you have an equity investment in your restaurant.

Investors are always interested in getting a good return on their money. So, as you are shopping your business plan, point out to potential investors that the restaurant industry is one of the few industries that continues to experience growth even during economic downturns and high gas prices because of very favorable changes in demographics and dining trends. Don't forget, owning a restaurant still has a certain amount of cachet and sex appeal. But you should be prepared to offer investors a higher return on their money than they would get in less risky investments. If you can't offer them good returns, they won't be interested.

If you tap out your savings, friends, family, and investors and still need more money, your next stop should be to approach a bank. Banks are notoriously conservative lenders. They not only shy away from start-up restaurants; they dislike pretty much all start-ups. Typically, banks won't lend a dime, even if you are prepared to personally guarantee the loan, unless you can offer some type of collateral, like equity in your home. What they will do, however, is partner with the Small Business Administration to help you get financing. Some bankers may also be able to introduce you to other potential investors.

SMALL BUSINESS ADMINISTRATION LOANS

The Small Business Administration (SBA) is a government entity that will become very important to you. While it does not actually lend money, the SBA provides loan guarantees for small businesses that would normally not have access to capital from conventional lending sources. Under its program, financial institutions that are designated SBA lenders—such as banks, economic development institutions, and other qualified lenders—issue the loans. Available amounts range from $25,000 to $2 million. To find a designated lender in your area, call 1-800-8-ASK-SBA or go to www.sba.gov/financing.

To qualify for an SBA loan, a start up restaurant must:
- Be independently owned and operated
- Have reasonable owners' capital or equity
- Be operated for profit
- Be operated in the United States or one of its possessions

SBA loan proceeds can be used for the following purposes:
- Working capital
- Renovation
- Construction

- Equipment
- Acquisition of an existing business
- Acquisition of a franchise
- Acquisition of land
- Leasehold improvements
- Inventory
- Machinery
- Refinancing certain existing debt

The following rules apply to the use of SBA loans:
- The SBA will not approve loans if the money will be used to pay distributions to shareholders or partners.
- While the SBA will approve loans to purchase a business, it will usually deny a loan request if there are any close family ties between buyer and seller.
- The SBA will not approve loans to refinance debt if the debt is already on reasonable terms, or the current lender will suffer a loss for which the SBA will later be liable.
- If the proceeds will be used to purchase a business, the purchaser must be buying 100 percent of the business.

SBA 7(A) LOANS

You will be happy to hear that the restaurant industry is the most frequent user of the SBA's 7(a) loan guarantee program. For fiscal year 2004, the SBA helped to provide $1.48 billion to an estimated 7,586 restaurants of various sizes through its 7(a) and 504 programs.

Because not all designated lenders use the same criteria to determine loan eligibility, it is entirely possible to be declined by one institution and approved by another. For example, when my partners and I opened Souper Dog, Citibank declined our SBA application but Banco Popular approved it later. If your first application is declined, ask why so that you can be better prepared when you reapply with another lender. But be careful not to shop around too much, since each time your application is declined it will be reflected on your credit report. Your best bet is to prepare a really good loan application and business plan.

As good as the SBA is, the money is not free. Loans are usually required to be personally guaranteed and collateralized by personal assets—such as real estate, stock, or bonds—and by your restaurant's future assets, such as equipment, accounts receivable, and inventory. The good news is that under this program, lack of collateral is not sufficient grounds for a lender to decline an application. For the SBA, the most important consideration will be your restaurant's ability to generate sufficient cash flow to repay the loan (now we know you're *really* glad you put all that work into your financial feasibility study). Other factors the SBA will consider are your previous job experience, especially restaurant experience, good character, good management ability, and the amount of personal capital or equity you are willing to contribute. Depending on the size of the loan and your creditworthiness, you may not have to pledge any of your assets, but you will have to personally guarantee the loan. When I later bought out my partners in Souper Dog, I was able to get a fifty thousand-dollar SBA loan that was secured by the equipment in the restaurant and my personal guarantee. It is important to note that any partner or investor with a 20 percent or more ownership interest in your restaurant venture must personally guarantee the loans also. Talk to your attorney or CPA about the best ways to structure your business entity in order to protect investors from any potential liabilities.

The SBA will not guarantee (become liable for) the full amount of your loan request; currently the SBA guarantees 85 percent of loans of $150,000 or less, and 75 percent of loans of $150,000 or more. For example, if you requested $150,000, the SBA would only guarantee $127,500 (that is, $150,000 × .85), and if you requested $155,000, the guarantee would be only $116,250 (or $150,000 × .75). In this case, it would make more sense to request the lower amount of $150,000, because the SBA would be guaranteeing a larger amount $127,500 instead of $116,250.

To use the program you must submit an application and supporting documentation (such as your business plans and tax returns) to a designated lending institution, where a loan committee will review it for appropriateness and then approve it conditionally. The lending institution will then submit your loan package to the district SBA office, which will review it for eligibility and creditworthiness. If your loan is approved, the SBA will contact the lender and your loan will be closed (finalized). If all of the supporting documentation is in order, the process could take three to four weeks. Lenders that are part of the SBA's certified and preferred lender programs can speed up the loan process considerably. Certified lenders perform some of the credit analysis for the SBA, making sure that the credit application is complete, and preferred lenders are authorized by the SBA to make all decisions regarding creditworthiness. With both certified and preferred lenders, the entire loan process can be reduced from three or four weeks to three days.

The three-day approval process will only apply to the amount of the loan request that the SBA will guarantee. In most cases, it will take additional time for lenders to approve the portion of the loan that will not be guaranteed. For example, if you were to apply for a $100,000 loan and were approved, only $85,000 ($100,000 times 85 percent) would be approved in three days. The bank would need additional time to approve the other $15,000. If you need to borrow money quickly, check with your local SBA office for names of certified and preferred lenders in your area.

The lending institutions usually set interest rates on loans, but they cannot exceed SBA maximums. Maximum rates are based on the size and term of a loan amount, and they are usually tied to the existing prime rate.

Although the SBA specifies maximum interest rates, lending among banks and other lending institutions is often competitive, so it is entirely possible to get rates that are lower than the SBA maximum. You should, therefore, talk to more than one lending institution about rates before making your final choice.

Though you will have to negotiate the term (length) of your loan with a lender, the final time period will be subject to the SBA's approval. One of the benefits of SBA loans is that in some instances your loan payments can be stretched out over a longer period of time than with conventional loans. The longer the loan period, the smaller your monthly payments will be. The current maturities (time over which a loan matures, or concludes) available are as follows:

- From seven to ten years for working capital
- Between ten and twenty-five years for equipment
- Up to twenty-five years for construction and acquisition of real estate

If loan proceeds (the actual loan monies) will be used for more than one purpose, each purpose will have a maturity schedule (loan term), and the maximum maturity will be the weighted average of the various maturities. For example, if you were to borrow $150,000 and wanted to use $50,000 for working capital (maturing in seven years) and $100,000 for equipment (maturing in 10 years), the weighted average maximum maturity would be as follows: 7 years × ($50,000 ÷ $150,000) + 10 years × ($100,000 ÷ $150,000) = 8.99 years, which would be rounded up to 10 years.

To offset the cost of its loan programs, the SBA charges lenders a fee for each loan that is approved. Lenders in turn are allowed to pass the fee on to borrowers, which is usually deducted from the guaranteed portion of your loan proceeds. The current fee structure is as follows:

- Loan amounts of $150,000 or less are 2 percent
- Loan amounts between $150,000 and $700,000 are 3 percent
- Loan amounts between $7,000,000 and $1 million are 3.5 percent
- Loan amounts over $1 million are 3.75 percent

If you were to borrow $100,000, for example, the fee would be $100,000 × .85 × .02, or $1,700.

In addition to the loan fee, the SBA has recently started to charge prepayment penalties for early repayment of loans having a maturity of fifteen years or more. To be subject to prepayment penalties, all of the following criteria will also have to be met:

- The borrower must be prepaying voluntarily.
- The prepayment amount must exceed 25 percent of the outstanding balance.
- The prepayment must be made within the first three years after the first disbursement (not approval) of the loan proceeds.

When the above circumstances apply, prepayment penalties will be calculated as follows:

- First year after disbursement, 5 percent of the prepayment amount
- Second year after disbursement, 3 percent of the prepayment amount
- Third year after disbursement, 1 percent of the prepayment amount

ADDITIONAL SBA LOAN PROGRAMS

In addition to the 7(a) business loan program, the SBA offers other guaranteed loan programs. Three such programs that are applicable to restaurants are the LowDoc Program, the SBA Express Program, and the SBA Community Express Program.

The LowDoc (low documentation) Program streamlines lending by simplifying the application process. Under this program, the application form is one page; the borrower fills out the front, and the lender fills out the back. The lender then submits a complete application to the SBA and receives an answer within thirty-six hours. To qualify for this program, you must meet the lender's requirements for credit. The maximum loan amount under this program is $150,000.

Terms, interest rates, collateral requirements, and uses of loan proceeds are the same as under the 7(a) program, but loans are not declined when insufficient collateral is the only negative factor.

Under the SBA Express Program, the loan process is further streamlined by allowing certain lenders to use their own forms and approval processes for loans up to $350,000. The maximum SBA guarantee for these loans is 50 percent. Lenders and borrowers can negotiate interest rates, which may be fixed or variable and are tied to the prime rate. For this program, SBA maximum rates are 6.5 percent over prime for loans of $50,000 or less, and 4.5 percent over prime for loans over $50,000.

Lenders are allowed to use their existing collateral policy for loans over $25,000 and up to $150,000. For loans over $150,000, SBA collateral policies must be followed. Lenders are, however, allowed to approve unsecured loans up to $25,000. The turnaround time after the loan application is received is thirty-six hours.

If your restaurant will be located in a low- or moderate-income area, or one of the SBA's new markets, you may be able to benefit from the SBA Community Express Program. This program is similar to the SBA Express Program, except that the maximum loan amount is $250,000 and the maximum SBA guaranty is the same as the standard 7(a) guarantee percentages. Under this program, applicants are required to receive free pre- and post-loan closing technical and management assistance designed to improve their chances of obtaining a loan.

OVERLOOKED FUNDING SOURCES

Often overlooked sources of funding are build-out allowances and rent-free periods from landlords. Depending on your concept and the overall condition of the local real estate market or a particular part of town, you may be able to get your landlord to offer reasonable rent-free periods or even to pay for part of your construction costs, commonly referred to as tenant improvements. Tenant improvements can significantly reduce the amount of capital you will have to raise. If, for example, a particular space has been empty for a long time and you can convince your prospective landlord that your restaurant will not only be able to pay its rent timely, but also that its success will add value to the property, the landlord may be willing to offer a certain amount of tenant improvements. Also, it is not uncommon for landlords to be looking for certain types of restaurant concepts to help anchor or increase the value of their property. When this is the case, landlords are often willing to offer a significant amount of tenant improvements.

EQUIPMENT LEASING

Another potential source of funding is equipment leasing. For first-timer owners, leasing equipment is an appealing alternative to buying equipment outright. For one thing, equipment leases are usually easier to obtain than conventional bank loans, and in many instances, when banks won't finance equipment for start-ups, leasing companies will. For example, in our early days, when our bank declined to finance the purchase of a new range, a leasing company stepped up to the plate. Also, as you become more profitable, there are significant tax advantages to leasing. You will not only be able to deduct all of your lease payments as expenses against your income, you also will be able to claim depreciation expense for the same equipment against your income over the equipment's useful life. With loans, while you can also depreciate the equipment over its useful life, you can only deduct the interest portion of the monthly payments.

That said, equipment leasing is generally more expensive than buying outright or getting bank financing. For example, while at a trade show right before I sold my interest in Zuni, I was offered an 11.75 percent five-year lease on a new $12,000 point-of-sale system. Had I accepted this lease, the monthly payments would have been around $319 and would have totaled $19,140 over the five years of the lease—an additional cost of $7,140.

Not prepared to pay that much of a premium, I went to our bank, which offered to lend us the $12,000 at 6 percent over the same five-year period, with monthly payments of $232.00. The additional cost in this case was only $1,920. We were offered a favorable interest rate because we had a relationship with the bank (which is not the case with start-ups) and our credit rating was good. Granted, the difference in rates between banks and leasing companies won't always be this large, but in general, leasing companies tend to charge higher rates because they will take a risk when others won't. Also, unlike most conventional loans, leases do not allow for early repayment of principal without penalty. Once you sign a lease, the entire amount of the lease must be paid. For example, had I signed the lease in the above example, I would have been liable for the entire $19,140, regardless of when I paid it. I learned this the hard way by not reading the fine print. When I started Wrapsody, I had to lease about $15,000 of equipment at 12 percent, only to discover that it could not be refinanced a year later when the business was doing well and interest rates at banks had declined significantly.

Other frequently overlooked and misunderstood fine print terms of leases include the following:

- Leases are no less enforceable than bank loans. They are legally binding contracts and are enforceable in the courts.
- Like bank loans, leases require collateral and personal guarantees. If you default, the leasing company can seize your assets.
- Equipment leases generally do not cover maintenance. Manufacturers are responsible for warranties just as if the equipment was purchased outright.

The biggest mistakes first-timers make when leasing are to resort to leasing only after they have realized that they are overbudget and undercapitalized, or to get talked into leasing either too much or overly expensive equipment by zealous equipment dealers eager to make a sale. This usually means that the new owners do not figure the lease payments into their monthly cash flow, and they are often surprised when they can't make them.

Don't let this happen to you. If you are considering leasing, think about it carefully and make it part of your overall financing plans by including the monthly payments in your conservative financial feasibility study. Also consider other alternatives of cheaper financing first, such as your bank—either personally or through the Small Business Administration program—or friends, investors, or relatives.

Finally, before you sign a lease, read the fine print carefully, and just as you would with any other loan, make sure that the following details are clearly spelled out:

- The amount being financed
- The length of the lease and the interest rate that will be charged
- The amount of the required deposit
- The required monthly payments
- The cumulative total of all of the payments

BUYING USED EQUIPMENT

One way to reduce start-up costs is to buy used equipment. When I opened my first takeout operation, my partners and I saved a few thousand dollars by buying used sinks, shelving, stainless-steel tables, stockpots, and sauté pans that were in excellent condition. We bought some at auction, and we got others from used-equipment dealers. In both cases, the sellers wanted cash only, and we had to arrange for our own delivery. That was a few years ago, but things may have changed with the advent of websites like eBay and Restaurantequipment.net.

Most used-equipment dealers buy their inventory at public auctions or restaurants that have closed up and gone out of business and clean them up for resale. The problem with a lot of used equipment is that it's difficult to know how old it is, how many times it changed hands in the past, and how well the previous owners maintained it. One way to determine the age of used equipment is to get the serial number and call the manufacturer. As you are checking on the equipment's age, you should also check for the availability of parts and service in your area, particularly for equipment requiring electrical components.

Used equipment is usually sold "as is" with little or no warranty, so look for equipment with a good reputation for performance and durability. Also, before you buy any piece, see it, touch it, and " kick the tires," particularly if it will be a workhorse piece of equipment such as a range. Generally, relatively new ranges and other types of cooking equipment that are all metal welded and constructed, are good buys and will last a long time. Two good brand names to look for are Jade and Wolf. These ranges are usually very expensive new, so if you can pick up one on the cheap it will be well worth it. Other guidelines for buying used equipment include the following:

- Compare the cost of the used equipment, including delivery, with the cost of buying new, including delivery and installation. If the savings are not significant, you will probably be better off buying new, considering that the used equipment will have little or no warranty.
- Try to get at least a thirty-day warranty.
- Check the equipment specifications, and make sure that it will fit into its intended space in your kitchen with the right amount of clearance. (Remember that one-inch measurement mistake that cost ten thousand dollars!)

Look for equipment that does not have movable parts and whose condition is obvious by looking and touching, such as tables, sinks, shelves, and pots and pans. This type of equipment is a lot more expensive than you might expect. You could save a lot of money with minimum risk if you buy it used

Many restaurateurs who have been unable to raise enough capital elsewhere have used small amounts of low-interest credit card debt. Some credit card companies offer as little as 0 or 4 percent for six months or more. If you must use credit cards, do so as a *last resort*, only after you have secured all of your other capital. Too much credit card debt will affect your ability to get SBA and conventional loans. Also, be sure to pay it off as fast as you can since one late payment, or the end of the low-interest period, will result in a huge jump in your debt-servicing costs.

WHY START FROM SCRATCH?

If you are unable to raise sufficient capital from all sources to build your restaurant from scratch, an alternative may be to buy an existing restaurant. Obviously, the decision to work with an existing restaurant will limit your location choices, though you must go through the same evaluation process as if you were starting from scratch. However, you can't ignore the fact that the two most cost-effective ways of getting into the business are to: (1) find a closed restaurant that is partially or fully equipped and reopen it, or (2) buy an existing operation. If you use either of these methods it will be quicker to get open, since you won't have to go through all of the zoning and regulatory red tape normally required for new construction and development. Also it is often possible to buy an existing restaurant or reopen a closed location for a lot less than it would cost to build one from scratch. For many first-time restaurateurs these are the methods of choice. As you may recall, I got into the business by leasing a space in which a previous restaurant had closed.

Very often sellers will agree to finance part of the purchase price; that is, they will take a down payment and allow you to pay off the balance of the purchase price with interest over a specified period using the restaurant and its lease as collateral. When I sold Wrapsody, I was able to get the best price using this method.

Getting seller financing could significantly reduce your start-up capital requirements and make it easier to get investors or bank loans. Once you come up with the down payment, it is often easier to get additional working capital financing through the SBA or conventional banks since you will have your investment equity in the restaurant along with its equipment and other assets to use as collateral. If you are buying an existing restaurant that is already profitable, you will be starting out with an existing cash flow stream, which always impresses investors and lenders.

But don't just figure on a fresh coat of paint and a new awning. Try to find out why the restaurant closed or is for sale. Particularly in so-called "cursed" locations. Very often, it's not so much that these locations are cursed as that the previous chosen concepts were ill conceived, or the previous owners were poor managers or lacked good business acumen. Sometimes, a fresh concept and a new approach to business can go a long way toward removing the stigma of being a cursed location. Also, when a restaurant site has a history of failure, landlords are often willing to offer very favorable terms.

Here are a few of the questions that you should contemplate before choosing a preexisting establishment:

- Is the asking price reasonable? Can you get a better price?
- Why is the owner selling this business?
- Will there be seller financing (that is, will the seller allow you to pay for the restaurant in installments)? If so, what will the interest rate on the note be?
- What is the condition of the existing plant, and how old is the equipment?
- Is any of the equipment leased? If so, what are the monthly payments?
- How much was spent on repairs and maintenance every year for the past three years? Ask for copies of tax returns or financial statements to verify this.
- How much are you prepared to spend on any necessary improvements to the property?
- How much is the restaurant currently grossing?
- Are you going to change the concept? If keeping, is the business growing, stable, or declining?
- In addition to looking at tax returns, did you personally observe the level of business at various times of the day for a couple of weeks or months?
- Does the level of business vary with the seasons? Look at monthly sales summaries or talk to other neighborhood restaurateurs or suppliers to find out.
- Did you check with the seller's major suppliers to find out if he is current with his bills?
- What are the total monthly occupancy costs, such as rent, taxes, and insurance?
- What percentage of gross sales are the rent and other occupancy costs?
- How many years are left on the lease; will the lease give you enough time to recover your investment and make a profit?
- What are the annual escalations in rent and taxes?
- Will your rent be at, above, or below market rates? A below-market lease creates equity for your business.
- What is the restaurant's seating capacity?
- Are there enough seats to maximize business during peak hours?
- Who are the current customers? What will you do to keep them and attract others?
- How big is the bar?

A Less Expensive Option

Rick Mitchell of Luka's Taproom and Lounge

After five hours as a tax attorney, I realized that the corporate life was not for me. Five years later, I followed my entrepreneurial spirit and opened a restaurant.

When looking for a space, I gave little regard to whether a location had previously served as a restaurant. I was banking on being able to identify an underserved market in Oakland. Although I was naïve and greatly underestimated my start-up costs, my instinct on location made up for those miscalculations.

I first focused my search on a certain small, well-placed, retail neighborhood district. But the district was too small and too well placed and nothing ever became available. Eventually a friend, who is now a partner in the business, suggested that I consider leasing an old hofbrau downtown that had been closed for nearly a year and looked like a windowless fortress of concrete and red paint. He told me that though a total dive, the hofbrau hosted a strong lunch service everyday before it closed, suggesting that nearby office workers were desperate for decent food. I inquired around and talked to a few bartenders who'd also served throngs of patrons before shows at the nearby Paramount Theatre. I also learned that the Oakland Hofbrau had been in continuous operation as a restaurant since at least the mid-1940s.

I set my mind on the space, and lucky for me, nobody else wanted to touch my dilapidated seventy-year-old building that was large enough and ugly enough to create its own blight zone. I invited a former restaurant employer over to inspect the site. He struggled to find a way to nicely tell me that I was in fact crazy. I didn't even read the (bleak) health department reports before I signed the lease. Well, good news: I got it for cheap. And good thing: low rent was second on my list after good location.

Having found a space, I tailored my concept around it. Then I made my best decision yet—to hire two very talented locals, Jacob Alioto and Byron Schostag, to serve as chef and bar manager. Build-out costs soared overbudget and we opened with our bank account deeply in the red, but we've been able to pay our creditors, keep the lights on, and still keep something for ourselves. More important, we were able to build something special for the community and create some decent jobs along the way. Caring about that is what separates restaurateurs from, say, tax attorneys for example.

- Will you be buying the lease and the company's other assets or stock? This is a very important question that you should discuss thoroughly with your attorney or CPA. If you are buying a company's stock, chances are that you will be assuming all of the old restaurant's outstanding liabilities in addition to acquiring its lease and equipment. Get an attorney to determine whether any of the equipment is leased. You may not want to assume the responsibility for these leases. In short, you want to make sure that you are not inheriting any unwanted liabilities.

A BUSINESS PLAN FOR SUCCESS

As I can't say often enough, one of the keys to getting funded is a well-researched and objectively prepared business plan. The work you have done on identifying a target market and tailoring your concept to it, combined with your budget and financial feasibility study, will put you well along your way. The business plan is simply a concise, clear way of conveying to potential investors the work you have already done and of convincing them of your restaurant idea's viability and potential profitability.

Writing your business plan will and should be challenging, and it will force you to think critically about the various aspects of your restaurant idea. It may even open your eyes to things you hadn't previously considered, both positive and negative, which could greatly increase your probability of success.

There are countless numbers of excellent guides on how to write business plans. SCORE is an excellent source for help with writing your business plan. In addition to having over 350 SCORE offices nationwide offering free advice and counseling on writing and preparing business plans, SCORE also offers a free downloadable business plan template online at www.score.org. At SCORE'S website, you will also find various spreadsheet templates you can download for free, which you can use to prepare financial plans, budgets, and forecasts. To reach SCORE by phone, call 1-800-634-0245. Another excellent source for writing a business plan is CCH Business Owner's Toolkit at www.toolkit.cch.com.

Essentially, your business plan will be your road map, which you will use to chart your business course and avoid pitfalls along the way. As you are writing your plan, put yourself in the shoes of a potential investor or lender, and ask whether you would want to invest in your project after reading your plan. With this in mind, your goal is write an objective, concise, informative, well-documented, easy to read, and convincing proposal.

Ask the bank that you plan to approach for financing what their required format is, and use that as a guideline for organizing the following topics. With the help of the material in previous chapters, you should be able to write a good and convincing plan. If you get stuck on any section, simply reread the relevant chapter. When you are finished writing your business plan, read it and reread it. Check it and cross-check it to make sure that it is free of obvious errors, makes a logical and compelling argument, and has all of your supporting schedules (properly cross-referenced).

Package it neatly and attach a cover page with the name of your restaurant; your name, address, and telephone number; and a table of contents listing topics and page numbers.

Ready? Let's go.

STATEMENT OF PURPOSE

The statement of purpose tells potential investors early on in your document what they need to know to start evaluating your proposal. Namely, it states clearly and concisely that your business plan will demonstrate the need for your concept in its market area and that your restaurant idea has the potential for high profitability at your chosen site and location. Then it summarizes your restaurant concept, including where it will be located, how much it is going to cost, how the money will be used, how much investment capital you are looking for, and how much risk you are going to take with them, that is how much of your own capital you are going to invest.

CONCEPT

Having set the table, you are now ready to serve up the necessary details to build a compelling argument for financing your restaurant. Start by describing your concept in detail, including its name, the type of cuisine (such as Italian, Mexican, or Asian), special menu highlights, design and decor ideas, the bar, the wine list, price ranges, and the level of service. In this discussion, you should articulate why you think your concept is particularly suited for your chosen neighborhood and location. For example, you might point out that your research shows a need for and a lack of your particular concept in the market, or that similar concepts in the area are very busy with long waiting lines during prime dining hours. Tell investors what's unique and special about your concept; describe your unique selling proposition (USP). Briefly describe the target customers—such as baby boomers, empty nesters, Gen Xers, or urban professionals—and say why they will choose your restaurant over other immediate competitors. Maybe it's the type of food you will offer or the way you will cook and present it, or maybe you will offer better food at more affordable prices. Chapters that would be helpful in writing this section are chapters 2 and 3.

MANAGEMENT

Once you've gotten their interest and they are beginning to see potential dollar signs, tell them about yourself and your management team. Investors do not only invest in businesses, they also invest in people. Tell them about your current and previous work experiences and how they have provided you with the necessary skills and talents to run a busy and successful restaurant. Talk about any previous restaurant experience you've had, if any, and your management and business skills. Also, if your concept calls for hiring a special chef, manager, or other uniquely qualified person to help run the business, describe his or her special talents, qualifications, and work experiences. In addition to food skills, talk about that person's attributes that will increase your probability of success. For example, it could be business savvy, understanding profit margins, adeptness at training and motivating staff, or a combination of these factors. To help investors verify work experience and job skills, provide them with resumes as support documentation.

BUSINESS AND MANAGEMENT PHILOSOPHY

Describe your business and management philosophy, and discuss your plans for running the business successfully and profitably. Here, for example, you could describe the factors that influenced your choice of meal periods and operating hours, and your plans for managing and controlling inventory levels and food, beverage, and labor costs. You might mention that there will be regularly scheduled deliveries, refrigeration will be properly maintained, and recipes will be standardized. Your management philosophy could also cover topics such as your commitment to serving only the freshest food and providing the best possible service, training and motivating staff, and treating employees respectfully and fairly. Explain how this philosophy fits in with your marketing strategy of building customer loyalty and repeat business. Finally you could talk about how giving back to your community is not only the responsible thing to do, it can also serve as positive publicity for your restaurant. Chapters to review before writing this section are chapters 15, 11, and 14.

MARKET OVERVIEW

Having read this far, investors should be convinced not only that your concept is good, but also that you have the knowledge and skills to run your business successfully. Now they will want to learn that you are also knowledgeable about local and regional economic conditions, and more important, that you have a thorough understanding of how well or poorly restaurants are doing in your target market area. This is where you will use the data you collected from your market studies to clearly and concisely give an overview of these market conditions and explain why your restaurant is likely to be successful in this business climate. For example, is the local economy slowing or growing? Will your concept and price points be affected by rising gas prices? You can obtain sources of data for this section from local and regional chambers of commerce, development agencies, restaurant associations, newspapers, residential and commercial real estate agencies, and various local city agencies. Types of information that you can include here are increases in restaurant sales tax collections and restaurant openings and closings. Use chapter 3 as a resource to write this section.

TARGET MARKET AND POTENTIAL CUSTOMERS

This is where you will get specific about describing your target market. Remember that you should consider your concept when defining your target market. As we noted before, the more upscale the concept, the larger the area that it can draw from. Not to be monotonous, but a diner's market range will be a one-mile radius, whereas a fine-dining establishment's market range could be a five-mile radius or up to a one-hour drive, in which case your target customers might live in more than one city. In this section, you want to describe the population size and density your restaurant will appeal to, that is, the population count(s) and the area in square miles of the city (or cities) in your target market area.

You should also specify your target customers' demographics here. For example, if your concept is upscale and your target customers are middle income and affluent people between the ages of thirty and sixty-four, you will want to state the area's total population, and the percentage of the population that falls within the targeted ages, and the median income for the area. In addition to residential target customers, you should talk about potential target customers from offices, theaters, shopping centers, and other special event seekers if applicable. At this point, you should repeat the characteristics of your concept and say why these target customers will find it appealing. Use chapter 3 as a resource to write this section.

LOCATION

Discuss the location of your restaurant's site in this section. Say what compelling factors influenced your decision to choose this location, such as competitors' sales, ideal demographics, or traffic flow. You should also talk about its physical characteristics. For example, it might be a corner location with wraparound glass frontage, in the middle of the block next door to a bank and surrounded by retail shops, or in a very busy shopping center. Describe your site's visibility, ease of access, and parking availability. If your plans are to provide on-site or valet parking, talk about how it will give your business a competitive advantage, particularly during breakfast and lunch hours when customers typically have a limited amount of time to eat and get back to work. Give pedestrian and vehicular traffic counts during hours of business whenever possible. Also be sure to talk about your site's proximity to traffic generators, such as office buildings, apartment buildings, and residential neighborhoods, and the ease with which potential customers could get to and from your site during business hours. For example, is it close to an exit that feeds off of a major highway or other major traffic artery? If your restaurant will be located at a site with spectacular views or in a historic district, mention this as well. Finally, if your location has any obstacles or disadvantages, tell what they are and how you plan to overcome them. Use chapter 4 as a resource to write this section.

COMPETITIVE ENVIRONMENT

List the names and locations of your top five primary competitors, and briefly describe their concepts. Tell how they differ from or are similar to your concept, and list their strengths and weaknesses. In addition to food, beverage, service, overall ambience, and price points, talk about their attributes, such as visibility, convenient parking, and ease of access. You should also describe how close they are to your site. Discuss how busy they are during different meal periods, particularly those that you will be competing in, and estimate their number of covers, sales volumes during each period, total annual sales, and overall profitability. Discuss how you plan to compete and why you think that you can take market share. Reiterate your USP, and tell why it will be more meaningful to target customers than the competitors' sales features. You may also want to talk about competitors' mix of customers during different meal periods and then say why your concept will be more attractive to one or more of these groups.

After discussing your primary competitors, describe your secondary competitors, such as restaurants that might be different in terms of overall concept but may compete solely on price. For example, if your concept is table service with an average lunch check of seven dollars, you may not only be competing with similar table-service concepts for lunch, but also with local delis, supermarkets, sandwich shops, and coffee shops. Use chapter 3 as a resource to write this section.

MARKETING AND PUBLICITY

Investors and lenders are very aware of the competitive environment in the restaurant business. They will want to know how you plan to get the word out that your restaurant exists and get customers in the door for the first time, and what your plans are to continuously market and promote your restaurant, taking customers from competitors and keeping them once they come in. Describe how you will use your concepts' unique characteristics to craft a marketing message—including pricing, location, ambience, special ingredients, and a bar, if applicable—that will appeal to your target customers.

Talk about your initial plans for getting the word out, including flyers, mailings, and press releases. Remember that word-of-mouth and positive reviews and write-ups in the media are the two best ways to attract first-time customers. Describe your plans for attracting the press and getting existing customers to talk often and favorably about your restaurant. Also, if you plan on having a bar, talk about where it will be situated and how it will be designed to capture the attention of passersby and entice them to come in. Discuss service and community involvement and how you will use them as marketing and publicity tools. Describe your website and/or blog, and discuss your plans for directing traffic to them and for keeping them fresh and current. If there is money in your budget to hire a public relations consultant, name the firm or individual and say what factors influenced your choice. You should also list some of their more successful restaurant clients. Use chapter 14 as a resource to write this section.

STAFFING AND PERSONNEL

List key personnel positions, if any. State the required qualifications and experience, and describe the skills, duties, and responsibilities related to these positions. Describe the local labor pool, and explain how and where you will find highly skilled people if necessary. List prevailing local salary and wage rates, and tell how they fit into your budget.

SPECIALISTS AND CONSULTANTS

Name your consultants—such as an accountant, attorney, architect, designer, or kitchen design consultant—briefly describe their qualifications and notable local accomplishments if any, and explain the services they will be providing for you. For architects, designers, and contractors, emphasize their knowledge of local codes and adeptness at dealing with local city officials and bureaucrats.

LEGAL AND ADMINISTRATIVE STRUCTURE

State your legal structure, that is, sole proprietorship, partnership, corporation, or limited liability company (LLC). List all of the necessary licenses, permits, registration numbers, insurances, and tax ID numbers that your particular restaurant will require, and note whether they have been obtained or applied for. Be sure to list federal and state tax ID numbers; beer, wine, and liquor licenses; building permits; health permits; certificate of incorporation; and fire permits.

Ask your prospective landlord to give you a lease that is contingent upon getting the necessary financing to open your restaurant, since most banks, particularly those that are part of the SBA program, will want to see a signed lease. I cannot emphasize this enough: do not, I repeat, do not sign a lease until you have the necessary financing to open your business. Use chapter 13 as a resource to write this section.

FINANCIAL FEASIBILITY STUDY AND CAPITAL BUDGET

Bankers and savvy investors are very meticulous about financial projections; for this reason, I recommend that you prepare a thorough and realistic draft of your pro forma profit-and-loss statement, and then hire a qualified accounting professional with restaurant experience to give it the necessary finishing touches. (Unless, of course, you are really good with numbers and details.) He or she will know the format and types of information that bankers and investors look for. Your financial feasibility study (pro forma financial statement) should show projected net income and cash flow for at least three years, and you should include supporting documentation of how you arrived at your numbers and conclusions. For example, you should show how you arrived at your average check calculations, projected daily and weekly customers by meal period, estimated food and beverage costs percentages, rates used to calculate payroll taxes and workers' compensation insurance, and commissions on credit card charges. Since you are applying for a loan, be sure to include loan repayments in your net income and cash flow projections.

A break-even analysis should accompany your projections, showing the point where sales and expenses are equal. A good break-even analysis will calculate daily and weekly break-even points in dollars and number of customers (covers) for each meal period and an overall break-even point. If your projected level of business shows that you will not be comfortably breaking even, banks and investors won't be interested. Emphasize that your estimates are conservative; don't just say this—it should and must be true. If investors see that conservative estimates are profitable, they will know that there is significant potential for even more profitability.

Other required financial data is your overall capital requirements budget, accompanied by supporting schedules for equipment (ranges, ovens, and refrigeration), smallwares (pots, pans, and so on), construction (plumbing, electrical, flooring, and drywall), and furniture and fixtures (chairs, tables, booths, and a bar). Include a schedule of kitchen and front of the house job descriptions—chef, sous chef, line cook, prep cook, dishwasher, porter, server, buser, manager, and so on—with pay rates and the projected number of hours to be worked daily and weekly. One of the most important items in your capital budget will be a healthy amount for working capital. Banks and other investors know that it can take a few weeks or months to build your business, and they will be impressed that you are smart enough to recognize this. Use chapter 5 as a resource to write this section.

PERSONAL FINANCIAL INFORMATION

Banks will also want copies of your federal tax returns for the previous two years and a copy of your personal financial statement. The higher your net worth, that is, the more your assets exceed your liabilities, the better. Banks can check your financial history instantly, so make sure that you disclose all of your outstanding liabilities and debts such as credit cards, student loans, auto loans, or mortgages. After doing all this hard work, you don't want them to think that you are dishonest; it will ruin your chances of getting funded. The way to avoid this is to get a credit report; if there are any blemishes, disclose and explain them thoroughly.

CHAPTER 13

SETTING UP YOUR BUSINESS

Food & Wine magazine named Rocco DiSpirito, chef and owner of Union Pacific restaurant in New York, one of the ten "Best New Chefs" in the United States in 1999. When the *New York Restaurant Report* asked him whether education played a big part in his success, he replied: "It did, but I never really had a problem with the creative part—that's always come easy for me. My struggle was with the business part, and it was my reason for returning to get my degree in hospitality administration at Boston University."

In this chapter, I'll explain the steps you need to take to set up your business's legal framework, including a commercial lease and a legal identity. Ready? Let's go.

SIGNING A COMMERCIAL LEASE

Signing a commercial lease is a major legal and financial commitment. It is a contract, which will bind you and your landlord for its duration. Therefore, you should thoroughly understand its terms and conditions. Rent will probably be one of your restaurant's biggest fixed monthly expenses, and it can make or break your business. More often than not, the right lease or real estate deal is the deciding factor as to whether or not a restaurant makes it.

Not surprisingly, leases are usually extremely complex legal documents. I cannot recommend strongly enough that you hire an attorney or other real estate professional with experience reading and negotiating commercial leases in your state and locality. This is not to suggest that you should not participate in the lease negotiation process. On the contrary, you should get intimately involved. Ask your attorney to explain in plain English the lease's key clauses so you will be able to understand and assess the legal and financial consequences of signing the document. The final decision to accept or reject any lease proposal should be yours.

Space availability and its purchase or rent cost varies considerably from city to city and from neighborhood to neighborhood. The more highly trafficked or otherwise desirable the location, the higher the rent will be. Rents also vary according to the national and local economies. In overbuilt markets and other markets with high vacancy rates, rent will be lower than in those with little available space and low vacancy rates. If you do your homework and become savvy about your target market areas, you may be able to pick up a good real estate deal. In most markets, a vacancy rate of 10 percent or more is considered to be good for tenants.

Before approaching a prospective landlord, check with local real estate brokers to find out vacancy rates and the going rate per square foot. Some brokers quote square foot rates on a monthly basis, while others quote them on an annual basis. For example, if you are quoted $5,000 per month for a 1,000-square foot space, your annual cost per square foot would be ($5,000 × 12 months) ÷ 1,000 square feet, or $60. On a monthly basis, it would be $5,000 ÷ 1,000 square feet, or $5. Knowing what's going on in the market puts you in a good position to negotiate a good deal.

Before you sit down to negotiate with a landlord, be sure that you have prepared a financial feasibility study showing the amount of rent and other occupancy charges that you will be able to pay and still achieve your desired profitability and return on investment. A well-thought-out and conservative feasibility plan should provide you with break-even and profitability benchmarks to work with. Most landlords are impressed by prospective tenants who are knowledgeable and well prepared, and in a competitive market, you may get the nod if you show up with a plan for your business's long-term success. As a rule of thumb, annual rent payments for table-service restaurants should not be more than 10–12 percent of projected gross annual sales. (Refer to your notes from chapters 5 and 6.)

The following are some key clauses in a commercial lease that you should consider carefully:

- **Lease term.** A lease's term specifies how many years a tenant will be legally allowed to occupy a space, expressed via a commencement date and a termination date. It is critical that your lease is specific about the date on which your rent payments will start. Before agreeing to a lease term, ask your potential landlord for a copy of the certificate of occupancy. Make sure that you won't be paying rent for space that has not been certified for occupancy by local building authorities. Also, if your landlord will have to make improvements to prepare your space, make sure that your rent does not commence until after the landlord has completed his or her work. You should not have to pay rent for unusable space. Negotiate a lease that is long enough to allow your business to grow and prosper and to make a good return on your investment. The lease term should be for at least five years, with options for one or more additional five-year terms, and it should contain a sublease and/or assignment clause (more about that clause follows).

■ **Renewal options.** A renewal option will allow you to renew your lease when it expires. These options are generally found in leases of five years or less. If your lease does not contain a renewal option, ask for one, since it is not unusual for a business to take a year or two to get established and develop a following. If you get a renewal option, make sure that its terms and conditions are reasonable and not substantially different form the original lease's terms. If the original lease was a gross lease, check to see whether the renewed lease switches to a net lease (see the gross versus net clause).

■ **Use and occupancy.** This clause specifies the types of business that will be permitted on the premises and the types of products that can be sold. Review your restaurant's concept carefully to make sure that any planned entertainment or sale of beer, wine, and alcohol will be permitted. Try to make your use and occupancy clause as broad as possible, so you will have flexibility in selling or subletting your lease if you want to. (See the sublease or assignment clause.)

■ **Rent.** As indicated earlier, rent is usually charged at a certain dollar amount per square foot, so make sure that every square foot that you will be paying for is useable. Take a tape measure to your space and check the actual square footage. You don't want to pay for unusable space, such as hallways, boiler rooms, or other areas that the landlord uses to maintain the property. In addition to specifying the starting base rent, most leases will include future escalations or increases. Scrutinize these increases carefully to make sure that your business will be able to afford them and that there are no hidden costs. Ask the landlord to prepare a schedule of future monthly rents in the years following the initial year, showing the new rent and the percent by which it will increase. Some leases ask for rent escalations based on an increase in a consumer price index (CPI). If this is the case, find out if it is a local, regional, or national CPI. This is an important distinction, because in some instances a national CPI is rising when rents and prices in your local market are stable or falling and vice versa. Check with your local chamber of commerce to find out what the local and national trends have been in recent years before making your decision. In most cases, you will be better off with a *reasonable* fixed escalation, one that you can budget for and plan your business around.

■ **Gross versus net lease.** There are typically two lease types: gross and net. In a gross lease, the landlord bears most of the risks of owning the property, such as real estate taxes, maintenance, and property insurance, and your monthly rent bill will consist only of base rent charges. In a net lease, on the other hand, in addition to base rent, tenants are asked to pay their proportionate share of the landlord's costs of owning and maintaining the property. These charges are referred to as *triple net* or *pass-through charges*. Such charges will typically include real estate taxes, property insurance, business license taxes, and common area (CAM) charges. CAM charges are generally included in leases where some space will be shared (such as lobbies, hallways, and parking lots), as found in office buildings, shopping centers, and malls. Common area charges are usually allocated to each tenant on a prorated basis, and they can include a tenant's proportionate share of heating, air conditioning, and general repairs and maintenance. In some instances, these charges can add up to hundreds if not thousands of dollars in additional monthly occupancy expenses, so to avoid any future surprises, ask the landlord for the dollar amount of current monthly charges, along with an itemized schedule of each charge. You should also ask for a calculation that shows how your share of each of these charges was allocated to make sure that you will not be paying for more than your proportionate share. If you will be operating in a city in which landlords get periodic real estate tax refunds from local taxing authorities, ask your attorney to insert a clause stating that you will be entitled to be reimbursed for your proportionate share of these refunds. The same should apply if your landlord gets discount rates for utilities purchased in bulk.

- **Percentage rent.** If you are planning to open your restaurant in a strip mall, a shopping center, or on the ground floor of a busy downtown office building, chances are your lease will include additional rent charges based on a percentage of your sales. The theory is that these rents are justified, since tenants are almost certainly guaranteed high traffic volumes via the presence of large anchor tenants and the landlord's ongoing advertising. Also, at locations other than malls, shopping centers, and office buildings, landlords may often charge lower-than-market base rents to attract tenants, but in exchange will ask for percentage rent. Before you decide to pay percentage rent, factor the asked-for percentage into your financial feasibility study to see how it will impact your projected bottom line. Whenever you are asked to pay percentage rents, try to negotiate lower base rent, since, in essence, your landlord will be sharing in your sales without taking any of the risks involved in owning and operating your business. You should also make sure that any percentage is based on net not gross sales; that is, it should exclude items such as sales taxes, employee meals, tips on credit card charges, and other sources of revenue not directly related to the sale of food and beverages, such as used equipment, T-shirts, and other novelty items. More important, make sure that the percentage charge does not kick in until after your net sales have reached the break-even point.

- **Alterations.** If you plan to do construction or make alterations to a space, make sure that the work will be allowed under the alterations clause. Also confirm that local building and zoning ordinances will permit it.

- **Insurance.** Many landlords require tenants to carry general liability insurance, typically referred to as an umbrella policy, to protect them from lawsuits that may arise during the normal course of their tenants' business, resulting from accidents and so on. Premiums can be quite expensive depending on the amount of coverage requested. Compare the requested coverage with that of other local restaurateurs running establishments with similar concepts to verify that it is reasonable. You may want to shop around for premiums since the cost of coverage can vary from carrier to carrier.

- **Sublease or assignment.** The sublease or assignment clause is a must-have in your lease; without it you will not have the right to sell or transfer you business or to sublease your space. This clause specifies the terms and conditions under which any future sale, transfer, or subleasing of your space will be permitted. Insist on this clause, which says that the landlord will not unreasonably withhold your right to assign your lease since there are any number of legitimate reasons why you may want to do so. If a property is in a desirable location, a *good* long lease will have value or equity if it contains a sublease and/or assignment clause.

- **Signage and facade.** In many cases, in order to maintain a certain aesthetic or look for their buildings, landlords will specify the size and type of signage and storefront that they will permit. Because your restaurant's signage and storefront will play an important role in its visibility and in the image you want to convey, make sure your intended signage and storefront will be permitted. This is a critical clause and should not be taken lightly. For example, just recently one of my clients spent thousands of dollars installing a new storefront and awnings only to have to remove them because his landlord decided that they were not consistent with the rest of the building. Local laws and ordinances may also regulate signage and storefronts.

- **Rent security.** Typically, landlords will ask for a security deposit ranging anywhere from one to six months' worth of the base rent. Depending on the base rent amount, these security deposits can require a significant outlay of capital, and you should negotiate them carefully.

- **Rent concessions and free rent periods.** In some cases, particularly in newly constructed buildings (raw space) or as an incentive to attract new tenants, landlords will allow a free rent period. This allows new tenants time to build out and prepare their spaces for business. *This is the norm and not the exception*, so don't be afraid to ask for it. A couple of months of free rent can save badly needed cash flow and go a long way toward helping to get your business off on the right foot. The amount of the concession will depend on the current real estate market and whether a landlord is looking for a particular kind of tenant—say, a restaurant. If you do obtain rent concessions, make sure that they do not begin before the landlord obtains a *certificate of occupancy.* Also, if possible, have the free rent period begin after you have obtained all your necessary building permits from the local buildings departments so you are ready to start your construction. It is not unusual for several weeks or even months to pass before you can obtain all the necessary permits.

- **Personal guarantees.** Very often, even if you will be operating your business under a separate legal entity—such as a partnership, corporation, or limited liability company (LLC)—landlords will require tenants to sign a personal guarantee. By signing a personal guarantee, you are promising the landlord that you personally will pay the rent for the entire duration of the lease even if your business fails. *This clause has serious future consequences, and you should negotiate it out of the lease if possible.*

- **Good guy.** A variation or substitute for a personal guaranty is a good guy clause. This clause basically states that the guarantor is personally liable for any unpaid base rent and other use and occupancy charges, such as real estate taxes and common area charges, up until the time that the premises are legally surrendered to the landlord.

- **Tenant's versus landlord's work.** Be sure that your lease clearly states who is responsible for certain types of improvements and repairs to your space. For example, in spaces located on the ground floor of apartment buildings, it is not uncommon for water damage to occur as a result of broken pipes in overhead apartments. At Zuni, this happened a couple of times over a twelve-year period. Fortunately, we had inserted a clause in our lease that stated that repairs of this nature were the landlord's responsibility. Landlords commonly pay for certain tenant improvements. The amount of tenant improvements your landlord might agree to pay for will depend on vacancy rates in your local market area, the space's physical condition, and how desirable your concept is. For example, your landlord may decide that your restaurant concept is just the type he needs for his space. If your landlord agrees to pay for tenant improvements, ask for an architectural rendering of the space, a schedule of the work to be done, and start and completion dates. You should also ask for a description of the scope of any work for which you will have to get prior approval. Make sure that the tenant's versus landlord's clause is not so restrictive that you will have to get prior approval to do ordinary, necessary, and regular repairs to your premises. A good way to do this is to set a dollar limit on the amount for which you will have to get approval.

- **Future work by landlord.** Ask your landlord to disclose whether there are any plans for future repairs or construction to the property that might negatively impact your ability to do business. If there are, try to include a clause stating that you will be reasonably compensated for loss of business or get rent concessions during the period of construction. This type of work is not uncommon in malls, shopping centers, office buildings, and apartment buildings. For example, as a result of scaffolding erected in front of Zuni while the landlord was constructing a new apartment building next door, our business declined by 20 to 25 percent over a ten-month period because of loss of visibility. With the scaffolding, it was very difficult for potential customers to see the front of the restaurant.

- **Cotenancy.** If your restaurant will be located in an office building, mall, or shopping center and will depend on the presence of one or more large anchor tenants for traffic, particularly if you will be paying percentage rents, insert a cotenancy clause. This specifies that you are entitled to rent concessions if traffic is reduced below the level you need to be profitable for an extended period of time due to the loss of one or more anchor tenants. The presence of anchor tenants is the reason landlords often use for charging percentage rents.

- **Indemnification and hold harmless.** Your lease should include a clause that states that you will be held harmless from claims arising from the landlord's or the landlord's agents' and contractors' negligence.

- **Arbitration.** Insert a clause stating that in the event of a costly litigation, you and your landlord will agree to submit *disputes* to arbitration and resolve them without having to go to court.

- **Recognition.** A recognition clause will protect you in the event that your landlord becomes bankrupt or sells the property. It should state that your rights and interests in your lease will be protected and that any new owner of the property must honor all of your leases' terms and conditions that you signed specifically with respect to your rent and the length or term of your lease.

- **Demolition or condemnation.** Include a clause asking for reasonable compensation in the event that the landlord's property is condemned or if the landlord elects to demolish the property for any reason prior to the expiration of your lease. At Zuni, we were able to negotiate a one hundred thousand-dollar demolition clause in our first lease. Considering that our business was successful, this was not a lot of money. Fortunately, a few years after we opened, the building was deemed to be a historic landmark.

- **Nuisance.** Most leases contain a clause that prohibits tenants from creating nuisances that will prevent other tenants or neighbors from the "quiet enjoyment" of the immediate area surrounding the premises. Since you are going to be in the restaurant business, ask your attorney to include a statement stating that "normal cooking odors are not considered as a nuisance," as long as they are in compliance with local laws. At Zuni, one of the neighbors complained to our landlord and the local Department of Environmental Protection about cooking odors. The complaints were dismissed since the exhaust system was installed with the landlord's knowledge and permission and was in compliance with local laws.

- **Hours of operation.** Leases, particularly those for spaces in shopping centers and malls, will specify the days and hours that restaurants can operate. Whether you will be in a shopping center or not, make sure that the hours specified in this clause do not conflict with your current or future business plans. Some clauses may require that you open for business on days and times that will not be advantageous for you to do so, while others may restrict the very times you will need to operate in order to be profitable.

SELECTING A LEGAL AND TAX STRUCTURE

Small business owners tend to either let legal and tax issues intimidate them as too complex and difficult to understand or completely underestimate their importance. They then make the mistake of ignoring these very important issues, often to their own detriment. The fact is, it's really in your best interest to understand the relevant legal and tax consequences when you decide to open a business, particularly if you are going to have partners. Fortunately, the basic issues are not nearly as hard to understand as you might think.

Your legal and tax structure will affect the tax returns you file with federal, state, and local taxing authorities, and, in most cases, the amount of taxes you will pay. It will also affect your legal liability and other administrative issues. Have an attorney advise you on selecting a form of business that provides the following:

- The best legal and tax benefits for your income tax planning purposes
- Advantages for your legal planning, particularly limiting potential liabilities, which could apply to you as a business owner

For income tax purposes, ask your tax attorney or accountant to advise you on the following:

- How can you and any investors in your business legally minimize or defer (put off until future years) income taxes on your business profits?
- How can you, your partners, or fellow shareholders, if any, use any losses from your business to offset other income you or they may have earned (and thus reduce your overall tax bills)?
- How can you best protect increases in your business's value from income and estate tax?

For legal purposes, your concerns should be:

- How can you and any other owners and investors in your business limit exposure to potential liabilities incurred by the business?
- What is the most efficient form of business from a management perspective?
- Which business form permits the most flexibility in the event that you and/or other owners and investors in your business want to sell or otherwise transfer their share to another party?
- Which business forms might limit the types of activities in which the restaurant can engage?
- Which form enables the best equity and capital financing arrangements?

Regardless of the outcome of any business venture—success or failure—the legal and tax consequences can be significant. I highly recommended that you consult a tax attorney or a CPA before making any decisions about the form of your business. As with other professionals, not all attorneys and CPAs are created equal. Some are better than others. To avoid paying for a learning curve, your best bet is to look for attorneys and CPAs who are familiar with business law and corporate taxes and who are familiar with the restaurant industry. To get referrals for real estate and tax attorneys and CPAs, visit your local restaurant association's website or ask other restaurateurs in your area.

The most common forms of businesses are sole proprietorships, partnerships, corporations, and limited liability companies. Let's run through how each works, its benefits, and its limitations.

SOLE PROPRIETORSHIP

A sole proprietorship is the easiest, least expensive, and, not surprisingly, most common type of business organization. In a sole proprietorship, the proprietor elects to own and operate a business as an individual, and consequently there is no requirement to form a separate legal business entity. In a sole proprietorship, the owner owns all of the property, conducts the business for profit, and is personally liable for all of the business's obligations and debts, which means that in most cases, his or her assets can be seized to satisfy the business's debts.

Although no separate legal entity is required, the owner may choose a separate or "assumed name" under which to operate the business. For example, if your name is John Brown, you don't necessarily have to name your restaurant John Brown Café; instead, your restaurant's assumed name could be The East Side Café. An assumed name is also known as a DBA or "doing business as" name. Some states and local authorities may require registration of DBAs or assumed names.

For tax purposes, since there is no separate legal entity, a business's net income or loss is reported as part of the owner's individual tax return on federal Form 1040 Schedule C, Profit and Loss from a Business or Profession. Net income may also be subject to self-employment and social security taxes.

PARTNERSHIPS

A partnership is an association of two or more persons who join together as co-owners and contribute capital or services to own and operate a business for profit. There are two types of partnerships: general partnerships and limited partnerships. In a general partnership, each partner owns an interest or share in the partnership, personally shares all of the business's risks and rewards, and has unlimited personal liability for all of the partnership's debts and obligations. Like proprietorships, general partners' assets can be seized to satisfy the partnership's debts.

A general partnership can be organized and operated with little formality. Generally, filing a certificate of partnership is not required to create a general partnership. The partners can simply agree to enter into a partnership agreement. Although state law will normally recognize an oral agreement, it is extremely important to prepare a written partnership agreement that details each partners' rights and obligations. In some states, if there is no written agreement, state partnership law will determine the partners' rights and duties. If your concept is successful and you want to expand it nationally, as a general partnership, you would only have to register it in your home state, not in every state in which you intend to do business.

A limited partnership must have at least one general partner who will be personally liable for the partnership's debts and obligations. The remaining partners will be limited partners, and as a result their liability for partnership debts and obligations will be limited to the amount of capital they invest into the partnership. Limited partners do not play an active role in the business's day-to-day management, and they usually do not receive salaries. They are, however, entitled to their proportionate share of partnership profits and losses.

General partners on the other hand, usually manage and control day-to-day business operations, and in addition to receiving their proportionate share of partnership profits and losses, they are typically paid a salary for running the business and assuming greater responsibilities. A general partner's assets can be seized to satisfy the debts of the business.

In some states, limited partnerships are subject to certain formalities, such as filing a certificate of limited partnership with state authorities and preparing a limited partnership agreement.

All partnerships are required to file Form 1065, Federal Partnership Tax Return. Most states also require partnerships to file state partnership tax returns. Partnerships do not pay taxes. Instead, any income or loss is passed through to each individual partner, who in turn must report the profit or loss on his or her own individual tax return.

Boilerplate partnership agreements are available at the Nolo Press website, www.nolo.com. Whether a partnership is general or limited, the partnership agreement should address the following:

- The amount of capital each partner will contribute
- The division of profits
- The partners' compensation
- The distribution of assets on dissolution
- The partnership's duration
- Provisions for changing or dissolving the partnership
- A dispute settlement clause
- Restrictions on the particular partners' authority to bind the partnership
- A settlement in case of a partner's death or incapacitation
- The business's name and the identity of the partners
- The nature and scope of the partnership business
- The duties of each partner in managing the partnership

CORPORATIONS

A corporation is an entity created by state law for the purpose of conducting business. It is regarded as a separate person having its own legal rights and obligations, which are distinct from its owners'. A corporation may be closely held (have one or a few shareholders) or publicly held (have a large number of shareholders with its shares publicly traded). Directors and officers manage corporations and are not required to be shareholders. Like a limited partner, an investor in a corporation enjoys limited liability, and is liable only to the extent of his or her investment in the corporation. This means that personal assets are generally not at risk. In closely held corporations, however, shareholders may be liable for any unpaid taxes.

Corporations are generally the most complicated form of entity to organize and operate. A corporation is required to prepare and file a certificate of incorporation, prepare articles of incorporation and bylaws, and pay filing fees. Actually filing the certificate of incorporation and paying the registration fees is not that difficult. Legal supply stores carry inexpensive incorporation kits, which include most of the required forms, and boilerplate articles of incorporation and bylaws. For almost any type of legal form, visit www.nolo.com. That said, your best bet is to consult a tax attorney or accountant to make sure you get things done right.

Along with federal tax returns, corporations are required to file state and/or local franchise tax returns in the state of incorporation, and they may be subject to taxes in other states in which they do business. If a corporation does business in more than one state, it must obtain a certificate of authority from and maintain a registered agent in that state.

A corporation can choose to be taxed either as a C corporation or as an S corporation. A big disadvantage of C corporations is that they are generally taxed twice, first at the corporate level and then again at the shareholder level. For example, if your restaurant operates as a C corporation and makes a net profit of $10,000, it would have to pay taxes on the $10,000 as a corporation at corporate tax rates, and when any of that $10,000 is paid out to you as dividends, you would have to report it on your individual tax return as dividend income where it might be taxed again.

One way to avoid the problem of double taxation is to have your corporation taxed as an S corporation. To elect S corporation status, you must file a federal Form 2353. S corporations are not taxed at the corporate level; that is, they do not pay corporate income taxes. Instead, like a partnership, any corporation income or loss is passed through to its shareholders and is reported on their individual income tax returns. S corporations must file Form 1120S, U.S. Income Tax Return for S Corporations.

In order to elect S corporation status, you must meet the following conditions:
- The corporation must be domestic, that is, a U.S. corporation.
- The corporation cannot have more than seventy-five shareholders.
- All shareholders must be individuals.
- All shareholders must be U.S. citizens or legal residents of the United States.

After forming and registering a corporation, it is highly recommended that the shareholders of a closely held corporation sign a stockholders agreement. I cannot overemphasize how important this is. Just recently, I had to spend thousands of dollars in legal fees to have my partner buy me out at a fair price, all because we neglected to properly execute our shareholders agreement.

The following are some of the major clauses that you should include in the stockholders agreement:

- Insurance
- Restriction on the distribution of stock during a stockholder's lifetime
- Purchase of stock upon the death of a shareholder
- Purchase of shares upon the termination of a shareholder's relationship with the corporation
- Purchase price of shares in the event of a shareholder's death or the termination of a shareholder's relationship
- Election of a corporate structure
- Involuntary transfer of shares due to judicial proceedings such as bankruptcy or divorce
- Additional capital contributions
- Events that would trigger the termination of the stockholder's agreement
- Permitted transfers of stock to shareholder's immediate family

LIMITED LIABILITY COMPANIES

A limited liability company (LLC) is created under state law. An LLC is a hybrid of a limited partnership and a corporation, and it combines the best attributes of a limited partnership with those of an S corporation. LLCs are governed by an operating agreement that establishes the rights, duties, and obligations of its owners, also know as members.

The primary advantage of a limited liability company over a partnership is the owners' lack of personal liability for the business. For example, while limited partners in a limited partnership may be sheltered from liability, at least one general partner must assume personal liability. In an LLC, members' liability is limited to the extent of any unpaid capital contributions. Also, an LLC offers more flexibility in managing the business. For example, in a limited partnership, limited partners are typically not allowed to become involved in the business's day-to-day operations, whereas members of an LLC can help manage.

Limited liability companies can also have significant advantages over S corporations. For one, the number of shareholders is not limited to seventy-five. Also, while only individuals, estates, and trusts can be shareholders of an S corporation, LLCs may have corporations, partnerships, and other entities as members.

A limited liability company is generally taxed as a partnership or as a sole proprietorship if it has only one member. When taxed as a partnership, you must file Form 1065, U.S. Partnership Tax Return, and any income or loss is passed through to members, who in turn report it on their own individual income tax returns. When there is only one member, any income or loss is reported on Schedule C Form 1040, Federal Individual Income Tax Return.

An LLC is organized by filing articles of organization, similar to the articles of incorporation filed with state regulatory authorities. Although not all states require this to be in writing, an LLC normally has an operating agreement similar to a limited partnership agreement, which details how the organization will be managed. A caveat: LLCs are not recognized in all states, so this may not be an option for you.

FEDERAL AND STATE IDENTIFICATION NUMBERS

Obtaining a federal ID number is critical. You will need it to file your tax returns, open bank accounts, get a sales tax ID number, apply for loans, and obtain almost any license you can think of. Every business that pays wages to one or more employees must have a federal ID number. To obtain your ID number you must file a Form SS-4, Application for Employer Identification Number with the IRS.

Only individual owners (sole proprietors), corporate officers, or authorized members of a partnership or LLC can apply for a business's federal ID number. If you want your attorney or CPA to apply for the number on your behalf, you must complete a Form 2848, Power of Attorney, authorizing them to do so.

Obtaining a federal ID number is actually quite simple. After completing Form SS-4, call your regional IRS processing center, give them the information, and they will assign the number to you over the phone. Once they give you your ID number, you must enter it in the designated space in the top right-hand corner of your Form SS-4, sign and date it, and mail it to the nearest IRS center within twenty-four hours. If you cannot get through on the phone because the lines are busy, you can fax or mail your application in, and they will assign you a number within five business days. To get the right phone and fax numbers for your area, call the general IRS information and ask for entity control.

ESTABLISHING BANK ACCOUNTS

If you will be operating as a sole proprietor, you will not need any special documentation to open a bank account. The process will be the same as when you open a personal bank account.

Corporations will require a federal ID number, a copy of their certificate of incorporation, and a corporate seal. You can obtain a corporate seal from most legal supply stores, but you must take a copy of your certificate of incorporation with you. Generally, only officers are allowed to open corporate bank accounts.

LLCs and partnerships will need a federal ID number and a copy of any other state or local documentation. The easiest way to get this information is to talk to your banker.

CHAPTER 14

TAKING IT TO THE STREETS

Getting your new restaurant opened on budget and on time will be quite an accomplishment, but it will be just the beginning. The real success will come only when customers start coming in frequently enough to make it a viable and profitable enterprise. Your job from opening day until the day you close your doors to the public will be to induce customers to come through those doors by choice, rather than by chance.

Occasionally, a new restaurant will open to immediate fanfare and attract lots of customers. This may be because the concept is new and unique to the area. More often than not, such instant popularity occurs because the owners launched an effective marketing campaign prior to opening. Attracting customers in the early weeks and months will not ensure that your restaurant will be successful over the long run. How often have you seen a new restaurant open, stay busy for a few weeks or months, only to close six, nine, or twelve months later when its novelty wears off? In today's competitive environment, to be successful, your restaurant must not only attract customers in the first weeks and months, it must build a strong base of repeat customers and continually attract new ones. You can accomplish this through steady and cost-effective marketing.

BRANDING

With a well-thought-out and well-executed marketing strategy, the various elements of your restaurant's concept (food, service, decor, ambience, name, and logo) will come together and create a unique brand. Your restaurant will become known for the unique selling points you offer, and this brand will generate a lasting impression and strong emotional connection with your customers, motivating them to frequent your restaurant regularly and recommend it enthusiastically to family and friends.

Most small business owners erroneously assume that creating a recognizable brand requires spending millions of dollars in print, radio, and television advertising. Many often think of Coke and Pepsi as examples. Well, I am here to dispel that myth and tell you that many very successful small businesses have created effective brand images without spending a dime on media advertising.

In my opinion, traditional advertising (print and radio) should be the last component of your marketing mix. You could easily spend thousands of dollars on this type of advertising and not get a significant response. At Zuni, for example, we spent about ten thousand dollars on newspaper and magazine advertising over a one-year period without any noticeable increase in business. Furthermore, print advertising works best when it's backed up with other types of marketing, such as public relations and promotions.

The truth is, you don't have to spend tons of money to conduct a targeted steady and effective marketing campaign. Two cases in point: Union Square Café in New York City and Chez Panisse in Berkeley, California, have both built strong brand images without advertising. While these restaurants serve great food and provide impeccable service, food and service are not what they are known for (their brands). Rather, Union Square Café is known for its hospitality, and Chez Panisse is distinguished by its organic and sustainable food. A more recognizable example is the many mom-and-pop coffee shops across the country that have been around forever because they are known for a basic meal and a "hardy howdy." Here again, their brand is not outstanding food, but hospitality.

Regardless of your concept, there are many inexpensive and creative ways to market your restaurant prior to opening, during the early weeks and months, and in future years. These methods use a combination of public relations (such as press releases and community involvement), promotions (for example, Web and blog sites, store postings, coupons, tastings, and samplings), and non-media advertising (including word-of-mouth, flyers, mailings, and door hangers), all of which (when done properly) can be very cost effective. Once you have adopted a marketing strategy, use it frequently and consistently. Research shows that frequency and consistency are key to effective and successful marketing.

Word-of-mouth advertising, or endorsements, is the oldest, cheapest, and most powerful form of advertising. As they say in the business, "A happy customer with a big mouth is the best form of advertising." Word-of-mouth advertising is particularly powerful because, unlike other methods, it is generally perceived to be objective and credible; it is assumed that people don't want to mislead listeners when they endorse a product or make a recommendation. If you can get customers to talk frequently and positively about your restaurant, you will achieve success beyond your wildest dreams! Later on, we will discuss specific ways to market your restaurant to create positive word-of-mouth *and* favorable press reviews. By the way, these two marketing methods are symbiotic; that is, they feed off of each other. Critics tell their readers that your restaurant is good, and happy customers tell critics to go to your restaurant because it is good.

The marketing strategies discussed here should not be applied universally to every restaurant concept in every market. Some strategies will be generic, while others will be more appropriate for a particular type of concept. For some restaurant concepts, advertising (such as flyers, coupons, door hangers, and colorful banners) is appropriate and cost effective, while for other concepts, public relations and promotions are the better choice. Your restaurant concept, its uniqueness, your type of table service (such as upscale or casual), your budget, and your target customers' demographic profile will all determine the amount and types of marketing that will be necessary to attract your target customers.

Let's consider some examples. If you have a corner site in a busy intersection and your concept is a family diner in a prime location, chances are you will not have to do much marketing in the early days to attract customers. Getting these early customers to return with friends would, more than likely, require some marketing. However, if your restaurant is the fourth or fifth such diner in the area and is located on a side street with poor access and visibility, even if you have the best food and service around, it would be foolhardy not to do some form of marketing. How else would customers know your place exists?

Now let's say you are planning to open a small brick-oven pizzeria on a crowded, busy urban street or off a busy highway. In these instances, the use of large colorful banners, announcing Grand Opening or Coming Soon, would be very appropriate, helping to create visibility and catch the eyes of passersby who might otherwise speed right by. But, more to the point, colorful banners are consistent with people's expectations of what pizzerias, fast food, takeout and delivery, and inexpensive family diners should use to market themselves.

If, in contrast, you are planning to open a sleek or formal upscale bistro on a similarly busy street, large colorful banners might not be appropriate, since they could send the wrong message. In fact, your restaurant's facade or storefront and signage should not only attract target customers' attention, it should also send a message about your establishment's food, beverages, service, and design that is consistent with people's expectations of a fine-dining establishment.

Similarly, if your concept is a casual upscale bistro in an urban area, a three-course moderately priced prix fixe menu would probably be a more appropriate and effective promotional tool than offering five-dollar discount coupons. If, on the other hand, your concept is casual, inexpensive, and family style, offering five-dollar discount coupons would probably be attractive and successful. You get the picture!

GETTING A RUNNING START

While most first-timer owners intuitively recognize the need to do some form of early marketing, all too often they wait until the last couple of days or weeks before opening, or even until after they have opened, to actually do something about it. What usually results is last-minute Grand Opening and Coming Soon banners, which are generally not enough to attract a steady stream of customers during the critical early days and months. A marketing strategy sufficient to attract numerous and repeat customers, not only in the beginning but also in successive years, takes time to formulate, plan, and execute.

To help your new restaurant hit the ground running, start to think about and plan a marketing strategy from the get-go, that is, as soon as you have selected a workable concept and a general location. For example, when you start shopping for sites, keep in the back of your mind that, when available and affordable, sites with high visibility, particularly corner locations, can be a source of free advertising. You should also consider how your restaurant's name, facade, signage, and logo will fit in with the image you want to project and how you can use them for marketing purposes. Think also about how they will resonate with your target customers. You may want a name that ties in with your concept, is easy to pronounce and remember, and can be turned into an attractive logo. For example, Iron Chef Mario Batali only names his Italian restaurants with words that can be spelled phonetically in five letters or less, such as Po, Lupa, Esca, and Babbo. Your restaurant's name could create a sense of place and tie in with its neighborhood. Examples of such names are Downtown, Museum Café, Windows on the World, River Walk Café, and Fifth Floor.

One of the benefits of having to prepare an objective and comprehensive business plan to raise capital for your restaurant idea is that you will be required to give a clear and precise description of your marketing plans. Why? Potential investors will want to know how you plan to position your restaurant to compete! So I suggest that even if you do not plan to get investors, you should take the time to write a marketing plan. Doing so will force you to think early and critically about how to promote and position your restaurant to ensure its success. This may sound like a broken record, but remember, "Those who fail to plan, plan to fail." Don't worry! There will be enough material in this chapter to make developing a marketing plan a breeze.

Remember what we said in chapter 2 about developing a unique selling proposition (USP) for your new restaurant? It's the four, five, or six unique aspects that you identified when formulating your concept, and they will form the building blocks of your marketing strategy. These characteristics should make your concept stand out from the competition and, at the same time, make it easy to identify and recognize your restaurant. If you can't think of four or five differentiating characteristics (for example, unique cooking methods or ingredients, impressive portion sizes, affordable pricing and value, outstanding service, excellent bar and beverage programs, interesting design and decor, great views, unusual packaging, or fun staff apparel) to build your marketing strategy around, then perhaps you need to rethink your concept. The more meaningfully unique your concept, the easier it will be to market. You may want to reread the section in chapter 2 on creating a USP.

STARTING A BUZZ BEFORE THE DOORS OPEN

Most, if not all, popular restaurants enjoy a certain amount of "buzz." Starting a buzz will be particularly important if your restaurant is a destination concept or is in a location with poor visibility and/or access. The sooner you can let your customers know that your restaurant, which is Coming Soon, has something special to offer, the better. Letting people know ahead of time that your restaurant will be opening works well in two ways. First and obviously, it announces your arrival on the scene. Just as important, being on the premises as you prepare to open, you will have an opportunity to meet potential customers and obtain their feedback about your concept. They may even give you some ideas about how to tweak your concept to better meet their needs.

To start an early buzz and get people talking, consider posting notices that will tip off your target customers about your upcoming menu offerings. For example, during build out and construction you could post a tentative menu in the window so passers-by can see the types of menu items you plan to offer. Along with the menu, you could post descriptions of any distinctive or unique cooking methods (such as wood smoking or thin-crust brick-oven pizzas) or any special and unique ingredients (such as house-cured meats or homemade breads) you plan to use. If you know that your target customers are environmentally conscious and interested in eating organic and sustainably grown foods, and you plan to offer them, post a mission statement about your commitment to use only the freshest and best organic produce, meats, poultry, dairy, and so forth. This type of marketing will not only be informative, it will help to create an emotional relationship with your target customers and make them more likely to support you. Also, if your chef had a following previously, post his or her name in the window along with where he or she worked and any favorable newspaper or magazine reviews. While you are at it, don't forget to post your URL (website address) or blog address, which you should already have (I will explain later).

Getting the attention of neighborhood passers-by is not enough; you will want to reach all target customers within your market range—a one-, five-, or ten-mile radius, or even larger, depending upon your concept. To this end, a few weeks before your scheduled opening, send press releases to the local media, announcing your restaurant's special features. (More about what to put in your press release later on.) Don't be intimidated if your restaurant is a hole-in-the-wall operation. Food writers and critics, similar to other reporters, are newshounds looking to sniff out the next scoop, and they will write about novel and interesting restaurants whether they are big or small, fancy or modest. If you can convince them to give you even a small mention in their food section, you will have accomplished, at little or no cost, what thousands of dollars in conventional print advertising would not. A small mention or write-up in a popular local newspaper or food magazine could reach thousands of readers, informing them of your pending arrival, piquing their interest, getting them talking, and helping to get your restaurant off to a running start.

If your market area has a vibrant food and restaurant culture, then as soon as you sign a lease your should consider asking friends to post messages on local food and restaurant blogs, revealing your coming restaurant and its unique features. In the San Francisco Bay Area, for example, many people, particularly foodies, often go to the popular Chowhound and Daily Candy websites to find out and chat about existing restaurants, as well as to discover interesting restaurants that are coming soon.

In your press releases and blog postings, try to create excitement without crossing over into hyperbole. Do not promise what you cannot realistically deliver. If bloggers, critics, or food writers later find out that you misrepresented or hyped your food and beverages' quality and/or uniqueness, they may start spreading negative comments by word of mouth. And as valuable as positive word-of-mouth advertising is, negative word-of-mouth attention can be equally devastating. In the business there is a saying, "If customers have a good experience, they will tell fifty people, but if they have a bad experience, they will tell a hundred."

Putting together press kits, writing press releases, and sending them out will require a lot of time that you may not have during the hectic preopening weeks and months. If you do not have the time or inclination but do have room in your budget, consider hiring a public relations agent. If you decide to take this route, look for an agent who has access to, and good relations with, the media and who will find the journalists and publications that your target customers are likely to read. Ask other restaurant owners whose agents have provided favorable results for a referral, or ask members of the media for referrals of agents or companies with whom they work well. Public relations or press agents can be expensive, but they can be a lot less costly and considerably more effective than print and radio advertising. The cost of hiring a public relations agent will vary according to your area—large urban, small urban, suburban—and the amount of work you want done. A good friend and client recently paid her agent $6,500 to publicize a small local operation and got fantastic results. On the other hand, a reputable agent quoted another large client in New York City $15,000 for preopening public relations work.

BUILDING ON YOUR BUZZ— SPREADING THE WORD EVEN FURTHER

OK, let's say that you've done a good preopening job—customers know that your restaurant exists, and they are anticipating good food, good service, interesting and unique flavors and textures, and, above all, good value for their money. Now the doors are open, and you have to present your brand image, that is, you have to deliver on your promises and keep the momentum going. All of your marketing so far has cost you little or nothing. We know that start-ups are tight on cash, so let's continue down this road.

You've hoisted your Grand Opening banner to announce your long-awaited opening. Target customers have perused the postings in your window, read about you on Chowhound and Daily Candy, visited your website, and read some small write-ups about you in the food sections of local newspapers and magazines. You've advertised that your food is exceptional, but most customers won't want to spend the big bucks until they taste it and know it's worth it. As they say, "The proof of the pudding is in the eating!"

One of the best ways to demonstrate your food's quality cost effectively, or shall we say on the cheap, is to do a tasting. By the way, according to market research, product demonstrations (in this case, tasting and sampling) is the most cost-effective form of marketing after word-of-mouth advertising and favorable food reviews. How you go about doing a tasting or sampling will depend on your concept. Let's give some examples. Say your concept is a small café and bakery, and all of your breads, cakes, and pastries are baked in-house. As soon as you open your doors for business, with the smell of fresh-baking bread wafting out the door, you could give away free samples at the counter or have one of your staff stand outside handing out free samples. Remember that market research we just mentioned? Well, it determined that at product demonstrations 51 percent of customers try products they normally would not try, and 79 percent of the people who sampled a product bought it later when they perceived a need for it. The moral of this story is: offering a tasting will induce customers to try your food and, more important, if they like it, they will come back for more.

You could also set up a stall at one or more local farmers' markets and street fairs to sell small portions of your signature dishes and offer free samples. While there, you can hand out flyers, business cards, brochures, and even coupons to be redeemed at your restaurant. I witness small restaurants doing this all the time at Berkeley farmers' markets with great success. This is not only a great way to spread the word beyond your immediate neighborhood, it's also an opportunity to meet and talk to new customers about your food and restaurant concept. I know firsthand that this type of marketing works. At Zuni, we would set up a stall in front of the restaurant every year during the annual Ninth Avenue International Food Festival to sell small plates, give free tastes of our signature menu items, and hand out promotional materials. The response was always very positive. Not only did we sell a lot, we got lots of new customers and our business increased by 15–20 percent for a few months after the festival.

Now let's say you are offering an upscale concept in a densely populated residential and commercial area. One way to introduce customers to your fare and ambience would be to throw an opening party or a half-price lunch and invite friends, local business workers, and the press. Another way to get potential customers to taste your food is to send complimentary boxed lunches of some of your signature dishes to employees of targeted companies. This will expose target customers to your food and alert them that you are open for lunch, and it will also help to promote your delivery service, should you offer one. Along the same lines, if your restaurant has an attractive bar, during the first couple months of operation, you could periodically invite employees from various target companies to come in for complimentary cocktails and appetizers.

If you start to get positive feedback about your food and beverages, you may want to go a step further and send free samples of signature menu items to local news, radio, and television reporters. If the radio and television reporters are impressed with your food and generosity, they will likely give you a mention on the air. But be careful when sending out food. Choose menu items such as salads, soups, and sandwiches, which will travel well. Cold and soggy meats and sauces won't create a good impression. Your goal here is not only to get customers in the door and expose them to your food and ambience, but also to make your restaurant look busy. People love busy restaurants! The busier and more difficult restaurants are to get into, the more people want to get in.

Where will you get all the money to throw parties and give away food, you ask? Partly from your vendors and suppliers; if you work with them to promote items that they want to sell in greater quantity or introduce to the public, they will team up with you. Wine, beer, and liquor sales agents often host free tastings, and most, if not all, major food vendors will offer deep discounts. Don't forget to invite them to your opening party!

This type of marketing is relatively cheap compared to print advertising, and it is ten times more effective. It will expose your name and food to the public *and* increase the probability that food writers and critics will discover your restaurant. *More important, this type of marketing leads to positive word-of-mouth advertising,* which I can't say often enough is *the* best form of advertising.

Other more conventional and more expensive ways to spread the word and attract customers after you are open is to distribute menus, flyers, and door hangers to targeted homes as well as to apartment and office complexes in your market area. For apartment, co-op, condominium, and office complexes, be sure to get permission from the management companies first. Also, most multiunit dwellers do not like their lobbies and hallways littered with flyers and door hangers and may get turned off by yours. You can do targeted mailings, but they are generally quite expensive. Many print shops sell mailing lists broken down into various demographic categories, such as family size, family income, age, and so forth. If you can obtain a list of names of residents who have recently moved into your zip code, use it to send your new neighbors a Welcome to the Neighborhood gift certificate or discount coupon. I know that this is possible since a few months after moving to Albany, California, I was the only one in my household to receive a gift certificate in the mail from a local restaurant. It worked! I redeemed the certificate, liked the food, and have gone back several times. Without the gift certificate, I probably would not have gone to that restaurant. Local realtors or the real estate section of your local paper can often be a source of information about new residents to your market area. Other sources of targeted mailing lists are the major credit card companies. For example, American Express, MasterCard, and Visa may be able to sell you lists of cardholders in your market area who regularly patronize concepts like yours. If you decide to buy mailing lists, make sure that they are current.

Your concept and hours of service should determine how far and wide to distribute flyers and send mailings. Recall from chapter 3, "Your Target Market," that the rule of thumb is: the more upscale the concept, the wider the market area. As a guide to estimating a flyer or mailing area, use the following two lessons noted in that chapter: according to the National Restaurant Association, studies show that, in most suburban areas, a standard table-service restaurant has a market area encompassing a one-mile radius, and anecdotal evidence suggests that 60–80 percent of a restaurant's customer base lives within a five-mile radius. Therefore, if your concept should happen to be a diner or a standard table-service restaurant, you may want to limit your mailings to target customers living within a one-mile radius of your location.

To increase the odds of gaining a high response, mail or distribute your flyers, mailers, or door hangers to the same customers repeatedly over a period of several months. The response rate to print advertisement is much higher with repetition. The response rate is also enhanced significantly when print advertisement is coupled with special offers, such as discount coupons, gift certificates, and freebies. Remember the gift certificate I received in the mail from a local restaurant? As I mentioned, I probably would not have gone to that restaurant without the discount coupon. To be effective, your discount should be at least 10 percent off; lesser discounts are often not enough of a draw.

Print advertising is most effective when it is credible, unique, and memorable. Keep these points in mind when you design your flyers and other printed materials. Apply the KISS (keep it simple, stupid) principle, and try to communicate a simple, single message. Just like your logo, letterhead, and business cards, flyers reflect your business. If you are creative, you can construct attractive flyers for next to nothing using your computer and a color printer. Remember that you want to create a consistent image in all of your advertising.

MAINTAINING WEBSITES AND BLOGS

In today's digital age, it would be a mistake not to have a website or a blog as part of your marketing strategy. Consider the following: a recent study conducted by the National Restaurant Association found that 46 percent of restaurant customers between the ages of eighteen and thirty-four used the Internet to find out about restaurants they had not visited before and that 33 percent of restaurant customers between the ages of forty-five and sixty-four used the Internet for the same purpose. Research also shows that customers who regularly spend more than fifty dollars per week in restaurants base most of their decisions on online information.

Most folks today, unless they live under a rock, are familiar with the Internet. Fewer people, however, are familiar with blogs. For those of you not up-to-date with the latest tech tools, a blog is essentially a website in a one-page format, which readers must scroll up or down to access various pieces of information. Blogs, unlike websites, do not have pages that can be accessed randomly by pointing and clicking on menu buttons. What blogs do have is an interactive aspect. Customers can post their comments on the site. From a marketing perspective, this is an ideal tool, enabling you to have ongoing, one-on-one conversations with your customers and read what other people are saying about your restaurant. Furthermore, you will be able to respond quickly to constructive criticism, which will help to build strong relationships with your customers, stem potential negative word-of-mouth advertising, and enhance your brand image.

Websites and blogs are potentially far more cost effective than conventional marketing and advertising, such as mailings, flyers, and newspaper and magazine advertisements. Not long ago, the cost of building even a basic website would run into thousands of dollars. Today, however, website costs have dropped dramatically. For example, Web.com currently offers to build and maintain small business websites for as little as $19.95 per month. The company also offers packages that cost $300 and $500 for three- and five-page sites, respectively. Web.com claims that their websites come with built-in point-and-click software, which makes them easy to update and maintain without having to be knowledgeable about HTML or other computer languages. Microsoft Office Live Basics offers a free website, a domain name, and e-mail accounts when you choose MSN as your Internet service provider for a monthly fee of $19.95. At these low prices, and given the potential as a marketing tool, there is absolutely no good excuse for not developing a website for your restaurant. Obviously, Web.com and MSN's website packages will not offer the most sophisticated state-of-the-art technology with lots of interactivity, eye candy, and bells and whistles, but they look quite presentable, offer good functionality, and can be a good place to start, particularly if your budget is tight.

Don't get me wrong; this is not to suggest that you should skimp on your website! On the contrary, your website should promote the best and most positive image of your restaurant possible. You should base the type and cost of your site on your concept, the image you want your restaurant to convey, and your budget. It should match your logo and other promotional materials, such as business cards and brochures. Also, your website or blog should be consistent with your restaurant's overall design, decor, and ambience. The objective is to launch your restaurant into virtual space and have it look and feel much the same as it does at its physical location. A poorly designed website, like a poorly designed restaurant, which is difficult to navigate and features unattractive images of food, cocktails, interiors, or frontage will send a negative message and quite likely turn off potential customers. On the other hand, be careful not to project an image or an experience that you can't honestly deliver. Remember, when customers think that they have been deceived, they are likely to start spreading negative critiques by word of mouth, and you certainly don't want that to happen!

To get ideas for your website design (as well as your business), check out the sites of successful restaurants that are similar in concept, look, and feel to yours. In fact, you should *definitely* check out the sites of your top five competitors! While you are on their websites, notice what they are offering and look for ways to create a competitive advantage. For example, look for things that they may *not* be offering, such as daily specials, food and wine pairings, or discount coupons. Also, consider features that you could offer on your website (such as interactivity) that will give it more pizzazz than theirs. Before you launch your website, ask for feedback from friends, other restaurateurs who will *not* be your competitors, and some of your potential customers. Once your site is up and running, ask some of your regular customers and those who found you through the Web for their feedback and suggestions. Try to spend a couple of hours every week, or at least every month, reviewing and reading the sites and blogs of successful restaurants to see what they are doing to entice traffic their way.

Blogs, in contrast, are easier to launch, easier to use, and considerably less expensive than websites. In fact, blogs require little more than basic word-processing skills to launch and use. Blog-hosting companies such as blogger.com, Wordpress.com, and typepad.com can get you started quickly and easily for little or no cost, or even for free. All three of these services provide templates and blogging tools to make entries, and they do not require any software installation. Since blogs are so inexpensive and can be built into websites, why not have both?

One note of caution: having a website or blog will not guarantee that people will visit them. To help guide potential customers to your site or blog, make sure that your URL and e-mail address are on your business cards, letterhead, flyers, coupons, brochures, outgoing message, and any other form of print advertisement or promotional materials. You should also submit your URL to search engines and restaurant-listing sites. Post special features about your restaurant on local and national food and restaurant blogs, as well. To make it easy for customers to research, locate, and come to your restaurant, be sure that your website or blog includes the following information about your restaurant: address, phone number, e-mail address, menus with prices, images, hours of operation, a map with directions, and the types of payment accepted.

Do not make the same mistake that many restaurants do of letting their websites get stale with old menus, images, and information. Remember, there is a good possibility that at least 46 percent and 33 percent of your customers between the ages of eighteen and thirty-four, and forty-five and sixty-four respectively, will go to your website to check you out before they decide to visit. Outdated information may turn them off. Instead, take this opportunity to impress and entice them to choose your restaurant over others. Keep your site fresh and interesting with copies of, or links to, favorable press reviews; current positive comments and testimonials from customers; printable menus; recipes for popular, new, and appealing menu items; novel and interesting cooking methods; special ingredients; community service awards; special promotions; current discount offerings; online reservation forms; blog or FAQ (frequently asked questions) pages to keep a dialogue going with your customers; and links to other food and beverage websites.

Needless to say, keeping your site fresh and current is going to require time and effort. If you don't have the time, gather the information and hire someone to update it for you at least monthly. Depending on your site's level of sophistication, you may be able to hire a local college or high school information technology student to maintain it at a reasonable cost. Be sure to review the updated Web pages before launching to make sure that they meet your standards. If you want a site with interactivity and music to effectively convey your message to the public, you will probably have to hire a professional to design, build, and maintain it. As you might suspect, these types of sites will probably cost upwards of a few hundred dollars.

KEEPING THE BUZZ GOING—
GETTING A WRITE-UP OR A REVIEW

Let's speculate that your pre- and post-opening marketing worked. Your restaurant got off to a running start. Right away, it was very busy, people were talking about it locally and on the food blogs, and a buzz was circulating about it. But the buzz is beginning to taper off now. You want to keep people talking about your restaurant and coming back to it, while attracting new customers. What can you do?

The best way to get lots of new customers and keep your buzz going is to be favorably reviewed in an influential local newspaper magazine or on a local television food show. I know firsthand; I experienced it. In 1995, Zuni received a favorable review from the *New York Times*. As a result, our business increased by 30-40 percent for about six months. People came not just from New York, but from all over the country. This review was more effective than the thousands of dollars we had spent in advertising. This is not just anecdotal evidence. A recent National Restaurant Association survey found that 70 percent of customers rely on restaurant reviews in newspapers and magazines when selecting a restaurant for the first time.

In addition to reviewing restaurants, the press reports on new and interesting cooking methods, special or seasonal ingredients, wines, cocktails, desserts, and design elements. This type of coverage also attracts the dining public's attention and, while it may not have the same impact as a favorable review, it will certainly get you a stream of new customers and keep people interested and talking.

The press also reports on special events that restaurants sponsor to benefit local schools, community organizations, and charitable causes. For example, in 1997, when Zuni raised twenty-five thousand dollars to help fight hunger locally in New York City, we received quite a bit of coverage from area media, which helped to attract a number of new customers. The press also likes to cover human interest stories. Recently, there was a write-up in *San Francisco* magazine's food section about my friend Paul Canales, the executive chef of Oliveto in Oakland, California, who applies management techniques he learned in his previous career as a corporate executive to training and motivating his chefs. While these types of stories are not food related, they serve a strong marketing function by reinforcing your image in the community and reminding customers who have not come in for a while that your restaurant still exists. Best of all, the press is free!

OK, you say. I am sold on the idea of food critics promoting my dining fair, but, so far, I haven't been lucky enough to have one of them wander in, and it seems that my friends and satisfied customers haven't gotten to them either. What can I do? The answer is: send them press releases (written announcements to the press) or press kits (a package including a press release along with pictures and other materials for distribution).

Earlier, we said that hiring a public relations' agent can be expensive, so let's talk about how you can go about sending out your own press releases and press kits.

Before you start putting together a press kit, you will have to do some homework. Your first assignment is to regularly read reviews and other food- and restaurant-related columns in popular local and regional newspapers and magazines. Food and restaurants, in particular, are now so popular that most major daily and weekly newspapers carry a dedicated food section. Major newspapers in large urban cities, in addition to having at least two reviewers or critics (one for upscale restaurants and the other for casual table-service and takeout operations) will also have several writers who cover all types of interesting and unique food and beverage topics and human interest stories related to restaurants. For example, if your chef is the lead guitarist in a band on his days off, reviewers may be able to find an interesting angle there; how about, "Guitar licks are as good as finger-licking-good BBQ!"

You may also want to start reading popular national magazines such as *Gourmet*, *Food and Wine*, and *Bon Appétit*. Critics and food writers for these publications cover all types of food and restaurant operations all over the country, from local dives in Biloxi to high-end temples of gastronomy in San Francisco. For example, when I owned Souper Dog, a tiny hole-in-the-wall soup-and-sausage operation in New York City, we got a very nice write-up in *Gourmet* magazine about our chicken sausages, which helped to attract lots of new customers, many of them tourists. The Food Network, one of the most popular cable TV channels (which was very instrumental in getting Zuni noticed) does stories on restaurants of all types and sizes. The objective of your homework assignment is to become familiar with the types of food- and restaurant-related stories that various local and national media are covering, and the names of the journalists who are covering them.

Once you have an idea of the types of stories that are being published, compile a list of the publications and the names of the critics and writers you think would be interested in your type of restaurant and concept. If, for example, you are doing new, cutting edge cuisine, look for publications, critics, and writers who are focusing on these types of trends. Similarly, if you are serving a particular type of ethnic food that's hot, look for publications, writers, and critics who regularly cover ethnic foods and restaurants.

With your targeted list of publications and writers in hand, put together a press kit that includes: copies of your menus; a business card; and a cover letter describing any unique and interesting details about your food, wine, cocktails, cooking methods, unusual ingredients; or chef (including his guitar wizardry). You may want to include a little eye candy, such as pictures of your food and restaurant. In your cover letter, do not promise the best or tastiest food or the best wine and cocktails. These types of promises can backfire. People and critics, in particular, tend to be skeptical of self-aggrandizement. Before sending off your kit, make sure that your restaurant's address, phone number, and URL are on your cover letter, business card, and menus.

Not all critics and food writers conceal their identities; many have their photographs displayed next to their columns. Look for them at various functions and events, such as restaurant trade shows and other food and beverage seminars, events, and conferences, or walking on the street. Introduce yourself, tell them about your restaurant, and ask whether you could send them a press kit. They are more likely to open your kit and read it if they have made a personal connection with you.

Many newspapers, magazines, and radio stations will do a write-up or a review in exchange for a certain amount of paid advertising. The problem with this arrangement is that it is typically quite expensive, particularly if the publication has a large circulation. What's more, since these reviews are paid for, they tend to be consistently favorable and therefore lack credibility. Think about it; would you pay for a negative review or write-up? This is not to say that if you can afford to purchase a review, you shouldn't, especially if the publication has a large circulation. Why? Because write-ups and reviews, objective or not, are more likely to be noticed than print advertisements.

Another way to get noticed and keep the buzz going is to get your restaurant listed and/or reviewed in prominent guidebooks. Currently, the most influential guidebook is the *Zagat Survey of Restaurants*, which is published in most major cities and covers restaurants of all types and sizes. Despite claims by some that the reviews are not always objective, many restaurant-goers swear by it and often use it to make their restaurant selections, particularly when paying a visit to a new city. Reviews in the guide are based on public opinion surveys and are usually quite entertaining and candid. It's also great for finding out what real people (not critics) are saying about your restaurant and about your closest competitors. To get more information about the Zagat surveys, go to www.zagat.com.

Chances are, you won't get a visit from a reviewer immediately after sending out your press kits. It can take weeks, months, or even a year before the writers come. But don't give up if you think your restaurant has something unique or special to offer! Instead, every couple of months, update your press kit with new and interesting things your restaurant is doing and send it out again. Whatever you do, do not become a nuisance by constantly calling or writing about the same angle or story. The critics will sense that you are desperate and be turned off. Be patient; once you do get a favorable write-up, review, or mention by one of the news media, the others will come.

As I mentioned previously, the media has a symbiotic relationship; that is, they tend to feed off of each other. Remember Zuni's *New York Times* review I mentioned earlier? Well, that came out shortly after we were featured on the Food Network for our unique Southwest cuisine. Coincidence you say? I thought so at first, but guess what? All of the media that we were trying to attract for months and even years started showing up after that one review. Fortunately, they all gave us good reviews. The extent of the media's feeding frenzy will depend on how influential your reviewing newspaper or magazine is, and how favorable the review is. Also, the more unique and interesting your food, cooking methods, special ingredients, and so forth are, the more likely you are to get wide coverage.

THE CRITICS ARE COMING!
THE CRITICS ARE COMING!

Most influential critics will come to your restaurant anonymously and often in disguise (for example, *New York Times* critic Ruth Reichl regularly wore wigs). They arrive incognito because they want to be served the same food and receive the same service as the rest of your customers, many of whom are likely to be their readers. If you happen to spot a critic in your restaurant, do not bend over backward to serve him or her better food or provide better service than you would your other customers. An astute critic is likely to notice that fellow diners are not getting the same attention and may either give a bad review or no review at all. The moral of the story is: if you are confident that you are serving really good food and providing great service, the best way to get a favorable review is to run your restaurant day-in and day-out the best way you know how, with passion and dedication. In short, prepare every day for your review by practicing on your customers.

Mind you, not all reviews are favorable. If they were, they would not be credible. Moreover, restaurant critics, like critics in other fields such as art, music, and architecture, often have varying opinions. In fact, it's not uncommon for one influential critic to rave about a particular restaurant's food, only to have another one come along and pan it. Case in point: many New York City restaurants that received favorable reviews from critics at the *New York Times*, *Zagat Survey*, and other influential publications, received average marks form the prestigious *Michelin Guide*. The good news is that most influential critics will visit a restaurant at least twice before giving a review. They also typically give new restaurants a few weeks or even months to get up to speed before paying their first visit, unless a restaurant is owned by celebrities or has a celebrity chef or owner.

Yes, positive reviews are great for business. But if your restaurant gets an unfavorable review, don't give up on promoting it. Remember, it will only be the opinion of one critic. Another one may come along and give you a favorable review. Though a poor review will sting and hurt your ego and your staff's ego, don't let it deter you. Continue sending out press releases and striving to keep your concept fresh and interesting for the critics who matter the most—your regular customers. Do this and when the next critic comes, you will be ready!

BUILDING A LASTING CUSTOMER BASE

Almost a year has passed, and your pre- and post-opening marketing campaigns have continued to work their magic. Customers are coming in the door and, from all indications, your concept is well received. Your goal now is not only to continue

Take It from a Food Critic

Amanda Berne of the *San Francisco Chronicle*

Once upon a time, the only review restaurants had to worry about were from restaurant critics. But in this golden age of technology and gossip, restaurants now have to look for reviews from food bloggers, major forums on foodie websites, the regular ol' reviews in magazines and newspapers (sometimes several newspapers), and gossip columns, both on the internet and in print. What's a restaurateur to do?

The critics, if they go by the code of ethics set forward by groups like the Association of Food Journalists (AFJ), will wait at least a month for the restaurant to open and smooth out kinks. After that, it's fair game.

A critic will visit not once, but at least two or three times, sometimes more to iron out any doubts. There will be an assumed name. Or two. Or three . . . each with different credit cards to match the new character. Friends will make the reservations so that the phone numbers can't be tracked and remembered by restaurant staff or the growing number of computerized reservation systems.

Then they slip into the restaurant, as casually as possible, and get comfortable. Some take notes. Most memorize their meals and immediately go home and write everything down. They always sit facing out so they can watch what's going on in the restaurant. They're constantly eating off their friend's plates or swapping mid-meal.

If a reviewer has been "made," or discovered, efforts to sway them with special treatment won't work. They'll look to see how you treat the people next to them or across the room. They'll dissect everything, even that extra bit of foie gras or that shaving of truffle you so lavishly tucked into their dish. They'll know that you're trying to woo them with luxe ingredients and will stop to wonder why you don't let the dishes speak for themselves.

If you get a negative review, don't despair. Take the criticisms to heart, decide what is worth changing, change them, and then let the reviewer know that things are shaping up. Chances are they will do an updated review to let readers know that things have gotten better, if they have.

As for the rest, food bloggers will come in early, trying to beat each other to post about the newest restaurant. No matter what, don't post scathing comments on their blogs—it only adds fuel to the fire. Same goes for food forum websites like Chowhound and eGullet. If you do choose to respond, do so, but don't do it anonymously and don't get catty.

The best thing a restaurateur can do is to always act in the most diplomatic fashion, welcome each and every customer the same, cook from the heart, and hope that people get it.

to attract even more new customers, but to get your regulars to return with their friends and family in tow.

Undoubtedly, the best and cheapest way to build a loyal customer base is to give your customers as many reasons as possible to talk frequently and favorably about your restaurant. This will be word-of-mouth advertising at its best. Don't take my word for it, but consider the following. A recent National Restaurant Association survey found that 90 percent of customers said they are likely to choose a full-service restaurant for the first time based on the recommendation of a family member or a friend. Also, a huge bonus of having customers talk often and positively about your restaurant is that it greatly increases the chances that the media will hear about it.

So how are you going to get customers to speak well and frequently about your restaurant? The answer is: you will have to continuously develop good relationships with your customers while providing food, beverages, and service that consistently meet or exceed their expectations in an environment that is clean and makes them feel comfortable. If you can do these things, you will give them perceived value for their money at any menu price level.

A key requirement in developing and building good relations with customers, regardless of your concept, will be getting all of your employees, particularly front-of-the-house and counter staff, to become an integral part of your team. Do this by educating them thoroughly about every aspect of your concept, including the food, beverage program, service philosophy, and type of restaurant experience you want your customers to experience. Remember, part of having a successful restaurant is meeting or exceeding customers' expectations. Treat your staff fairly and respectfully, and reward and compliment them for good work. Your staff, in turn, will be motivated to provide the best possible service to your customers. And they will recommend your restaurant to their friends, family, and acquaintances, too! (Of all the aspects of your business, excellent service is probably the one that's best for helping to build a strong brand image.) At this point, you may wish to review chapter 11.

One of the best ways to develop solid relationships with your customers, particularly regulars, is for you and your staff to go the extra mile to make them feel special. Greeting regular customers by name, remembering how they take their drinks (with an olive or a twist), and remembering their favorite table can go a long way in making their dining experience a good one. You can also create goodwill by giving regulars—particularly when they bring friends—a complimentary treat. When you recognize customers in the presence of their friends, they feel special, which can help to build an emotional relationship and lead to customer loyalty. Here's one possibility: if you are running a table-service operation, send your regular customers something special—a complimentary bottle of wine, a plate of appetizers, or a plate of desserts—with every fourth or fifth visit. I know of one restaurant that offers its customers recipes of dishes that they particularly enjoyed, or if customers at one table seems interested in a dish served at another table, servers will take them a sample to try. You can also develop a customer list and use it to track birthdays, anniversaries, and holidays or to send thank-you cards to loyal customers. Most POS (point-of-sale) systems offer features that will make these tasks easy.

You should also get involved in your neighborhood and community, supporting local charities and those of your regular customers. If you have the room and can afford it, consider hosting special events to raise money for local charities. If your restaurant has downtime between meal periods (between lunch and dinner) or if it has a private party room, offer to serve as a meeting place for local professional groups and charitable organizations. When customers know that you appreciate their business and you care about the community in which you are doing business, they are more likely to become vested in your success, become loyal customers, and reward you with frequent visits.

As you develop good relationships with your customers, encourage them to give you feedback on your food, beverages, service, and overall ambience. This will give you the opportunity to quickly identify potential problem areas and correct them before they develop into a situation that could create negative word-of-mouth talk. According to statistics from the U.S. Department of Commerce, for every registered customer complaint, there are another twenty-six customers with the same complaint. The big payoff for nipping negative word-of-mouth comments in the bud is that, very often, some of the best word-of-mouth endorsements result when customer complaints are quickly and satisfactorily resolved.

The restaurant experience, regardless of the concept, is as much an emotional experience as it is an eating and drinking experience. People don't only go to restaurants for sustenance, they often go to share meals in a place that is welcoming and makes them feel comfortable. Once you start seeing lots of the same faces regularly, you will know that your restaurant has a successful brand, having become known for something special, and that it has made an emotional connection with your customers. Your marketing efforts, whatever they are, are working.

CHAPTER 15

OPENING DAY
AND BEYOND

OK, you're up and running, your menu is priced to perfection, your marketing plan is working, and lots of customers are coming in the door. Yet after the first month of operations, profits and cash in the bank are substantially less than they should be. What could possibly have gone wrong?

The most likely culprits are one of or a combination of the following: spoilage, waste, employee theft, or labor costs—caused by a lack of proper controls over inventories, purchasing, receiving and storing food and beverages, and staff scheduling. By properly controlling these vital elements of your business, you will be able to effectively reduce or substantially eliminate these costs and put your business back on the road to your desired level of success.

Before we get into some of the details, let me give you an example of the potential losses that could occur if you do not work quickly to implement proper controls. Let's assume that your projected first-year sales are $500,000, and as a result of poor labor, waste, spoilage, and theft controls, you lose $.05 of every sales dollar, which by the way, according to some estimates is the national average. If you think that this won't add up to much, you are very wrong. Take a closer look, and you will see that it's really $500,000 × .05, or $25,000 annually! Now let's assume that this continued for ten years. Guess what? Without considering interest lost, you are looking at losing $250,000. Got the picture?

In order to take charge and implement proper controls over your business, you will have to: establish standards and procedures, train your employees to properly perform their respective jobs, monitor employees' performance, make quick and timely corrections, and compare your results regularly to expectations to see whether you are meeting your goals. That said, policies and procedures won't mean a thing without good management, which means that, from the get-go, you must roll up your sleeves and get actively involved in your business's day-to-day operations. There is no better way for you as a first-time restaurateur to learn and appreciate the ins and outs of the restaurant business.

This does not mean that you will have to run a formal and rigid shop, but it will require time, effort, and good leadership on your part. This may sound clichéd, but you are going to have to lead by example; as the adage goes, "The fish usually stinks from the head." Your game plan for success should be to set standards high and manage low (nice and easy). Your daily work habits, attitude, behavior, manner, and ability to take corrective actions when necessary will set the tone for your employees. For example, if you help with plating and consistently overportion, your employees are likely to do the same. Similarly, if you receive deliveries and do not check properly for quality and quantities, why should you expect your employees to act differently? All right, let's get started.

INVENTORIES

Before placing your first food or beverage order, you should determine the minimum amount of each food and beverage item that you could hold in inventory without compromising your ability to keep things running smoothly. One of the most common mistakes that both experienced and inexperienced restaurant owners make is to overstock food and beverage inventories. Some people are lured by volume discounts offered by zealous distributors and vendors eager to make a sale, while other owners are reluctant to monitor their inventories diligently because they think that it is too difficult or time consuming. Unquestionably there will be times when it will make sense to take advantage of volume discounts and stock up on particular inventory items. As a rule, however, it is never a good idea to overstock any inventory item by more than 5 or 10 percent for the following reasons:

- Carrying higher-than-necessary inventories needlessly ties up valuable working capital and reduces cash flow; that is, the more money you have tied up in inventory waiting to be sold, the less you will have available to run the other day-to-day aspects of your business.

- Carrying excess inventories can lead kitchen and bar employees to become careless with overportioning. Having adequate but minimum inventories will also make it easier to notice when employees are overtrimming. In most restaurant operations, overportioning and waste (overtrimming) are major causes of inventory loss and consequently of high food costs.

- Carrying larger-than-necessary inventories will make it harder to notice missing items, thus encouraging employee theft.

- Large inventories increase the risk of spoilage of perishables such as meat, fish, poultry, and produce in the case of possible power outages, refrigeration failure, and unanticipated slow periods. In these situations, you will lose a lot less with smaller inventories. Small well-managed inventories will also keep perishables fresh, which will help to maintain high food quality.

Instances when it may be necessary to overstock are: delivery interruptions due to holidays or weekends; special holidays such as Easter, New Year's Eve, or Mother's Day, when it may be necessary to stock up to cover additional business; price discounts on food and beverage items that are usually expensive; anticipation of a price increase in a high-volume inventory item, or compliance with vendors' minimum orders. Minimum orders typically occur when vendors will not ship an inventory by the piece, such as one or two bottles or cans of an item.

The keys to efficient purchasing and maintaining small but adequate inventories are: accurately estimating business volume; scheduling timely deliveries; properly rotating stock, particularly perishables; and keeping accurate and up-to-date inventory records. In your restaurant's early weeks and months, anticipating sales volume and consequently inventory needs will be tricky, but over time, daily, weekly, monthly, and seasonal sales volumes will become a lot more predictable.

A good way to guard against overstocking, while maintaining a sufficient amount of inventory, is to establish par levels for each item. As discussed in chapter 9, the par level of any inventory item is the amount necessary to meet anticipated demand plus a safety amount to cover better-than-expected business volumes or delivery interruptions. The first step in establishing par levels is to divide your inventory into two categories: perishable high-turnover items, such as meat, fish, poultry, dairy, and produce; and low-turnover items that are purchased in bulk, such as spices, dry goods, and canned goods. For beverages, high-turnover items would typically be well drinks and house wines (wines sold by the glass), and low-turnover items would be premium wines and spirits.

The formula to calculate par inventory for any particular item is as follows: estimated weekly use plus safety stock divided by number of weekly deliveries. Estimating initial inventories and safety stocks will be a little challenging, but if you have done your homework—establishing a realistic estimate of your top competitors' level of daily business and successfully marketing, promoting, and advertising your restaurant—it won't be that difficult. For starters, I would suggest that your initial safety stock for any item should not be more than 10 percent of your estimated weekly volume, unless deliveries are not regularly available, in which case you would want to increase that amount.

To illustrate the par calculation, let's assume that you will be running a steak house: your estimated weekly sales is 70 steaks; your desired safety stock is 10 percent, or 7 steaks; and your butcher will deliver Monday through Friday. Using the formula, your par level for steaks would be (70 + 7) ÷ 5, or approximately 15. In reality, weekly sales of 70 steaks will not occur evenly at the rate of 10 per day (70 ÷ 7), but will more likely be 40 percent Monday through Thursday, or 28 steaks, and 60 percent Friday through Sunday, or 42 steaks, since most restaurants are busiest on weekends. This means that except for Friday, when you will have to stock up for Saturday and Sunday (because there are no deliveries on these days), the amount of steaks in inventory should seldom be more than par, or 15. A good estimate for inventories on Friday would be 49 steaks—42 for anticipated usage Friday, Saturday, and Sunday, and 7 for safety stock.

The size of safety stocks will depend on deliveries. Frequent and reliable deliveries will require low safety stock levels and vice versa; infrequent and unreliable deliveries will require high safety stock levels. For example, if you will be located in a rural area where deliveries are only available a few days a week, your safety stocks will have to be larger than if you will be operating in an urban market with deliveries available five or six days per week. The level of predictability of your business volume will also affect the amount of safety stocks. Erratic business volumes will require high safety stock levels; predictable volumes will require low safety stock levels.

Determining the level of safety stocks for low-turnover inventory items will not require the same level of attention as high-turnover items, first because they tend to be lower in value than high-turnover items, and second because they are usually not as perishable. Items such as canned goods, dry goods, and spices are typically nonperishable and are generally purchased in bulk, such as by the case, usually once or twice per week. Depending on the size of can or number of containers in a case, you may want to establish a policy of reordering when you are down to one or two unopened containers. Other items that may fit into this category are fifty- or one hundred-pound bags or cases of carrots and potatoes for making stocks, soups, and sauces. These, however, are perishable and should be refrigerated immediately. That said, not all low-turnover inventory items are low in value; some such as caviar, certain types of oils and spices, extra virgin olive oil, saffron, and vanilla beans are very expensive and should be securely stored and overstocked only when it's advantageous to do so.

In addition to minimizing the amount of cash tied up in inventories and helping to maintain tight but adequate inventories, maintaining a par system will also help you to do the following:

- Control spoilage since only the par amount of any item will be on hand
- Quickly check inventories and make accurate replacement reorders since once par levels are established, the amount of each order can be easily determined
- Reduce storage space requirements
- Make inventorying less labor intensive and tedious since only necessary amounts of inventory will be kept on hand

In setting par levels, it is important to understand that inventory usage will fluctuate with increases and decreases in business volume and that you may have to adjust your par levels periodically. Signs that par levels may be too low are frequent shortages, regular emergency deliveries, and reorders that are consistently larger than the par amount. On the other hand, signs that par inventories are too large are increased spoilage and reorders that are consistently less than par. Increased spoilage could also be a sign that perishable inventories are not being properly rotated on a first in, first out (FIFO) basis with old stock (first in) remaining in the back.

If you are like most first-timer owners, you probably will need to delegate some purchasing responsibilities to members of your staff, such as a chef or bar and beverage manager. One way to establish controls over staff's overbuying is to set dollar limits on purchase orders. For example, you could instruct your chef and or bar manager to only place orders for say five hundred dollars or less, getting your permission for all larger orders. Another method is to limit spending on purchases to the amount necessary to return inventories to par. Yet another way is to set the purchasing limit to your weekly food costs estimate. For example, if the previous week's food sales were $10,000 and your targeted food cost is 28 percent, spending to restock would be limited to $2,800 ($10,000 × .28). The same would apply to the bar manager.

PURCHASING

Two factors that will directly influence the quality and quantity of your food and beverage purchases are the portion sizes of your menu offerings and the specifications of the products required to create your various menu items. But before you can do any purchasing, you will have to make lists of the various foods and beverages that will be required to create your menu items. As you might expect, your recipes will be the basis for your lists. For example, assume that one of your menu items will be Italian meatloaf and the recipe is as follows: twelve ounces of ground beef chuck, twelve ounces of ground beef round, two cups of finely diced onions, one cup of bread crumbs, two-thirds cup of ketchup, two-thirds cup of finely diced parsley, three large eggs lightly beaten, one teaspoon of ground thyme, two cups of shredded mozzarella cheese, one cup of grated parmesan cheese, three tablespoons of finely diced garlic, two teaspoons of dried oregano, and salt and pepper to taste. Using this recipe, you would create a separate list for each of the ingredients: meats (ground chuck and ground round), eggs, cheeses (mozzarella and parmesan), spices (thyme, oregano, salt, and pepper), produce (onions, garlic, and parsley), and dry goods (bread crumbs and ketchup). Using your other recipes, you would then add items to these various lists and create additional lists as necessary. For example, if you had a recipe for grilled steak and french fries, you would add steak to your meats list, potatoes to your produce list, and frying oil to your list of oils.

To make ordering more efficient and to ensure that you consistently get quality products that are best suited for your preparation methods and menu items, you also will have to establish product specifications. Product specifications refer to the grade, trim, and fat content of meats, poultry, and seafood, and to the brands, sizes, packaging, and degrees of freshness of your produce, dry goods, and canned goods.

For example, if you were going to offer a steak and baked potato entrée, to make sure that you consistently served the same size steak and potato with each order, you would have to tell vendors exactly what size steak and potato you want. In this case, your potato specification might be a fifty-pound case of Idaho 80s, meaning eighty Idaho potatoes to the case. The steak specification could be strip loin, bone-in, ten-inch cut, ranging between fourteen and sixteen pounds, with one to three-fourth's of an inch of fat. Specifying the brand, Idaho, and the number of potatoes in each fifty-pound case would ensure that each customer consistently gets roughly the same size potato. Similarly, specifying the cut, size, and fat content of each strip loin would ensure that you could consistently serve every customer the same size steak. An example of a canned goods specification would be: organic Roma peeled tomatoes in juice, thirty number-ten cans per case.

Creating product lists with specifications is not only useful for establishing product quality and portion sizes, it also helps you do the following:

- Get different vendors to submit bids for the same product based on the same specifications
- Avoid misunderstandings between you and your chef and vendors when placing orders
- Make it easy for other staff members to call in authorized orders if you or your chef are not available
- Make products easier to check in when they are received
- Make sure that appropriately sized and quality products are available before deciding to create a menu item

After compiling your required list of food and beverages and then establishing product specifications, your next task will be to find the right vendors to supply them. Look for reputable distributors who are known for supplying quality products and who are knowledgeable about your concept. For example, if your concept will call for lots of frying, look for an oil supplier who knows about the smoking point of different oils, so he or she can advise you on the product that will provide the best quality, taste, texture, and price. If you are planning on doing cutting-edge cuisine, look for vendors who will introduce you to new and interesting products when they become available. Remember, updating menu items can help to catch the attention of food writers and critics. Also, as the organic movement continues to grow, you may want to consider working not just with vendors, but also with local farmers and ranchers to find good deals on fresh seasonal products.

As a small start-up, you should also look for vendors who understand the economics and finances of independent restaurants and will accept and deliver small orders. In addition to inquiring about product quality, ask about their level of service, dependability, and frequency of deliveries. The more frequently they can deliver the better. Remember, frequent deliveries will help keep inventories low, reduce waste and spoilage, keep foods fresh, and help to maintain good cash flow. A vendor's willingness and ability to make emergency deliveries is also a plus.

To find good vendors and suppliers, look to see who is supplying local successful restaurants, particularly those that are similar to your concept.

Once you have identified potential vendors, don't be afraid to ask them for references; they will definitely get references on you before delivering anything on credit. Ask to visit their storage facilities to see that they are clean, well organized, properly refrigerated, and well run. You should also find out if their operation is profitable. Vendors who are not doing well financially may be inclined to cut corners.

From the get-go, establish and maintain friendly, professional, and trusting relationships with your vendors and suppliers. More than banks, they will carry you during slow periods. Once you are up and running and have established a good payment track record, many vendors will extend payment terms from cash on delivery to payment every two weeks or even monthly in some cases. Many will also work with you on deals to do special dinners and other promotions and will inform you when an item that you use a lot of is either going on sale or going up in price. Good vendors can also be part of your word-of-mouth marketing network.

Inflation is a fact of life, and prices of most products fluctuate and increase over time. You may not always be able to pass on the increases to your customers. That said, you should always check to make sure that you are getting the best prices and looking for opportunities to get discounts, without overstocking of course. Keep vendors honest by letting them know up front that you will periodically review their prices and solicit bids from other vendors. In your first year of operation while you are building relationships with vendors, consider using the following bidding intervals: monthly for seafood, meat, poultry, and produce; quarterly for groceries (canned goods and nonperishables); every six months for dairy items; and once per year for paper goods and cleaning supplies. Reassure vendors whom you trust and work well with that small price differences will not matter as long as they continue to provide quality products, good service, and timely deliveries.

Pay attention to and try to take advantage of seasonality when purchasing and creating new menu items. While it is true that prices will fluctuate during the course of a year, it is also true that prices of red meats are usually lower in the spring and higher in the summer, and produce prices are lower in the spring and summer and higher in the winter. With this in mind, you may want to consider changing your menu seasonally.

Finally, beware of vendors offering special deals and lower-than-market prices. Sometimes vendors looking to offload slow-moving products won't care if they are right for your method of preparation or portion sizes. If a particular vendor is offering a special deal, be sure that the product or products being offered meet your specifications in terms of size, quality, and freshness. If getting these products will require excess preparation time or trimming to comply with your specifications and portion sizes, it will not be worth it.

RECEIVING, STORAGE, AND INVENTORY MANAGEMENT

All your plans for maintaining efficient inventory levels and purchasing will not mean a thing if your food and beverage products are not properly received and stored. It is not uncommon for many restaurants, large and small, to experience a significant amount of theft and spoilage because of poor receiving and storage practices. Don't let this happen to you! Always check to verify that you are getting the quality and quantities of goods you ordered at the prices you agreed to pay.

RECEIVING GOODS

The best way to ensure that you are getting quality products, particularly perishables, is to have a trained staff person (usually you or your chef) inspect them as soon as they are received. Not only should you inspect perishables for freshness, you should also refrigerate them as quickly as possible to prevent higher food cost due to spoilage. Consider the following: bacteria count doubles every six days when held at thirty-four degrees, and doubles every six minutes when held at seventy-two degrees. What's more, it is estimated that a head of lettuce will lose one day of shelf life for every hour that it is not refrigerated. Think for a moment of the potential losses that could occur by not having your food stored properly and quickly!

Problems with deliveries and delays in proper storage of food and beverages often happen when deliveries arrive just before or during service. Although this situation is not always avoidable, the best way to prevent it from happening regularly is to arrange to have deliveries made during slow or off hours. If this is not possible, it may be worthwhile to add an additional employee to work on days when you expect a lot of deliveries. It will be money well spent; you will save a lot of money in spoilage and salvage that subtle difference, freshness, which makes food taste better.

Losses often occur because of short deliveries. Keep a working scale (preferably digital) close to where you receive food items that you purchase by weight. Weigh most or all of your high-value items regularly, and match the weight to the invoiced amounts. You should also count all items and match them to their respective invoices. Notify vendors of shortages and other discrepancies immediately; if they know that you are checking they are less likely to be dishonest. Also, don't take for granted that you are being invoiced at the agreed-upon prices. Periodically check prices on invoices to those you were quoted when you placed the order. Vendors may periodically increase prices between the time an order is placed and the time it is shipped. Occasionally check the price extensions (quantity times price) on invoices, as well, especially those that are not computer generated, before paying them. If these types of errors occur, they could distort your cost of sales calculations, sometimes materially. Over the years, I have found a number of quantity, price, and extension discrepancies.

In chapter 10, I talked a lot about the various pieces of storage equipment needed in a kitchen, such as types of refrigeration and shelves. Let's talk now about ways to make storing and taking inventories manageable and efficient on a daily basis.

To facilitate counting and to make inventorying less tedious and time consuming, keep storage areas neat and organized. Store similar items in the same section. Label shelves to prevent products from being stored in different locations; this makes it easy to locate items during inventorying. Also, when products are stored in different locations, they can often be overordered, left to spoil, or stolen.

Use columnar preprinted count sheets. A preprinted count sheet can have a column for each of the following: item name, specification, unit size, par amount, quantity on hand, cost, and value. List items on the count sheets in the same order as they are found in the storeroom.

For purposes of weekly cost of sales analysis, focus on counting key high-value items. Usually, as much as 70-80 percent of the typical restaurant's inventory is made up of high-value items, such as meats, seafood, poultry, dairy products, wines, spirits, and beer.

SPOILAGE AND WASTE

I have already touched on the amount of potential spoilage that could occur when perishables are not placed in refrigerated storage quickly, something that happens a lot more than most restaurant operators like to admit. And guess what? Waste and spoilage, much of it easily avoidable, are actually two of the main causes of excessive food costs in many restaurants.

SPOILAGE CULPRITS

A common spoilage culprit is refrigerators that aren't sufficiently cool. Look at how the problem can compound: first, perishables aren't stored quickly enough, and then they are stored in refrigeration that's not sufficiently cool. For the record, required storage temperatures are 34 to 36°F for fresh meats, produce, and dairy products; 30 to 34°F for fresh fish and seafood; and 0 to 10°F for freezers.

The cheapest and easiest ways to avoid unnecessary costs due to spoilage are: set up a regular maintenance program for all of your refrigeration (see chapter 10 for more details), install curtains on all your walk-in boxes, train receiving staff to refrigerate perishables as soon as possible, and invest in a vacuum packer. Vacuum packing removes air from storage bags and will extend the shelf life of perishable food items. Vacuum packing also prevents freezer burns on food. A good vacuum packer can easily reduce food costs by one or two percentage points and will quickly recoup its cost.

UNNECESSARY WASTE

Now that you have some ideas about how to eliminate unnecessary spoilage, let's turn to the other food cost culprit, waste. While it is important to eliminate waste, it is also important to understand that a certain amount of waste is unavoidable in food preparation. But recall from chapter 6 that you took care of that by including a waste factor in your menu pricing. Your next step is to substantially reduce or entirely eliminate unnecessary waste.

A majority of waste and consequently high food cost is usually caused by over portioning, over trimming, and a lack of use of standard recipes in food preparation. Before we get into some of the solutions to these problems, let's see how costly overportioning and overtrimming can be. Assume your kitchen staff consistently overportioned a menu item that costs $7 per pound by $1/2$ ounce. No big deal, right? OK, let's do the math: $7 \div 16$ = roughly $.44 per ounce, or $.22 per $1/2$ ounce. Now let's assume that you sold 20 of these menu items each day, or 140 per week (20 × 7). This would add up to $30.80 of lost profits per week (.22 × 140), or $1,601.60 per year ($30.80 × 52) on this item alone. Guess what the cost would be if you had 20 such items on your menu? In a single year, it would be $1,601.60 × 20, or $32,032! A similar calculation can be done for overtrimming, with equally if not more startling results. Can you imagine what the costs could be if each item on your menu was not only overtrimmed, but also overportioned! OK, I made my point; let's talk solutions.

Waste and over portioning does not happen deliberately. Most of it happens either because employees haven't been properly trained or because they have become lax. What usually happens is that the opening kitchen crew is trained, and subsequent employees, if they are trained at all, are given a crash course with very little emphasis placed on the proper use of standard recipes, proper trimming, or proper portioning. This often happens in kitchens with high staff turnover. If your kitchen becomes a revolving door, there will be little time to train key employees properly. Treat your employees respectfully, and reward them for good work. Do not try to wring every dollar of profit out of your business on the backs of your employees. Pay them as well as you can and train them fully; the cost savings in reduced waste will more than offset the cost.

A common misconception on the part of many restaurant employees is that busy restaurants are very profitable regardless of waste and spoilage. Dispel this notion by educating your employees about the business's financial aspects. Only then will they understand that their seemingly harmless errors are really very costly. One way to do this would be to walk them through the exercises we did earlier in this chapter to demonstrate the costs of overportioning. In addition, teach them to think in business terms by explaining that any increase in costs, waste, and so on, without a corresponding increase in sales, results not only in high food costs, but also in a loss of overall profits. Tell them that the more profitable you are, the more you will be able to pay them, and demonstrate it by giving raises and paying bonuses when profits are good. What's more, it's now well accepted that creating a positive work environment will not only reduce employee turnover, it will also reduce the incidence of theft, both of which can be costly. High turnover can result in high recruiting and training costs, and theft of course will result in loss of financial resources.

Don't just establish standard recipes; train your chefs and cooks to use them. Over time, many chefs and cooks become complacent and start to eyeball recipe ingredients and portion sizes, especially proteins, meat, and fish, when plating. I can't tell you how often I have gone into the kitchen and seen this happening.

In addition to training your kitchen staff, make sure they have the right tools and equipment to do their jobs properly and efficiently. Correctly sized measuring cups and spoons are essential for including the right amount of each ingredient in a recipe and getting a consistent taste. Similarly, properly sized serving utensils will ensure consistent portions. For example, if you are going to run a burrito joint and want to make sure that each burrito gets four ounces of each ingredient, using a four-ounce serving spoon will not only ensure consistent portion sizes, it will also make assembly quick, easy, and efficient. Using properly sized serving utensils will take the guesswork out of portioning sauces, dressings, and side dishes made in advance and will allow for quick service and consistency of taste, texture, and plate presentation.

When it comes to trimming and portioning meats, fish, and poultry, a portion scale is an invaluable piece of equipment. These menu items typically make up the lion's share of a restaurant's food costs, and, as we calculated, mistakes can be costly. Invest in a good scale and make sure that it is properly calibrated. Even small errors can be costly. Another good way to ensure proper portioning is to periodically weigh some of the protein portions that have been prepped for service yourself. You should also take a look in your garbage bins occasionally to see if there are excessive meat and/or vegetable overtrimmings. Also, pay attention to plates going back to the kitchen. Lots of plates with lots of scraps may be an indication of overportioning.

EMPLOYEE THEFT, REVENUE, AND SALES CONTROLS

According to published reports, employee theft averages anywhere between $218 and $500 per employee per year, to as much as $.05—yikes!—out of every sales dollar. If it's any consolation, restaurants are not unique in suffering from employee theft; the retail industry as a whole reported about $15.1 billion of employee theft in 2002. What makes restaurants particularly susceptible to theft is the fact that food and beverages are not only easily consumed, they are also easily transported. Another problem is that many restaurants deal in cash, which is always a temptation to dishonest employees. My experience is that not every employee will steal the equivalent of $218 to $500 in cash, food, and beverages every year, but there are almost always a few individuals who, despite your best intentions and efforts, will either feel undervalued or underpaid and will unfortunately resort to theft. In chapter 9, we discussed employee theft in bar operations and will therefore limit the discussion here to the front of the house and the back of the house.

Employees steal or "get over" on their bosses or the owners in numerous ways, the most common of which are: giving free food and beverages to family and friends; giving customers free drinks and sides in order to boost tips; pocketing cash from sales; taking, eating, and drinking food and beverages without paying; charging regular prices, ringing up lesser amounts, and pocketing the difference (padding checks); voiding tickets and keeping the proceeds; and recording over-rings to cancel actual cash sales.

The problem with the three most common forms of theft—giving free food and drinks to family and friends, unauthorized eating and drinking, and padding checks—is that most employees don't see these acts as theft or consider them to be ethically challenging. A good friend who works as a server recently told me that she and most of her fellow servers don't see how "giving away" or "taking" a little food here and there could really hurt the boss; after all, he makes so much money! It was not until I explained how seemingly small amounts of petty theft committed regularly over a period of time can add up to a lot of money that she understood. My experience is that the majority of employees are honest, and when they are educated about the compounding effects of petty theft, many will do a lot less of it. Also, as mentioned in chapter 11, establishing a policy of employee discounts for family and friends will go a long way toward increasing morale and setting a good example, particularly if you plan on routinely treating your own family and friends. Staff discounts should, of course, be planned for and budgeted into your cost of operations.

An effective way of deterring service and counter staff from taking special care of friends and family and from eating and drinking unauthorized items is to establish a policy that food and or beverages are not to be issued to servers without approval. You can require staff to present a "dupe" (duplicate copy) of a guest check to the kitchen or bar, and then periodically reconcile the number of items, particularly high-value items, sold in the dining room or at the counter with the number of those items the kitchen issued. For example, if examination of guest checks for a particular dinner shift shows that thirty salmon entrées were sold, there should be thirty dupes in the kitchen with requests for salmon entrées. To detect possible collusion between service and kitchen staff, you should also periodically reconcile your entrée inventories with sales. For example, let's assume that inventory records show that there were five orders of salmon on hand at the start of the day and an additional thirty-five orders were received and prepared for service. This would mean that forty orders were available for sale. Since guest checks show that thirty orders were sold, the kitchen should have ten orders left in inventory at the end of the day. A count of fewer than ten remaining salmon orders, with no record of waste or spoilage, would indicate that some orders were either given away or stolen. Doing these types of checks and balances manually in an operation with more than a few menu items and moderate to high volume will be very time consuming and tedious; I know because I did it for a while. A much better alternative is to use a computerized POS system, which is discussed in more detail later in this chapter.

Clues that service staff and cashiers may be planning to pocket cash are: keeping pens, pads, coins, or a calculator near the register, which are usually used to track the amount of theft (charge the customer, ring up a no sale, put cash in the drawer, use pen and paper to track dollar amounts of no-sales placed in the register, and then remove the cash from the register before closing out at the end of the shift), lots of voids, and cash registers left open.

To safeguard foods, you can purchase security locks with most walk-in refrigerators, freezers, and storage systems. You should also keep your back door locked unless deliveries are being received or trash is going out. If, despite your best efforts, theft remains a problem, consider installing security cameras in the kitchen and storage areas. If you opt for these measures, inform your employees prior to installing them so that they will know that your intention is not to snoop, but to catch or deter thieves. Not long ago, this type of technology was quite expensive, but now it can be purchased relatively inexpensively as part of a computerized point-of-sale (POS) system. With these systems, you will be able to view all the areas in your restaurant from virtually anywhere using your computer (more on computerized POS systems later in this chapter).

Other common sense steps that can be taken to curb theft are: keep a minimum amount of cash at risk by periodically removing excess cash from registers; implement specific policies for voids and no sales, such as requiring approval; insist that all employees come and leave through the front door, periodically inspect employee bags, and limit access to storage areas, particularly those with high value items. Finally, to send a message that theft will not be tolerated under any circumstances, establish a zero tolerance policy by firing anyone caught stealing, even if he or she is your best employee.

COUNTING BEANS, NOT COOKING THEM

We have already established that as a first-time owner, being hands-on will greatly improve your chances of success. But the problem for many independent operators is that they get so caught up in day-to-day operations that they often forget to follow through on the last, but very important, part of the control formula—regularly checking the numbers to see if sales and expenses are what they are supposed to be. Sure, there are lots of things to do as a hands-on boss, but don't let this happen to you! While you are mastering the operational side of your business, you should also take the time to become familiar and comfortable with its financial aspects. Only then will you be able to nip problems in the bud that, if left unchecked, would significantly reduce your overall profitability and could actually ruin your chances of turning the corner to success. It's important to realize that lost profits are not recoverable! No amount of corrective actions can recover money that has already gone down the drain. So the sooner you get on the ball working with your numbers and the more frequently you check them, the more likely you are to be profitable. I can also tell you from my experience that successful restaurant operators who check their numbers weekly are almost always more profitable than those who check them monthly or even less frequently. I am confident that my previous experience as a numbers cruncher allowed me to spot early warning signs and was very instrumental in Zuni's survival and ultimate success.

The numbers that you should pay particular attention to are food, beverage, and labor costs and sales. Check and reconcile food, beverage, and labor costs at least weekly. You should investigate variances of 2 percent or greater from your target costs immediately. Keeping an eye on these particular costs is important; not only will they consume the lion's share of your sales dollars—typically $.60 to $.65 out of every sales dollar—but recall from chapter 5 that unlike fixed costs such as rent, insurance, utilities, and garbage collection, they are controllable, which means that with careful monitoring, you can keep them from getting out of control. Rent, insurance, loan payments, and utilities—typically the next largest expenses after food—will remain the same every month. There is very little you can do operationally to lower them.

Track sales daily and weekly for budgeting and cash flow purposes—so you can pay bills and decide when to give you and your staff a little raise—and also to see which menu items are selling and which are not. You should remove items from the menu that are not selling well as quickly as possible. Ingredients for menu items that do not sell, especially those that cannot be cross utilized—used in other menu items—end up as waste and increase food costs. Alternately, if an item is selling very well, you may be able to increase your profit margins by increasing its price slightly.

COST OF SALES

Let's work now on calculating that all-important weekly food cost number I've talked so much about. It's really quite straightforward once you get organized. The formula for calculating weekly food costs, or cost of sales, is: beginning inventory (the dollar amount of food inventories at the start of the week) plus the total dollar amount of food purchases (meats, seafood, poultry, dairy, produce, dry goods, and canned goods) during the course of the week, minus the total dollar amount of food inventories at the end of the week. Put simply, it's beginning inventory plus purchases minus ending inventory.

You can obtain the total dollar amount of your weekly food purchases by compiling and totaling a list of the dollar amounts of each of your food vendors' invoices. If an invoice includes nonfood items as well as food items, subtract the nonfood items from the total invoice amount before including it on your list. From your total, subtract any credit memos you may have gotten for product returns, and add the amount of any emergency food purchases you made during the week with cash taken from the cash register. This will give you your total weekly purchases.

The next step is to calculate the dollar amount of food inventory at the end of the week. You do this by taking stock, making a list of perishables in refrigerators and freezers and of dry and canned goods on storage shelves, and then totaling it. If you are using a par system and following the instructions I gave earlier for maintaining inventories, this will be a cinch. Get someone to count, and you write down the numbers, and it will go a lot faster. To make counting even easier and less time consuming, end your week on Sunday or any other day when your inventories are at their lowest. In most restaurants, inventory levels are at their lowest on Sunday night or Monday morning. To calculate the dollar amount of inventory, multiply the weight or unit amount of each inventory item by its most recent invoice price. For example, if you had ten pounds of chicken breast on hand and the most recent poultry invoice showed that you paid two dollars per pound for chicken breast, the dollar value of the inventory would be 10 × $2, or $20. Similarly, if you had five cans of crushed tomatoes on hand and the most recent invoice showed that you paid $1.50 per can, the dollar value of this inventory item would be 5 x $1.50, or $7.50.

The dollar amount of beginning inventory for any period will be the dollar amount of ending inventory at the end of the previous period. Put another way, the ending inventory for week number one becomes the beginning inventory for week number two. Now that you've got that straight, let's walk through an example. Assume that at the end of week number one, the dollar value of inventory on hand was $1,000, and that for week number two, total food purchases were $4,000 and ending inventory was $500. In this scenario, your food cost would be beginning inventory ($1,000) plus food purchases ($4,000) minus ending inventory ($500), or $4,500, and the beginning inventory for week number three would be $500.

Once you have determined your food cost number, you can then express it as a percentage of sales to see whether you are achieving your targeted food cost percentage. For example, if sales for the week totaled $15,000, your food cost percentage would be 4,500 ÷ 15,000, or 30 percent. If this was your targeted food cost percentage, your food cost total of $4,500 would be right on target, and an investigation would not be necessary. But remember! If there is a negative variance from your target food cost of 2 percent or greater, investigate it immediately. You can do similar procedures and calculations to calculate and check your beverage costs.

LABOR COST

As your weekly and monthly bills come due, you'll quickly realize that the restaurant business is a people business in more ways than one. Don't be surprised if your combined people (labor) costs—salaries, wages, workers' compensation, and payroll taxes—is your single largest expense. Check weekly to make sure that you are not overstaffing. After the first couple of months, your business patterns should become fairly predictable. Pay attention to business volumes during various days of the week, and check your staffing schedule to make sure that you are staffing efficiently, that is, scheduling fewer employees during slow periods and more during busy periods. Calculate the ratio of total labor cost to total sales (total labor cost divided by total sales) to get an idea of how much of each sales dollar is going to labor costs. This information will help you to determine whether your methods of preparation are too labor intensive.

You should also periodically check to see whether jobs can be combined to reduce staffing, but be careful not to understaff and overwork your employees for the sake of a buck. Too few kitchen and or service staff will not only result in poor service, it can also cause poor morale, which in turn will lead to high turnover and become counterproductive. The cost of constantly hiring and training new employees will eat up any cost savings you get by having fewer staff than seems necessary.

KEEPING UP WITH INFLATION

If there is one thing that you can be sure of, it's that your operating costs will increase every year, because of inflation. Too many operators are afraid to increase prices for fear of losing customers to competitors. However, as we saw earlier, small increases in costs can quickly erode your bottom line. Since you can't increase your prices each time your supplies cost increase, a good approach is to increase your overall prices at least two or three percent annually. Small percent increases that result in small changes between $.10 and $.25 are seldom noticed by customers and can add up to a substantial increase in sales. For example if you are operating in a price sensitive environment and one of your menu items sells for $4.75 and you increase it by 3 percent or $.15, the price would become $4.90 and would probably go unnoticed by customers. On the other hand, a price increase of 10 percent or roughly $.50 ($4.75 × .10) would increase the price to $5.25 and would definitely be noticed by customers. Similarly, in a casual to mid-scale operation a $15 item can be increased by 3 percent to $15.50 with little or no notice from customers. The compounding effect of these price increases over the years will help you to stay ahead of inflation and protect your overall profit without alienating your customers. For example if your gross annual sales is $500,000 and you increase your prices by 3 percent annually your gross sales over two years would increase by $30,450 to $530,450.

HELP WITH CRUNCHING THE NUMBERS— POINT-OF-SALE (POS) SYSTEMS

There's no question that being hands-on while staying on top of the numbers can be tedious and time consuming. But with a good point-of-sale (POS) system, both tasks will be a lot less daunting. When properly used, a POS system will not only allow you to make timely decisions based on readily available and accurate information, it will also free up more of your time to do the really important work of taking care of customers, properly managing and supervising staff, and growing your business.

Compared to standard cash registers, POS systems are not cheap, but their use in helping to save costs is very cost effective in the long run. Prices vary according to restaurant concept and size and can range from $3,000 to $50,000. The more functions and bells and whistles added, the more expensive. For example, one of my clients was recently quoted $3,000 for a one-terminal one-printer system for their café, which grosses about $300,000 annually; another client whose restaurant and bar is projected to gross $2.5 million will pay $20,000 for a system with three terminals, three printers, plus additional bells and whistles. The cost of the system works out to be about 1 percent of sales (3,000 ÷ 300,000) for the smaller operation, while the larger operation's cost works out to be less than 1 percent of sales (20,000

÷ 2,500,000). If they both use their systems to save $.03 of waste, spoilage, and theft combined out of every sales dollar annually, the cost savings will be tremendous. The café would save $9,000 annually (300,000 × .03), and the restaurant and bar would save $75,000 annually (2,500,000 × .03).

While a POS system's primary function is to track sales, it's the instant access to sales data that will allow you to do the types of analysis necessary to track problems, make sound business decisions, save time, and become more productive. For example, at the press of a button a basic system will provide some of the following sales data:

- Total sales daily, weekly, monthly, quarterly, and annually
- Total sales by shift or meal period, per server, per table
- Number of orders (menu mix) of each food and beverage menu item sold
- Sales in dollars of each menu item
- Number of customers and average check per customer, per meal period, daily, weekly, monthly, quarterly, annually, and so on
- Average sale per server for each meal period
- Total daily, weekly, and monthly sales broken down by cash and charge
- Total dollar sales broken down by food and beverage

You can utilize the generated sales data to help prevent excess waste, spoilage, employee theft, and labor in some of the following ways:

- By having sales numbers at you fingertips, you will be able to quickly and easily calculate weekly cost of sales percentages (total food cost divided by total food sales), which in turn will allow you to catch any negative trends before they become a problem.
- By having sales-by-menu-item readily available, you will be able to easily identify and remove slow-moving items from your menu, which will help to control waste and spoilage.
- By knowing the number of each food and beverage item sold daily and weekly, you will be able to quickly compare units sold to inventory to check for theft.
- Having accurate daily, weekly, and monthly information—such as number of customers, sales-by-meal-period, and sales-per-server—will make it easier to schedule staff more efficiently. For example, fewer fast servers can be scheduled during rush hours, which could help to reduce server hours and overall payroll costs.
- Having servers log in and out helps track employee hours and prepare payroll.
- By not having to compile all that data with a pencil and paper!

In addition to facilitating various types of financial analyses, POS systems make running day-to-day operations a lot faster and more efficient and can even reduce labor needs. For example, because the system sends customer orders directly from the service station terminal to the kitchen and bar, fewer trips and possibly fewer staff will be necessary when ordering food and beverages. A few of a POS system's other functions that will save time and improve efficiency are as follows:

- Eliminating check pricing and totaling errors; food and beverage menu prices are automatically assigned once an order is entered into the system, and checks are automatically totaled when closed out
- Tracking complimentary, staff, and promotional meals
- Tracking tips by server for IRS reporting

The biggest time saver, however, will come at the end of the day when it's time to close out and prepare daily sales reports. Without a POS, gathering sales data has to be done manually with pencil and paper. Having done this, I can tell you that this process takes hours, is very tedious, and is often fraught with errors. For this reason, many restaurant operators who opt not to use POS systems, seldom if ever gather the very information that could help to save them thousands of dollars.

The more sophisticated and expensive POS systems offer even more functions and bells and whistles, such as: inventory management; customer databases with the ability to capture marketing information, such as customer name, address, phone number, e-mail address, and favorite foods; digital security surveillance; time and attendance checks, having employees use badges to check in and check out of work stations and eliminating the need for a time clock; an ability to interface with measured-pour bar systems; an ability to interface with accounting and bookkeeping software such as QuickBooks; print and track gift certificates; and settlement flexibility, with the ability to split checks. Currently, the two most popular systems are Aloha and Micros, but there are several other providers on the market.

Depending on the size of your operation, investing in a POS system can require a fairly large capital outlay so make sure to do your homework before deciding on any one particular system. Here are some guidelines to follow:

- Make a list of the features that you think will be most useful for your size and type of operation. Don't let salespeople talk you into unnecessary extras.
- Talk to people who are using the systems you are considering. Ask for advice, and find out what they like and dislike about their system.
- Get comprehensive demonstrations of the features that you think are a must-have for your operation.
- Avoid customizing; it's very expensive, and service can be spotty.
- Ask salespeople what assistance is provided during installation, what training is included prior to installation, what additional training will cost if necessary, and what specific service programs are offered.
- To avoid sticker shock, get a quote on the total system, including computers, software, cash registers, and cables.

I don't want to leave you with the idea that if you start out woefully undercapitalized or with the wrong concept in the wrong location you could somehow control or plan your way to success. But should this be the case, with good controls and by paying attention to your numbers you at least will be able to identify problems, stem losses, and preserve some capital to keep your dream alive and start again, better prepared with a new concept. After all, this is essentially what happened to me!

The Triple Bottom Line

Mark McLeod of The Downtown Restaurant

Over the last couple of years, I have become increasingly intrigued with the concept of the triple bottom line (TTBL or 3BL)—a term coined in 1994 by John Elkington, cofounder of the business consultancy SustainAbility. The TTBL argues that to be successful, a business must measure not simply its financial performance, but also its environmental performance and its social performance. For a restaurant to have long-term sustainability, it must be committed to the highest possible level of performance in all three categories.

The Downtown Restaurant is fortunate to be located in a county that has a rapidly deepening understanding of the environmental bottom line. There are a number of agencies committed to helping businesses realize that the three bottom lines are irreparably bundled. You cannot work successfully on one without simultaneously working on the other.

One such TTBL-driven agency is Sustainable Berkeley, which is committed to helping businesses keep their eye on the environmental bottom line. Sustainable Berkeley has chosen restaurants as one of their early partners. The energetic and ebullient Leila Khatapousch, Sustainable Berkeley's restaurant liaison, came to us in 2005 and helped us to understand how we could send money to our financial bottom line by operating our restaurant in such a way that we would be sending points to our environmental bottom line. With Leila's assistance, we learned how to run our restaurant in an environmentally respectful manner—how to light our restaurant, how to heat and cool the restaurant, how to reduce our water usage, how to recycle 100 percent of our waste—all the while sending several thousand dollars each year to our financial bottom line which otherwise would have gone to the bottom line of several public utilities companies.

Another TTBL-driven organization is Ingrid Severson's Rooftop Resource Project in Oakland, California, which is part of a larger organization called Baylocalize. Ingrid has shown me how our restaurant can use its 30,000 square foot flat rooftop to grow herbs, fruits, and vegetables year-round; capture and store rainwater (which we can then use inside the restaurant and for irrigating rooftop gardens); and install solar heating grids. All of these rooftop uses significantly diminish the building's contribution to global warming and climate change.

As a restaurateur, what I think is most wonderful about TTBL is that by adopting the concept, we're promoting a set of operational procedures that not only helps to sustain the environment, but also helps to sustain our community, the enjoyment we derive from serving that community, and the persistence of the restaurant business overall. Heed TTBL, and we all have a chance to prosper, remain healthy, and enjoy ourselves for many decades. Ignore TTBL, and we had better pack up our marbles and catch the next flight to the moon!

Index